RAYMOND WILLIAMS

'There are ideas, and ways of thinking, with the seeds of life in them, and there are others, perhaps deep in our minds, with the seeds of a general death. Our measure of success in recognising these kinds, and in naming them making possible their common recognition, may be literally the measure of our future.'

Raymond Williams, 1921–1988

RAYMOND WILLIAMS

Critical Perspectives

Edited by Terry Eagleton

Northeastern University Press
BOSTON

Library of Congress Cataloging-in-Publication Data
    Raymond Williams : critical perspectives / edited by Terry Eagleton
    p.   cm.
    Bibliography: p.
    Includes index.
    ISBN 1-55553-060-5
    1. Williams, Raymond—Criticism and interpretation.
    I. Eagleton, Terry, 1943–
    PR6073.I4329Z87   1989
    828'91409—dc20

Manufactured in Great Britain

CONTENTS

ACKNOWLEDGEMENTS

I am grateful to the editor of *New Left Review* for granting permission to reprint from that journal the essay by Francis Mulhern, which appears in lightly revised form as chapter 4 in the present volume, and my own Introduction; these first appeared in the issues of November–December 1984 and March–April 1988 respectively. I must also thank the editor of the *New Statesman* for permission to reprint an interview with Raymond Williams which first appeared in that journal on 7 August 1987, and which is reproduced here as chapter 10. The essay by Stuart Hall which appears here as chapter 3 was first published in *Screen Education*, Spring 1980, no. 34.

My thanks also go to all those who kindly gave permission for the reproduction of photographs, as detailed in the captions.

Terry Eagleton

NOTES ON CONTRIBUTORS

Tony Pinkney is Lecturer in English at Trent Polytechnic, Nottingham, and editor of *News from Nowhere,* the journal of Oxford English Limited. He is the author of *Women in the Poetry of T. S. Eliot,* and of a number of forthcoming studies of modern criticism and literature.

Dai Smith is Professor at the School of History and Archaeology, University of Wales, College of Cardiff. He is the author of *Lewis Jones* and *Wales! Wales?*

Stuart Hall is Professor of Sociology at the Open University and former Director of the Birmingham University centre for Contemporary Cultural Studies. He is the author of numerous articles on political and cultural theory.

Francis Mulhern is Lecturer in English at Middlesex Polytechnic, and author of *The Moment of 'Scrutiny'.*

Fernando Ferrara teaches English and cultural studies in Naples, and is the author of numerous articles in both fields.

Robin Gable helps to produce *New Left Review.*

Lisa Jardine is a Fellow in English at Jesus College, Cambridge and the author of a feminist study of Shakespeare, *Still Harping on Daughters.*

Julia Swindells is author of *Victorian Writing and Working Women,* and works with Lisa Jardine in Cambridge.

Bernard Sharratt is Reader in English at the University of Kent, and author of *Reading Relations* and *The Literary Labyrinth*.

Edward W. Said is Professor of English at Columbia University. His publications include *Beginnings, Orientalism, The Question of Palestine* and *The World, the Text and the Critic*.

Terry Eagleton is Lecturer in Critical Theory at the University of Oxford, and Fellow of Linacre College, Oxford. His latest book is a novel, *Saints and Scholars*.

Alan O'Connor is Assistant Professor to the Department of Communications, Ohio State University. He is the editor of *Raymond Williams on Television: Selected Writings*.

INTRODUCTION

—— *Terry Eagleton* ——

Raymond Williams and I arrived in Cambridge simultaneously in 1961, he from a long stint in adult education to a college Fellowship, I from a year's teaching in a northern secondary modern school to an undergraduate place. It was hard to say which of us was more alienated. Williams had made the long trek from a rural working-class community in Wales to a college which seemed to judge people (as I was to find out later to my cost) by how often they dined at High Table. He looked and spoke more like a countryman than a don, and had a warmth and simplicity of manner which contrasted sharply with the suave, off-hand style of the upper-middle-class establishment. He never got used to the casual malice of the Senior Combination Room, and was to write years later, in a fine obituary of F. R. Leavis, that Cambridge was 'one of the rudest places on earth ... shot through with cold, nasty and bloody-minded talk'. I found myself marooned within a student body where everyone seemed to be well over six foot, brayed rather than spoke, stamped their feet in cinemas at the feeblest joke and addressed each other like public meetings in intimate cafés. It was a toss-up which of us was going to make it.

I knew of Williams's work then only vaguely, mainly through association with Richard Hoggart and the so-called Angry Young Men of the 1950s, now mostly dyspeptic old Tories. Hearing him lecture was an extraordinary personal liberation: it was like seeing someone stand up in the most improbable place, formal and begowned, and articulate with enviable ease and eloquence all the struggling, smouldering political feelings you had yourself, but which were not so to speak official or academic, and which one had simply not expected to hear given voice in such an environment. It was as if a dispirited juvenile offender in a remand home (an experience not far removed from that of an early 1960s Cambridge college) was suddenly to realize to his astonishment that the Governor speaking up there at the front was sending out oblique but unmistakable messages that he was an offender too, a kind of fifth columnist in the prison service. Part of the delight of this, of course, was to hear one's own values and instincts argued far more subtly and beautifully than one could ever have done oneself – converted to a marvellously intricate intellectual case without any diminution of personal conviction. Williams was a man of remarkable grace and dignity; and through the medium of this authority I felt somehow authorized to speak myself, and through me all those relatives and friends who could never speak properly, who had never been given the means to say what they meant, whom nobody ever bothered to ask what they meant. It was as though one's most spontaneous gut reactions, which one wouldn't really have been able to defend, were suddenly out there in the public arena, dignified and justified at the level of tenacious argument. And all this seemed to be less a matter of academic debate than to spring directly from the slow personal ruminations of Williams himself, as though the ideas were just the more public, audible bits of an unusually rich and deep identity. I think everyone who met Williams was struck by what I can only call his deep inward ease of being, the sense of a man somehow centred and rooted and secure in himself at a level far beyond simple egoism. I wondered then where this inner balance and resilience came from, and how I might get hold of a bit. I was to learn as I got to know him that it came essentially from his class background – indeed that the whole of his lifelong political project was secretly nurtured by a formative early experience of working-class solidarity and mutual support which had left him unusually trusting and fearless. But I couldn't understand this quiet authority at the time, or the way he seemed at once so gentle and so rugged, and put it down, I suppose, to middle age, though in fact he was only forty. I asked myself where this man was coming from, and how he could speak out on behalf of the powerless in this place, with the degree of shrewdness and sureness. I understood about a third of what he said, and resolved to get to understand the rest.

Leavis was still lecturing across the road, just on the point of retirement. 'Queenie did it all in the Thirties' was his comment on Williams's work, conveyed to me by Williams himself with his customary dry amusement. George Steiner was at Churchill College, telling his students that the trouble with Williams was that he didn't appreciate the chastening power of human tragedy. Most of the rest of the English Faculty seemed to see him as some kind of sociologist who had strayed through the wrong departmental door and inadvertently got caught up in the Metaphysical poets. They, of course, dealt with the essentially human; Williams was distracting himself with historical red herrings, with class and industry and politics and all of that, and even worse with film and advertising and the popular press. I think this was probably the deepest irony of all, because the most evident difference between Williams and most of his colleagues was indeed a matter of humanity, but as it happened the other way round. Williams's discourse rose straight from a human depth which seemed to put almost everyone else, oneself included, in the shade; it was the *level* at which he spoke, not just what he said, that marked the real distinction. You couldn't separate what he said from the sense of a whole rich hinterland of experience informing his words. Long before the slogan 'the personal is political' became fashionable, Williams was living it, in the complex, intimate relations between his life and work. He never seemed to credit anything he hadn't personally assimilated, absorbed gradually into his own being; and he lived in a kind of slow, steady, meditative way, again very like a certain kind of countryman, taking the whole of his experience with an intense, unwavering seriousness quite removed from the portentous. This seemed quaint, amusingly archaic, to some of the hard-boiled cynics around him, to the young men on the take and on the make whose depth of experience seemed from the outside about that of a Disney cartoon. There were the predictable friendly-malicious comments about the flat cap and the farmer's boots, the kind of talk which Williams himself always rightly saw as a kind of sickness. Even one of the obituaries, tenacious to the last, managed to drag out the word 'nostalgia' to characterize a man who wrote a major work entitled *Towards 2000*. Quite unwittingly – for he was the kind of man you had to work very hard on to make him feel negatively about someone – Williams made people feel uneasy about their own glibness and stylish political scepticism, and they were sometimes not slow to strike back in their anxiety.

Williams's own Cambridge experience had not been primarily one of stamping, braying six-footers. It had been the experience of war: the interrupted English course, the armed struggle in Europe (he was a tank commander in France), then the young servicemen, those who had survived, back on King's Parade to take up their studies again, as a Labour government moved into power. It had also been for Williams the experience of the Communist party, of which he was briefly a member. When he returned to Cambridge in 1961, after years of teaching adults in village halls around the south of England, he found it hard to get used to the supervision system, to teaching the children of the privileged, and kept a wary distance from the system. Yet it was the outsider, in a familiar paradox, who upheld the most creative traditions of the place. I mean the best traditions of the Cambridge English Faculty, which Williams personally incarnated for years, among Faculty colleagues who often hardly knew what he was talking about. Williams brought together in a new conjuncture the two distinctive currents of Cambridge English: close textual analysis on the one hand, 'life and thought' on the other. But what they called 'close reading' or 'attention to language' he called historical linguistics, and what they called 'life and thought' he called 'society' or 'cultural history'.

If this was a fertile conjuncture, it was not without severe tensions. The close analysis, he well knew, was by no means ideologically innocent: it was the learnt habit of a specialized, separated intelligence, deeply dependent on unconscious ideological consensus and radically dissociated from how most people actually had to live. To bring that to bear on so-called 'life and thought', on a whole social and cultural formation, was thus to risk becoming caught in an immediate political contradiction. How do you analyze your own people from the outside?

Does't the very form of that cognition run somehow counter to the content, as Matthew Price of *Border Country* suspects, and Peter Owen of *Second Generation* fears? It is a duality which crops up in Williams's work in all kinds of guises, and one I dismissed with the brisk impatience of relative youth in *Criticism and Ideology* (1976). It is there in the running battle between 'common' and 'educated', between the 'knowable community' and the harsh world of capitalist production, between country and city, Milton and Donne, isolated civilized subtlety and a general common humanity. Williams picks up just this conflict in the work of Leavis, in his obituary – Leavis who 'committed himself heavily to . . . one form of the discontinuities, the detachments, the cold wit of Eliot, yet was seized, always, with especially strong feelings of continuity, of commitment, of the everyday substance of English provincial life'. Williams is surely here speaking obliquely about himself as well; he had a lifelong fascination with modernism, despite the 'realist' label I and some others too facilely stuck on him, and saw just how modernism's radical estrangement of the ordinary was at once a creative political experiment and a disabling deracination. Unlike some others, he wasn't going to come down too quickly on either side of that particular fence. If he came in effect to abandon the lineage of 'close analysis' in his later work, it was not because he was not good at it (he was very good at it) but because the political price came to seem to him too high. *Culture and Society* is a courageous, breathtakingly original attempt to bring that current of trained textual analysis to bear on a common social history; but it is therefore an acute instance of the conflict in question, and for all the acclaim it received as a radical text it was written in political isolation in the Cold War years, the book of one still having to negotiate the tension between Leavisism and socialism. 'First-stage radicalism' was how Williams would later characterize this most seminal work, in a calculated self-distancing.

He was always haunted by the border he had crossed from the 'knowable community' to the life of educated intelligence, and lived in border country the whole of his life. When he moved from Hastings to a brief spell in Oxford he homed in unerringly on just the same dilemma: *Second Generation* opens on Oxford's conveniently named Between Towns Road, where you can look one way to the spires of the university and the other way to the roofs of the Cowley car factory. Williams never of course believed for a moment that this contradiction, embedded as it is in a class-divided society, could be somehow intellectually resolved, and never in any case viewed it as a simple opposition. One of his earliest essays is entitled 'Culture is ordinary', in which he argues that nobody who understands the Welsh working-class respect for learning and literature could imagine that it was a sheer break to cross the border from Abergavenny to Cambridge. He also remarked in an interview I did with him towards the end of his life that one of the things his Welsh comrades valued most about him, when he came back to Wales, was exactly the fact that he had crossed the frontier and made his way in the metropolitan institutions. It wasn't just a case of 'culture' on one side of the border and 'society' on the other: what Williams grew up in, what nourished him, was a culture if anything was, and like Hardy's Jude in Oxford it didn't take him long to perceive that it was in all sorts of ways more precious than the nasty, cold-hearted talk he was to encounter in so-called civilized Cambridge. Williams helped to bring the very concept of culture to Cambridge, often enough to have it thrown back in his face by the cultivated. It was't a question of some nostalgic backward glance to the valleys and the hillsides: *The Country and the City* takes the 'organic society' illusion and undoes it with deadly, devastating insistence. He once said disparagingly of Nye Bevan that it took one Welshman to know another. I never knew anyone who had a deeper respect for rational enquiry than Williams, and that from a man who knew as well as anybody that reason is not, in the end, where it is at. He never underestimated the value of the intellectual tools of which his own people had been deliberately deprived; it was just that he took the instruments which he had been handed and turned them against the educators. He used them instead to create the finest body of cultural work of twentieth-century Britain, on behalf of those who had not enjoyed the privilege of arriving in Cambridge to be told by E. M. W. Tillyard that his boots were rather large.

Williams was not only ungrateful enough to bite the hand that fed him; he was truculent enough to do it more and more as he grew older. Those liberal critics who had welcomed *Culture and Society* with open arms were rather less enthused by his later talk of Third World insurrection and the brutalities of capitalism. A striking feature of Williams's career is that he moves steadily further to the political left, in a welcome reversal of the usual clichéd trek from youthful radical to middle-aged reactionary. The left reformism or left Leavisism of the very early Williams of the journal *Politics and Letters*, when he was out in the political cold of post-war Britain, yields to the quickening solidarity of the early New Left and CND, where he could find friends and supporters. The little book *Communications* of 1962 proposes with casual boldness and in some practical detail the social ownership and control of the communications media, and by the time of *Modern Tragedy* in 1966 the gradualist discourse of *The Long Revolution* has turned, five years on, into the long tragedy of armed struggle against imperialism. Around this time Williams began to turn backwards so that he could keep moving forwards, re-exploring his Welsh heritage in a deliberate distancing from both 'English' literature and the brave new world of a Labour government whose idea of culture was C. P. Snow. Like many an exile, he had to discover, reinvent almost, his own social history, fight his way gradually past the English and Eng. Lit. identity he had partly adopted, in order to find out who he was. He had purged some of the pain of leaving Wales in *Border Country*, and could now return. That whole dimension enters into *The Country and the City*, a work which he had more trouble in getting finished than probably any other, since its themes touched him to the quick. A new tone, almost a new sensibility or structure of feeling, emerges in that strange, profound, unclassifiable work, which takes a long steady look at the English country estate and reads in its ceremony and elegance one long history of fraud, crime and violence perpetrated against working people. This is a Williams who has now lived through Vietnam and the student movement and the crass utilitarianism of the Labour government, and the change is there in his voice: less courteous, gently reasonable and cautiously circumspect, more dry, steely and saradonic. His writing becomes coldly angry and implacable in those politically turbulent years, and as far as his liberal supporters are concerned he has clearly gone over the edge. 'Sullen' was Frank Kermode's revealing class-epithet for *Modern Tragedy*.

The formal rapprochement with Marxism arrived four years later with *Marxism and Literature*, and the formulation of the doctrine of 'cultural materialism'. But this is done in a way which suggests less that he has finally been appropriated by Marxism than that he has coolly appropriated it. ('Cultural materialism', he declared cautiously, was 'compatible' with Marxism.) He will out-Marxize the Marxists by going the whole hog, extending materialism full-bloodedly to cultural practices too; but in thus pressing Marxist logic to an extreme, he will by the same stroke undo the 'base'/'superstructure' distinction and so retain a certain critical distance. That was always Williams's way: he was not only deeply suspicious of orthodoxies, but rarely even quoted another thinker or paused to note an influence. The work was somehow as much all *his* as the life; he gave off a rock-like sense of self-sufficiency which sometimes merged into solitariness, though he was paradoxically the most social and public figure one could imagine. It was not the quirky introspection of one shut out so much as the arresting originality of one out in front; you had a sense of having struggled through to some theoretical position only to find that Williams had quietly pre-empted you, arriving there by his own personal, meditative route. He was a kind of 'Bakhtinian' social linguist when the Bakhtin industry was still only a gleam in the eye of Slavicist semioticians; he anticipated by several years some of Jürgen Habermas's major theses on communicative action. He wasn't what one would think of as a particularly feminist writer, yet *Second Generation* is as searching a study of the relations between work, politics, sexuality and the family as one could envisage. As early as *The Long Revolution*, well before the emergence of the women's movement, Williams was speaking of the centrality of what he then termed the 'system of generation and nurture', ranking it on a level with the political, economic and cultural spheres. He refused to be distracted by the wilder flights of Althusserian or post-structuralist theory and was still there, ready and waiting for us, when some of us younger theorists, sadder and wiser, finally re-emerged from one or two cul-de-sacs to rejoin him where we had left off. He had seen the 'Road Up' signs, but didn't believe in barracading a route.* I don't think I ever heard him use the word 'theory' in the sense current now in left cultural circles, and though he had a large, devoted following throughout the world he never made the slightest attempt to form a 'school'. I have had American left critics beg me to persuade him to visit the United States, where his work has widespread, enthusiastic support, but he refused to do so during the Vietnam war and made only one or two visits there afterwards. He wasn't interested in academic stardom, he had little or no sense of himself as part of a 'profession', and preferred to get on with his work at home.

I think there were limits as well as strengths to this independence. It led him at times into a certain magisterial isolation, imposed the odd Olympian tone or over-defensive gambit on his writing, and frustrated some of his supporters who wished him to launch a more trenchant, collective project. Perhaps he had grown too used to working on his own in the years of adult education; or perhaps he was wary of what had happened at Cambridge to the Scrutineers. Sectarianism bored him, and he had a way of combining the most pluralist, unsectarian approach to politics with a socialist commitment so deep and unyielding that you sometimes felt he literally could not imagine how anyone could believe otherwise. If a contained sardonic anger was one aspect of his work, the other was a trust in human potential so generous and steadfast that he could be almost physically shocked by the political right's routine cynical disparagement of people. This was not some sentimental optimism: there was a hard cool streak of realism about Williams, which came out in some unlikely ways – in his impressive abilities, for example, as an administrator and political coordinator. It was just that he knew from his own experience what ordinary unheroic people were capable of, and it drove him to smouldering fury to hear them slighted and demeaned. Tragedy for him was not the death of princes but the death of his railway signalman father, whom nobody would ever have heard of had it not been for his devoted son. It was not of course that he believed that these fundamental values, of love and compassion and solidarity, would inevitably politically prevail; how could such an astute political analyst in a dark period have credited such a view? It was rather that he refused to be shifted, whatever the immediate loss or set-back, from the faith that these values were in the end the only ones that mattered, that they might not win out but they were what it was all about, that if you abandoned this then you abandoned everything. He had known what community could be, and would not rest until it was recreated on an international scale. He had a remarkably quick sense of how easy it is to blaspheme against humanity, and the best of what he inherited from Leavis could be summarized simply as reverence. He knew from his study of Welsh history what unbelievable fortitude and resilience an oppressed people can manifest in the cruellest conditions; and this is one reason why it would not have been possible for him to do what so many have now done, scale down his hopes and trim his political sails, face reality. What he faced *was* for him reality; and his deep personal patience allowed him always to take the long perspective, to avoid, as he once dryly commented, 'making long-term adjustments to short-term problems'.

Some of the borders which Williams respected least were those which ran between conventional academic disciplines. In the end it was impossible to give his project a name: it was not quite sociology or philosophy or literary criticism or political theory, and it was quite as much 'creative' and 'imaginative' writing as academic work. In a list of his own keywords, 'connecting' could come high in the ranks, along with 'active', 'complex', 'difficult', 'changing'. He was a librarian's nightmare, and had been practising the current fashionable deconstruction of the 'creative' and 'theoretical' for a good thirty years. Language was one of his intellectual passions from beginning to end, from *Culture and Society* to *Keywords*, but his sense of what it signified ran so deep, shaded off in so many directions, that one hesitated to call him a linguist. Words for him were condensed social practices, sites of historical struggle, repositories of political wisdom or domination; he had a Celtic feel for them, for their rich texture and density, and he himself spoke pretty much as he wrote, weightily, rhetorically, constructing and composing his speech rather than slinging it provisionally together. If he was a political theorist it was less in the sense of a short-term analyst (though he could organize sharp political interventions on particular issues) than in the manner of the figures from Blake to Morris of his own Culture and Society tradition, prophetically discerning the forms and movements of a whole culture. In this sense he belonged to the lineage of the classical intellectuals, those who eschew a single 'discipline' for a sense of intellectual responsibility to a whole social order; but if he avoided the myopia of the specialist he also sidestepped for the most part the amateur moralism of the traditional sage, if only by virtue of his literary sensitivity to the concrete and particular. Whereas Leavis had accommodated certain social and cultural issues by a literary colonizing of them, Williams came steadily to reverse this logic and 'decentre' literary studies into a wider field of cultural practices; but he never apologized for the fact that his first and persistent interest lay in writing – he simply transfigured the meaning of the category. It was ironic that some colleagues should view him as a reductive 'contents analyst' of literary works, for to him what brought everything together was form. His criticism rescued cultural forms from the formalists and discovered in them structures of social relations, histories of technological possibility, precipitations of whole socially determined ways of seeing. He could trace a change of ideological perception in a shift in stage technique, or detect the rhythms of urbanization in the very syntax of a Victorian novel.

Williams had, I think, an unusually strong sense of himself as an historical figure. If he could be aware of the massive importance of his own work without the least personal vanity, it was in part because he had a curious ability to look on himself from the outside, to see his own life as in a Lukácsian sense 'typical' rather than just individual. He lived everything he did from the inside, saturating his thought with personal experience; yet he also seemed able to place himself impersonally, judiciously, as 'an ordinary life, spanning the middle years of the twentieth century' (*Modern Tragedy*, p. 13). That he was at once ordinary and exceptional was one of the many paradoxes about him. Though he was personally the most generous and humble of men, with a warmth so radiant as to be almost tangible, it was perhaps this 'historicity' which helped more than anything to divide him from his colleagues. They were individual dons, working on this or that; his work was an historic project, of an intensely personal yet strangely impersonal kind. He had a quite extraordinary sense of the overall consistency of that work, and of the life in which it was rooted. He lived his life deliberately, vigilantly, as a committed act or coherent task. Others may write a book or two or even twenty, but Williams was engaged on a different sort of enterprise altogether. You had the strong sense that it would have got done somehow whether he was an academic or not; what some left academics sometimes like to feign – that they are merely passing through the system, dipping in and out, fundamentally detached – was in his case oddly true, even though he spent most of his working life as a Cambridge Fellow. He didn't need to apologize for being a don, in some access of radical guilt, because it was palpably obvious that that was not at all the centre from which he lived. As far as the dons went, he was quite evidently not their kind of man, which sometimes bemused the well-intentioned and estranged the politically hostile even further. He assumed his place in Cambridge naturally, with dignity, as though he had a right to it, which of course he did; it was somewhere to carry on the work, and he didn't waste time complaining about the incongruities which that brought in its wake. He had the well-nigh universal respect of his colleagues, but not their collaboration; his collaborator from first to last was Joy Williams, 'virtual co-author' of *Culture and Society* as he writes in the preface to that book. The most intense intellectual partnership, and the deepest sharing of personal life and love, would for Williams naturally go together.

Almost single-handedly, he transformed cultural studies from the relative crudity in which he found them to a marvellously rich, resourceful body of work. In doing so, he altered irreversibly the intellectual and political map of Britain, and put hundreds of thousands of students and colleagues and readers enduringly in his debt. He could do this because he never relinquished his belief in the utter centrality of what he liked to call 'meanings and values'. He fought all his life against various left-wing reductions or displacements of these things, and believed that language and communication were where we lived, not just what we used to live. In this sense, he had held all along what some others on the left came gradually to discover sometime later, through Gramsci or discourse theory or psychoanalysis or the 'politics of the subject'. And then, just when everyone else had caught up with him and was busy pressing this case to an idealist extreme, he turned on his heel and began to speak of material modes of cultural production, of the social institutions of writing, of – in a word – cultural materialism. He had got there before us again, as he would no doubt have done several times more, if his premature death had not taken him from us and left us impoverished and bereft.

This book was first conceived as a tribute to a man who was then still alive, in the midst of writing a major novel (*People of the Black Mountains*) in which, one imagines, his theoretical and fictional interests had finally converged totally into a single work. This present book, sadly, has now been turned into a memorial volume. Most of the essays were written while Raymond Williams was still alive, and there seemed no need to invite the contributors to revise their essays in the light of his death. The present tense of the collection, so to speak, testifies to the many ways in which he is still with us. Like all editors I have my regrets, and my deepest one is that Raymond Williams cannot now contribute the Afterword to this symposium which he was eager to write. He followed the development of the book with keen interest, and made a number of valuable suggestions which I have taken up. I also regret the absence from the volume of one or two of Williams's key associates, such as his close friend and political comrade E. P. Thompson, and the former editor of *New Left Review*, Perry Anderson. These and a few others were unable to write because of other commitments. I am sorry also that there are only two women contributors; several other women were requested to write, but for one reason or another felt unable to do so at the time. A full feminist engagement with Williams's work is thus still to come, as one of the most pressing projects he has left us.

The essays here range widely over diverse areas of Williams's writing, from politics, drama and Wales to fiction and cultural theory and from more personal to more theoretical reflections. One of the contributors, Edward Said, has chosen to honour Williams by writing on a literary and political topic close to his interests, rather than commenting directly on his work. I am particularly grateful to Robin Gable for his devoted labours in producing the photographic essay on Williams, and for the generous cooperation of Joy Williams and others in making this project possible. I am also indebted to Alan O'Connor for allowing me to use a selection from his admirably well-researched bibliography of Williams's writings, the first, to my knowledge, to have been completed. The full bibliography will appear in O'Connor's forthcoming book on Williams from Basil Blackwell.

In the absence of a Postscript from Williams himself, the volume itself may stand as an afterword to him, whose words will continue to have a rich afterlife in the generations to come.

---

*A fuller word of explanation is perhaps in order here. I do not mean to suggest that all of the theoretical developments of this period were by any means cul-de-sacs; and Williams himself, while sharply critical of some of them, drew valuably on others. That his own work benefited from the flowering of a Marxist culture in the 1970s, even when it found itself at odds with some of those currents, is, I think, indisputable. My own critique of Williams's work in *Criticism and Ideology* grew out of those new trends, and was felt by some to be unjust or even faintly scandalous. This was not, for the record, Williams's own view. While dissenting from some of my criticisms, he concurred with others – a logical response from a thinker whose work was in continual evolution, who could himself be astringently critical of some of his own earlier positions, and who welcomed vigorous argument rather than obedient discipleship. Some of those who generously leapt to his defence at the time, or who still do so, are thus perhaps not entirely at one with his own more shaded, self-critical attitude. I would still defend many of the criticisms I made of Williams's work in *Criticism and Ideology*, though I would advance them today in a more nuanced style, and in a different tone. Some of my formulations, in the struggle to distance myself critically from a body of work which had meant more to me than almost any other, were unacceptably acerbic and ungenerous, and for these I apologize.

1

RAYMOND WILLIAMS AND THE 'TWO FACES OF MODERNISM'

—— Tony Pinkney ——

'He lives in Llanidloes or in Europe, I can't remember which'

The Fight for Manod

'Perhaps the only English [sic] Marxist able to hold his own with his continental peers'; 'no English comparison is even remotely relevant ... must be referred for comparative assessment to the aesthetic production of a Lukács, Benjamin or Goldmann'; 'fully the equal and in some crucial respects the superior of [his] counterparts elsewhere in Europe'.[1] Such claims, even where they remain no more than gestural, are by now almost mandatory in any discussion of Raymond Williams's work; and the purpose of this essay is to test out the most familiar of these continental comparisons in relation to the question of artistic modernism – which is where it seems to me to have had its most distorting effect. However, since (as the Oriental proverb has it) you use one axe handle to hew another, I shall close not with a raw and unmediated Williams but with yet another Western Marxist metaphor, another European 'as if', which may more adequately register the scope, nature and inner logic of Williams's achievement.

The 'English' or British Lukács: the phrase has been invoked often enough, and has even up to a point been endorsed by Williams himself – 'I feel very close in approach to Lukács over the realist novel' (*Politics and Letters*, p.349). The comparison usually serves to buttress a critique of Williams's 'provincialism', both spatial and temporal: an excessive attachment to British as against European literary traditions, an excessive attachment to the nineteenth-century realist novel as against its modernist successors. Williams's notably un-Lukácsian enthusiasm for Joyce is noted, but as a minor quirk, perhaps a marginal gesture of Celtic solidarity; it is not allowed essentially to interrogate the overall account of his cultural nostalgia. Alike in their constructions (or constrictions) of the history of the novel, both Williams and Lukács are found wanting in the eyes of what we might term British Brechtianism; yet of the two, Williams is the less 'guilty'. For Lukács to have been Lukács required a perverse self-distantiation from the turbulent cultural energies and experiments of early twentieth-century Europe, a gruesome and self-inflicted lobotomy of the spirit. But for Williams to have been Lukács was much more in the natural order of things; his supposed provincialism is then the inevitable consequence, or expression in miniature, of the general British parochialism around him.

To dub Williams the 'British Lukács' is simultaneously, if implicitly, to project an interpretation of the literary culture of the 1930s from which he emerged – a reading of the decade which we are now becoming able to see as a drastically partial one. The case has been argued, with characteristic trenchancy, by Terry Eagleton, who in his *Walter Benjamin* paints in broad brush strokes the literary-historical 'infrastructure' of the powerful account of Williams in *Criticism and Ideology*. Sketching some of the 'astonishing moments' of avant-gardiste activity in post-revolutionary Russia and Weimar Germany, Eagleton notes, by way of contrast, that:

> To those who inquire what was happening in England while the European *avant-garde* was at its height, it might be suggestive to reply that we had E. M. Forster. The English surrealist movement, which appears to have flourished and died somewhere around summer 1936, is one index of English culture's relative impermeability to such trends.

If there wasn't an English avant-garde, nor, by much the same token, was there ever really an English modernism. What there was of it is, on this showing, 'mostly a foreign implantation', occurring in such 'peculiarly ephemeral, marginalized and reactionary form' that we would do better to speak of 'the missed moment of modernism'. And 'by the 1930s, with Auden and Orwell, realism was firmly back in the saddle'. So it is that, in this cultural desert, the Marxist critics of the 1930s, 'taken together with Williams for this purpose alone ... may be described in a rough sense as the English equivalent of Lukács'.[2]

But though such an answer is indeed 'suggestive', is it dialectical? Or does it not rather, in so vigorously propounding a necessary part-truth about this cultural phase, risk obscuring its full complexity – and indeed richness? Should we not on principle be wary of an account which unwittingly dovetails with the dominant culture's *own* dismissal of the literary radicalism of the 1930s – all the way from Auden's 'low dishonest decade' onwards? We now have two specific advantages over the 'men of 1968' (to adapt Wyndham Lewis's phrase) who first opened the debate in the pages of *New Left Review* about the significance of Williams's work and, more generally, the availability of native socialist intellectual resources.

First, a diminished 'anxiety of influence', at least in relation to Williams himself – less of a need to diminish the 'Europeanism' of this commanding precursor so that our own should burn the more brightly. Second, a welter of new historical evidence. As we move through the fiftieth anniversaries of all the great struggles of the 1930s, there has been a spate of memoir-writing and autobiographical reminiscence (some of it from Williams himself) which demands a revaluation of the radical culture of the decade and of the view that anything like a 'British Lukács' could emerge from it.

The fact that English modernism is largely the product of expatriates, of 'exiles and emigrés', has sometimes been offered as evidence of how little it 'took' in the culture at large. But, as Raymond Williams has recently reminded us in *Culture*, there is nothing exceptional about this situation, which is neither a 'missed moment' nor a freakish 'peculiarity of the English' but rather the very condition of possibility of modernism as such. Certain facets of avant-garde culture have, Williams contends,

> to be analysed not only in formal terms but within the sociology of metropolitan encounters and associations between immigrants who share no common language but that of the metropolis and whose other (including visual) received sign-systems have become distanced or irrelevant. This would be a traceable social factor within the often noted innovations in attitudes to language and to the received visual significance of objects.[3]

Eagleton himself has more recently tended to see the expatriatism of 'English' modernism as a socially generalizable phenomenon.[4] But if 'colonial modernism' is indeed premised upon experiences of dislocation, exile, deracination, then might we not have expected the young Raymond Williams – eighteen year-old Welsh immigrant in ruling-class Cambridge – to gravitate instinctively towards *it*, rather than to the more settled, if not positively monumental, forms of Lukácsian realism? In *Politics and Letters* Williams declares himself a 'Welsh European', evoking experientially exactly the linkages between regional rootedness and epochal cosmopolitanism, marginality and modernism, the 'less' and the 'more' of the individual nation-state, that he has theorized elsewhere. His interviewers, themselves men of 1968, seem surprised by the fluency and ease of the transactions possible within the 'border country' of such colonial modernism: 'Your father's politics grew in a very direct sense out of his immediate work experience and family situation. Yet from what you have been saying it seems that much of the pressure and focus of your teenage politics was international.' And Williams confirms this assessment: 'to us international actions were much more involving and interesting' (*PL*, p. 32). Indeed, he suggests that *New Left Review's* attempt to return his father's commitments to 'immediate experience' is itself reductive, narrowing politics to phenomenology. For in Williams's account of his boyhood rural community 'the railwaymen were a modernizing element' (*PL*, p. 24). The railways for him retain, some seventy years on, all that turbulent, transformative, liberatory but also ambivalent dynamism which they had in those famous pages of Dickens's *Dombey and Son* which he cites at length in *The English Novel* as a major instance of 'the mobility, the critical mobility, which was altering the novel'.[5] The signalmen in particular are not plumped full with the positivity of a settled, Hoggartian working class (as the *New Left Review* interviewers suggest), but are rather the 'empty', busy nodes of some great communications network, Saussurean signs that are constituted by differences rather than positive terms: 'they talked for hours to each other on the telephone – to boxes as far away as Swindon or Crewe ... they were in touch with a much wider social network, and were bringing modern politics into the village' (*PL*, p. 24). If much of Williams's work has evoked the values of a traditional rural community as a critique of the atomized *Gesellschaft* of contemporary capitalism, we must none the less also insist that, at least in relation to the railways of his childhood, he evinces a well-nigh Futurist exhilaration in mechanical power and mobility (Matthew Price, in *Border Country*, has at one point to 'recover slowly from the power of the train'). And the railway itself is a metaphor for the more general problematic (non-)identity of the 'border country', since 'there was a curious sense in which we could speak of both Welsh and English as foreigners, as "not us"' (*PL*, p. 26). Cut away from both national and nationalist identities, the lines of communication were open from the most locally intimate and rooted experiences to the most internationalist dimensions of contemporary reality. A curious image of this is Williams's encounter with the Soviet pavilion at the Paris International Exhibition of 1937. The symbol of international revolution, 'a massive sculpture of a man and woman with a hammer and sickle on top of it', reaches directly into the linguistic immediacies of the home community, bypassing the disinfected, distancing nomenclature of the metropolis: 'I kept saying: "What is a sickle?" – I had used the damned thing and we called it a hook' (*PL*, p. 38).

If, then, we can locate a predisposition to modernism on the side of the subject, if the young Raymond Williams would have, actively and in a sense against the grain, to *become* Lukács rather than being born with a realist spoon in his mouth, so too can we trace such a predisposition on the side of the object– particularly in the radical student and working-class cultures of the 1930s. For the modernist or avant-garde options were certainly available, as potent living cultural traditions, to be seized and developed. Recent memoirs of the late 1920s and early 1930s have revealed to us far more various, adventurous and cosmopolitan a culture than the depressing myths of a 'return' to a decent native realism allow for; not everyone was a Larkin *avant la lettre*. Here, for instance, is James Klugmann, Communist Party member and Modern Languages student in the Cambridge of the early 1930s:

> the journey to Berlin, study in Germany, cultural visits and so on, were second only to the journey to Moscow ... The ideological influence of the revolutionary or

rebel culture was very deep and wide, whether it was in painting, drama or other fields. Names like Brecht, Tucholsky, Kaiser and Toller I remember especially, because I had studied German at university and was a great addict of German expressionist theatre. There was a little theatre club down Villiers Street by Charing Cross station, the Gate Theatre, where I used to go, and then there was the Festival Theatre in Cambridge. These were things we hung on to, and which influenced us tremendously, and warmly and well.[6]

If the Cambridge student body had thus jettisoned its genteel Bloomsbury heritage ('we had E. M. Forster'), so too did dissident students at Oxford round angrily upon the classicist, Arnoldian traditions of their own university. At the very moment when, in Julian Benda's La Trahison des Clercs, Arnoldian ideals of disinterestedness received a powerful European restatement (thereafter becoming a crucial element of the Scrutiny synthesis), the young W. H. Auden announced: 'I knew no German and no German literature, but I felt out of sympathy with French culture, partly by temperament and partly in revolt against the generation immediately preceding mine, which was strongly Francophile.'[7] He then set off to Weimar Berlin, the 'bugger's daydream', in the footsteps of Christopher Isherwood. Auden saw an early performance of The Threepenny Opera and studied Brecht's poetry; Isherwood declared that 'the films were the most interesting in Europe.'[8] The fruits of such enthusiasm included Auden's Dance of Death, produced by the left-inclining avant-garde Group Theatre and which Williams describes in Drama from Ibsen to Eliot as 'exciting to English audiences in its use of various expressionist techniques which are always well suited to satire', and the Auden–Isherwood collaboration, The Ascent of F6 (1936), which in Williams's view shows 'the very direct influence of Toller'.[9]

Nor did you necessarily have to make the journey to Berlin to gain access to the radical and other modernisms of the 1920s and 1930s. Literary expressionism made its way over as the Muirs indefatigably translated Kafka throughout the 1930s; works by Edward Upward and Rex Warner register his presence, in a tense novelistic dialogue. In the non-commercial theatre, Expressionism was also a potent force. Ashley Dukes's version of Kaiser's From Morn to Midnight 'played a vital role in the little theatre movement in England, particularly the Stage Society and the Gate Theatre'; and Toller's presence was even more commanding, for 'by the mid-thirties all of [his] major works were available in translation. His plays were enthusiastically reviewed in the journals, and were pointed out as a "stimulating model for the young dramatist"' in the Criterion in July 1936.[10] And Expressionism's more politicized successors were not far behind. Herbert Marshall of Unity Threatre had studied in Moscow with Eisenstein and Meyerhold, and André van Gyseghem spent a year there under the auspices of the International Union of Revolutionary Theatre, of which Erwin Piscator was then director. The many private film societies (set up to beat the political censorship) were a major inlet for both the German and Soviet avant-gardes: Pabst's film of

The Threepenny Opera and *Kuhle Wampe* were shown by the London Film Society in 1931-2, and the works of Eisenstein, Pudovkin and others were shown repeatedly up and down the country. In 1933 three productions of the Brecht/Weill ballet *Seven Deadly Sins* were given at the Savoy Theatre, as was a single performance of *Mahagonny*; even the BBC broadcast an English version of *The Threepenny Opera* in 1935. By 1936 theoretical writings by Brecht had begun to appear in *Life and Letters Today* and *Left Review*, and his *Senor Carrara's Rifles* was performed by Unity Theatre in 1938. As Williams himself acknowledges, discussing Brecht in *Politics and Letters*, 'if you care to look back there were ways of knowing about his work, if distant and specialized ones' (215-16).[11]

Not, however, as distant and specialized as all that. For as the German emigration intensified, many avant-garde artists turned up in person in England, for longer or shorter periods. Brecht was in London in late 1934, where he made contact with the Group Theatre, and again in 1936, staying at van Gyseghem's flat and meeting members of the GPO film unit (including, it seems, W. H. Auden). So too did Ernst Toller turn up in England, where he persuaded both Auden and Spender to translate his work. Nor was the influx confined to literature. In 1934 Walter Gropius, Marcel Breuer and Eric Mendelsohn arrived in London as refugees; László Moholy-Nagy joined them in 1935, Naum Gabo and Mondrian in 1938. In that same year the Belgian surrealist E. L. T. Mesens also arrived here to play a crucial role in the fortunes of English surrealism, a movement which lasted not – *pace* Eagleton – for a single summer, but from 1935, when David Gascoyne drew up a manifesto of English surrealism and published his *A Short Survey of Surrealism* (whose entire first printing sold out in a few months), to 1944 when, as its best recent historian concludes, 'the movement in England, for a number of reasons, was moribund'.[12] Once again, the men of 1968 have downplayed the significance of this modernist emigration. Perry Anderson's powerful account of the 'White' emigration to England in his 'Components of the National Culture' is the pre-eminent example of this, bleaching the culture clean of a 'red' cosmopolitanism so that *New Left Review's* own European orientation arises, splendidly autonomous and unfathered, in the 1960s. But even when the English sojourns of the Reds and modernists were indeed – in Anderson's phrase – 'brief and obscure' (and they were by no means always so), they were often pregnant with consequences for a subsequent native modernism.[13]

In his most recent discussion of Raymond Williams in *The Function of Criticism*, Terry Eagleton acknowledges the rich diversity of the radical working-class culture of the 1930s, its constitution of a proletarian 'counter-public sphere.' The contrast between Weimar Germany and Britain is now less painfully stark: the proletarian 'theatres and choral societies, clubs and newspapers, recreation centres and social forums' of the former are now counterposed, not to E. M. Forster, but to British '*agitprop* groups, the Unity theatre, the Workers'

Film and Photo League, the Workers' Theatre Movement, workplace branches of
the Left Book Club, the London Workers' Film Society and a range of other
institutions'.[14] But the account is too brief to dispel the lingering assumption
that, politically admirable though such a counter-culture may indeed have been,
its aesthetic practices are dourly Orwellian or Audenesque, with realism firmly
back in the native saddle. In fact, however, the radical modernist experimentation
I have sketched above was never confined to small circles of Oxbridge or
metropolitan intellectuals but rather – in a series of interchanges near
unimaginable in our own 'mass-cultural' days – found its base within the popular
radical movement. A few instances only must suffice here. The works of Kaiser
and Toller were a standard part of the repertoire of the proletarian theatre, as
were the expressionistic dramas of Eugene O'Neill. Ken Worpole, in a brilliant
piece of literary-historical excavation, has demonstrated the existence of a
vigorous line of Expressionist experiment in native working-class fiction in the
1930s.[15] The labour movement found access to Brecht less 'distant and
specialized' than did the young Raymond Williams: in March 1936 several
performances of *Die Massnahme* were given by the London Labour Choral
Union, and the Workers' Music Association published the scores of Brecht/Eisler
songs for performance by its members. Intellectuals and workers alike clamoured
to see the films of Eisenstein *et al.* – a conjunction symbolized, say, by the
Scottish USSR Society, with its large working-class following, and the New Art
Cinema Movement joining forces in Glasgow in 1932 to organize a season of
Soviet films. Even surrealism achieved something like a mass base in – of all
places – the Mass-Observation movement. This movement, which might have
seemed to be the most grimly 'factist' of all the decade's projects, was organized
by the English surrealist Charles Madge, and was conceived of by him (if not by
all the rest of his colleagues) as 'a symbology of the mass-unconscious', a
technique for unleashing 'the surreal content of ordinary minds'.[16]

It was into this very culture I have been evoking – combative, cosmopolitan,
experimental, eclectic, modernist and avant-garde by turns – that the young
Raymond Williams was inducted by what he later terms 'the intense subculture
of CUSC' (Cambridge University Socialist Club). If a 'British Lukács' was here
already in the making, no-one, it seems, had bothered to alert Williams himself to
that fact:

> our interests were very much more in modernism ... by the second year Joyce was
> without question the most important author for us. *Ulysses* and *Finnegans Wake* –
> which had just appeared in 1939 – were the texts we most admired, and we
> counterposed to socialist realism ... But our modernism was not by any means
> defined in exclusively literary terms. We were also drawn to surrealism, especially in
> the cinema. We thought that Vigo was quite as interesting as Pudovkin or
> Eisenstein – whom we anyway interpreted quite unorthodoxly. Jazz was another
> form that was important to us (*PL* pp. 45–6)

In an earlier essay in *My Cambridge* Williams underlines the cultural centrality of avant-garde cinema: 'more than anything else the films. Virtually the entire sub-culture was filmic. Eisenstein and Pudovkin but also Vigo and Flaherty . . . .'[17] Later in *Politics and Letters* he adds the name of German Expressionism to the litany, since 'in the late thirties admiration for *Dr Caligari* or *Metropolis* was virtually a condition of entry to the Socialist Club at Cambridge' (*PL* p. 232). Drawn into the orbit of these various experimentalisms, the young Williams affiliated himself to the group termed the 'Aesthetes' within CUSC and contributed to its journal, *Outlook*: 'we consciously represented a cultural stance in opposition to what we by then would call "party attitudes" to literature – which we criticized as narrow and stuffy' (*PL* p. 46). Nor was this Cambridge subculture only determinant upon Williams for a couple of buoyant undergraduate years; immediately after the war, too, 'I was still attempting to maintain the productive cultural emphasis of the thirties' (*PL*, p. 64). Its strong internationalism clearly shaped the work of a man whose memories of his English Tripos sometimes seem to consist entirely of the works of Henrik Ibsen. His post-war practical and theoretical interests in film obviously stem directly from it; the research that went into *Drama from Ibsen to Brecht* was very specifically an attempt to return to and think through the late nineteenth- and early twentieth-century roots of the mixed avant-gardisms of the late 1930s; and, on a slightly different tack, there seems a strong, perhaps direct, carry over in both substance and tone from the wartime crisis that broke German Expressionism's early Fauvist exhilaration in the non-representational use of colour and turned it into the sombre, tormented thing of its major phase, and that post-war crisis which turned Williams himself from brash, youthful modernist into the more problematic, troubled, evasive self of his later writings.

But if there are – even when registered in this somewhat impressionistic fashion – strong continuities between pre-war British radical modernism and post-war Raymond Williams, we then need to enquire how it was that the 'British Lukács' tag could come to seem not just an interesting heuristic comparison (which it is), but an almost blindingly self-evident and final – and often dismissive – account of this intellectual project. The answer, of course, is over-determined, and I shall tease out various strands of it as this essay proceeds: it is a complex mixture of plausible and less creditable motivations, in which a Bloomian desire to diminish a commanding precursor plays a not insignificant part. One of its major strategies, however, can be outlined at once. Make *Culture and Society* and *The Long Revolution* take a backward somersault over and behind *Drama from Ibsen to Eliot* and *Preface to Film*, implicitly reverse the order of their composition and publication in the very structure of one's discussion of Williams, and you magically produce a deeply-rooted native social theorist, as 'essentially English' (in that key Leavisite phrase) as the very intellectual lineage he discusses, but whose quaint, engaging, marginal hobby is collecting twentieth-century dramatists – which might indeed as well be butterflies, postage stamps or silver teaspoons for all the bearing they have upon his general social concerns. This is the approach silently adopted in *Politics and Letters* (II. Culture, III. Drama), in Eagleton's *Criticism and Ideology*, where the early work on drama 'could not carry him very far, could not touch the specificity of what he sought', and in J. P. Ward's 'Writers of Wales' monograph, where it emerges as an explicit principle; we are there informed, extraordinarily, that 'it seems best to see [the] two books of dramatic criticism as part of the second period.'[18] Such manoeuvres are presumably truthful enough as it were phenomenologically, since most of us will have encountered Williams's work first in the social criticism and then, under the potent spell of that, have turned to the earlier dramatic writings. But given that so many of the 'men of 1968' have assailed Williams for the limitations of his *Scrutiny*-inspired insistence on the 'lived', on 'felt thought' and immediate experience, there seems peculiarly little excuse for their projection of their own biographies as readers as the innermost structural secret of his oeuvre itself.

If then – and this is the essential wager of this essay – we take *Drama from Ibsen to Eliot* and *Preface to Film* as definitive of the early Williams, how does the comparison with Lukács fare? And moreover how, in the light of this shift of emphasis, will it stand up in relation to even those parts of Williams's later writings where it does indeed seem to have a *prima facie* plausibility? One ground for the comparison is a certain shared lofty equanimity of *tone*, which is a matter of having been born – like little Father Time in *Jude the Obscure* – already old; one tends to forget, remark the *New Left Review* interviewers of *Culture and Society*, 'that it is actually a young man's book' (*PL* p. 98), and this remark could certainly be extended to the earlier writings, where it would be even more acutely the case. Such mouthfilling Olympianism is, it is implied, the equivalent at the level of prose texture of Williams's supposed predilection for novelistic realism at large; he writes much as George Eliot narrates, and nothing could be more removed from the nimble, swift-moving, busily aphoristic styles of a Benjamin or an Adorno. Yet all accounts of Williams's style or tone have registered an essential contradiction: its measured public stance is shot through with obscure private resonances and impulses, which it only just holds in place. Terry Eagleton best captures this sense, in a wonderful page of *Criticism and Ideology* that verges on pastiche or parody of its object: 'what appears at first glance the inert language of academicism in in fact the stage of a personal drama ... a style which in the very act of assuming an unruffled, almost Olympian impersonality displays itself (not least in its spiralling modifications) as edgily defensive, private and self-absorbed.' And J. P. Ward analogously registers 'the tension in *Border Country* ... as though the whole would burst apart if the author had one lapse in concentration'.[19] In *Politics and Letters* Williams elaborates candidly on the crisis of personal and political breakdown and withdrawal within which these early works were written: 'when I was working on European drama after the war, in a very disturbed condition, I really did feel as I was reading that my life was being put in question' (*PL* p. 332). Nothing, in the event, could be further than Williams's prose from the lucid, disinterested, 'Attic' utterances of the realist narrator which, in a founding transcendental gesture, have bracketed out emotional disturbance and turbulence, even *substance*, which are thereafter the soiled, grimy, inferior possessions of the characters alone.

It could perhaps be shown that Lukács's style too is less suavely self-possessed than it would like to think itself, but we need, in Williams's case, to relate the formal disturbances of the prose to the explicit critical judgements articulated in it – which are consonant with that disturbance and decidedly *anti*-Lukácsian. With the advantage of historical retrospect, we can see that *Drama from Ibsen to Eliot* intervenes in two critical debates, neither of which it could have been fully aware of at the time of writing. Completed in 1948, the book was published in 1952 – the same year as Donald Davie's *Purity of Diction in English Verse*. Davie's book was the first full-length theorization of the rejection of Anglo-American modernism already practically under way in the early writings of 'the Movement': it saw the modernist stress on defamiliarizing metaphor, on 'making it new', as leading directly (in Pound above all) to the irrationalism of Fascist politics, and called for a resumption of Arnoldian disinterestedness and Augustan civility. The case against modernism was then prosecuted with even more vigour and precision by Frank Kermode in *The Romantic Image* (1957), which attacked the elitism of the Symbol and demanded – in a curiously Williams-like phrase – that poetry now acknowledge 'the commonalty of the means of discourse'.[20] Williams's own book, with its bold defence of the dramatic experiments of Yeats and Eliot as a necessary break with naturalism, thus constitutes a rejoinder *avant la lettre* to such arguments, and evinces a commitment to modernism so strong as to refuse to make – at least at the time of writing, for Williams has since recanted in *Politics and Letters* – essential cultural-political distinctions within it.

But Anglo-American modernism is not the only hero of *Drama from Ibsen to Eliot*, just as Davie and Kermode are not its only 'antagonists'. 'It is very common, in England,' Williams writes, 'to be patronising about the expressionist experiment, and to remind readers that it was mainly *German* expressionism, which presumably settles its inferiority' – but these are not judgements in which he is prepared easily to concur. In this displaced way, then, the book engages the great Expressionism debates of the 1930s, and displays the 'British Lukács' assiduously eluding in advance the labels his critics would seek to attach to him some twenty years later. This is true first of all at the level of critical method. Far from constructing a Lukácsian 'ideal type' of which the actual texts then seem so many derivative and uninteresting instances, Williams insists, with Leavis looking over his shoulder, on the specificity of the individual work, the need for close 'practical criticism', in relation to which overall generic judgements can never be more than tentative and provisional. None the less, he has some substantial generic judgements to make. Ibsen's *When We Dead Awaken* and Strindberg's *Road to Damascus*, for example, are not degenerate naturalist plays, whose inferiority is to be attributed to authorial weariness or insanity, but positive and powerful instances of a major new mode: 'Ibsen has here written what came to be called an expressionist play', Strindberg has effected a 'complete rejection of the representational stage for a kaleidoscope of imaged expressionist themes'. In Williams's account of Toller, Expressionism is rescued from charges of subjectivism and psychic extremism – 'the landmarks of expressionist theatre are primarily social plays' – and pronounced 'a real attempt at vitality and seriousness'.[21] Certainly Williams has his reservations, about the occasional externality of expressionist devices of spectacle and its relative devaluation of dramatic speech, but these are only qualifications within a deep overall endorsement. It is worth noting that in rewriting these passages for later editions of the drama book, Williams tends to downgrade the reservations and upgrade the statements of Expressionist achievement.

This radically anti-Lukácsian view of the matter is reinforced in *Preface to Film*. At first sight, however, the book seems to afford an opportunity to *extend* the Lukács–Williams comparison, to flesh it out with still more detail. For Williams here is as nostalgic for the integrated totalities of ancient Greek civilization as was the author of *Theory of the Novel*; he ruefully counterposes the integrated tragedies of classical Athens to the dire dissociation of sensibility, 'this very separation into distinct forms', of our dramatic modernity. Yet the Lukács parallel here bizarrely inverts itself into its opposite. The answer to the alarming autonomization of the components of the drama is not to reinvent the lost epic unity in the realist novel or its naturalist theatrical counterparts; the latter, indeed, are precisely part of the problem. Evoking the ideal of 'total expression' (which already secretly announces where the answer is to be found), Williams discovers the Greeks of our time to be, ironically, the Goths: 'The kind of film which has most nearly realized the ideal of a wholly conceived drama, in which action, movement and design bear a continuous and necessary vital relationship, is the German expressionist film of the twenties.'[22] Again there are significant qualifications to be made, but these are not remotely comparable to Lukács's wholesale writing-off of the Expressionist phenomenon. In *Politics and Letters* Williams is equally forthright in declaring his aesthetic predilections in this period, when 'my own thinking was derived from the cinema of the twenties' (*PL*, p. 233).

I don't want to deny the pertinence of the Lukács comparison, but merely to insist that it needs a much more complex and differentiated analysis than it usually receives. A British Lukács would have to be *made*, not born, and that active process of making would always be far from complete, never involving more than a partial rupture with 'my friends the modernists' (*PL*, p. 385) and always the bearer – in my view – of other and more fundamental anxieties. The first major emergence of the Lukácsian problematic in Williams's work is the chapter on 'Realism and the Contemporary Novel' in *The Long Revolution* – a book which is prepared to dismiss Expressionism, for the first time, as 'this always potentially opaque form'. The realist totality, integrating the social and the individual, splits apart, leaving us with the abstract extremes of the novel of exacerbated individual sensibility and the novel governed by a social formula, *Mrs. Dalloway* and *Brave New World*; it is a classic Lukácsian schema. Only, as we have seen, Raymond Williams never *had* been a realist in the first place; it is the split itself which preoccupies him, not some putative realist unity which has come unravelled. Tolstoyan harmony is only a provisional heuristic device whereby we can take a first set of bearings on the new tensions and transitions of modernist culture itself. And these first bearings – neat to the point of glibness – are by no means Williams's final ones, which we must now elucidate.

The crisis is not a matter *internal* to modernism, with Zola and Mallarmé or Huxley and Woolf confronting each other stonily across a great divide, but concerns its relation to social reality at large. Modernism only 'splits' when post-war capitalism appropriates whole dimensions of it as the very mode of its own existence; even those elements which it does not confiscate then also mutate decisively. Williams has written of the 'glossy futurism' of the 'stylish consumer society which would be the new form of capitalism'; and Richard Hoggart, lamenting the loss of the traditional working-class community in *The Uses of Literacy*, fulminated against 'the shallower aspects of modernism', 'the nastiness of their modernistic knick-knacks', the 'cheap gum-chewing pert glibness and streamlining' of the new consumerism.[23] Once the exhilarating dynamism of modernist culture is incorporated in these ways, packaged within and *as* the sex appeal of the commodity rather than being – as originally with Italian Futurism – the Dionysiac social energies that would sweep away bourgeoisie, utilitarian calculation, commodities and all, so too does the function of the modernist rump, expressionist rather than futurist, also change, naturalizing and ontologizing those experiences of alienation, breakdown and non-communication which it had once critically presented. In *Culture* Williams wryly notes 'the contradictory character of the history of the avant-garde movements', as their 'sharp and even violent breaks with received and traditional practices' become 'the dominant culture of a succeeding metropolitan and paranational period'. In *Towards 2000* he extends the analysis, seeing the grounds of the eventual containment of modernism as lying in its original social conditions of possibility – the negative freedoms and new technical media of the great metropolitan centres.[24] Yet this most recent account tends to neglect the role of 'consumer modernism' and to paint the modernisms of the turn of the century as homogeneously doom-laden and angst-ridden. Williams speaks of the two 'faces' of modernism – its original critical charge and its subsequent rationalizing and ontologizing mutation – infelicitously using a synchronic term to cover a diachronic process. It would, however, be more precise to designate two 'phases' of modernism, *each* of which contains two 'faces' (Futurist and Expressionist, consumerist and ontologizing). For the second face of the second phase, Williams has reserved his most Lukácsian invective, speaking in *Politics and Letters* of 'a period of really decadent bourgeois writing in which the whole status of human beings is reduced' (*PL*, p. 392).

As modernism mutates under the pressures of post-war capitalism, so it splits the working class in its wake: 'an internal division in the working class was occurring, separating the politically and industrially active sectors of it from the rest of the class' (PL, p. 286). If this split sounds uncannily like the fissure that is presumed to have afflicted the realist novel, it is no accident that one of Williams's earliest attempts to evoke it, in an account of that 'structure of feeling' in contemporary working-class consciousness whereby 'a displacement of class relations from their necessary centrality' led 'to a curious mixture of a certain real unloosening and a particular style of consumption, which was itself merely a shift in the market' (PL, p. 173), should have come in Part Three of *The Long Revolution*, which immediately follows the analysis of 'Realism and the Contemporary Novel'. If the Lukácsian doctrine is at one level a rather desperate clutching for some stable literary model, however regressive, as the modernism which is much more the stuff of Williams's cultural being enters a disturbing and not immediately focusable new phase, it also constitutes a code whereby to ponder, in displaced fashion, the dislocations that are afflicting but also partly liberating the post-war working class. The realist totality becomes the secret utopian home of a comprehensive proletarian activism which no longer exists as such. From now on, certainly, the rhetoric of realist revival becomes a substantial component of Williams's work, and gives the Lukács-minded comparativists the evidence they need to press home their case.

Three caveats need immediately to be entered, however. First, Williams has on the whole spoken of the necessity to resume the realist *project*, rather than the realist novel *tout court* – and this broader formulation allows substantial technical and formal licence. The term can indeed, on occasion, contain within itself great swathes of modernism itself, as when Williams argues that 'to realize the full possibility of the naturalist project, as a new secular view of personal character and social relationships, drama had to move on to other forms' (PL, p. 205). This argument is, moreover, a precise analogue of the case advanced by the modernistic Aesthetes group in the Cambridge Socialist Club of the 1930s, since 'we would probably have denied that we were against socialist realism. We would have claimed that much more complex and dynamic techniques were needed for it than those which were officially recommended' (PL, p. 46). Secondly, just as Williams's public mode of address is infiltrated by subterranean currents of anger, anxiety and crisis, so too do some of his most 'Lukácsian' productions reveal, on closer inspection, strangely wayward impulses at work. The Dickens of *The English Novel from Dickens to Lawrence* is not only a prodigious totalizer, but a major Expressionist precursor, effecting 'a breakthrough in the novel from which those other novelists of cities – Dostoyevsky and Kafka are the most immediate names – in their own ways learned'.[25] The George Eliot Williams here values is not the serenely capacious *Middlemarch*, but the more uneven early novels. Discussing his book in *Politics and Letters*, he specifically rejects form 'perceived only in a rather integrated classicist sense', which we might have expected a

British Lukács precisely to have clung to, and declares his allegiance to 'the formally disturbed novels of early George Eliot or the essentially confused forms of Dickens's novels' or the 'bad writing' of Thomas Hardy (*PL*, p. 264) – all of which we might well be inclined to see as versions of historical Expressionism. Moreover, there is a recurrent tendency in Williams's discussions of realism to slip from a 'mature' Lukácsian definition of the term – the successful integration of individual and society – to an earlier version of it – an individual grindingly encountering society as an objective outer limit to the attainment of personal desire. The *New Left Review* interviewers alertly pinpoint one such moment of slippage, when 'you seem to be using a new definition of realism now' (*PL*, p. 222). This 'new' definition, derived from Lukács's *Theory of the Novel*, was dismissed by him in later comments on the book as being, precisely, Expressionistic.

There is a third limit to Williams's commitment to realism, perhaps the deepest of all. The modernism which 'splits' the proletariat is in some sense its own product, since it had formerly split apart realism in its turn. In *Politics and Letters* Williams throws out, as a somewhat casual hypothesis, the suggestion that 'the arrival of an articulate, newly organized and modern working class presented qualitatively new problems to the kind of integrated and extended social vision which had been the major achievement of the bourgeois realists' (*PL* p. 262). But clearly some deep intuitive sense of this off-the-cuff observation has funded his literary oeuvre throughout. No socialist could, on this showing, be a realist novelist in any straightforward sense, and certainly Williams's comments on this issue in *Politics and Letters* are ambivalent, at times evasive, even – one might say – tormented. And his novelistic practice too, enacting in this the realist paradigm of *Theory of the Novel*, forces us painfully up against the objective limits set by the form itself on the *desire* of the individual socialist writer. In *Border Country* the formal structure of the novel is exactly congruent with the structure of the political defeat at the book's heart – to the point, indeed, where one is inclined to posit causal relations between them. A socialism addicted to such cultural forms perhaps *could* not achieve more than it is here shown to do in the political field. Most writers on *Border Country* have registered the extraordinary metaphorical austerity of the book's prose, far removed from Williams's undergraduate enthusiasm for Joyce in particular and modernism at large. At its best, the style recreates the experience and rhythm of work in the community itself, dogged, sparing, tight-lipped and dry-eyed, a tenacious effort to win a small margin of freedom from an often difficult Nature; a notable example is afforded by the pages recording and enacting Matthew Price's insight that 'this was not anybody's valley to make into a landscape. Work had changed and was still changing it' – pages which tackle and defeat a long Romantic tradition of aestheticizing the rural environment. Yet this same purged style ultimately, in its systematic exclusions, entails other and less desirable commitments: close to the community in one sense, it marginalizes or even abolishes it in another. In *Politics and Letters* Williams reportš his desire to avoid 'the Welsh style that had got established in England', with its extreme verbal exuberance, free-associationism and metaphorical virtuosity (*PL*, p. 279). But to do so was to enact the founding gesture of the realist novel itself, which first moves *into* the local community, since it is there that it will effect its social-democratic extension of 'sympathy', but then steps radically *out* of it, in its construction of the universal, disinterested, linguistically transparent Reason of its own narrative level. To renounce metaphor or the signifier is no innocent, local gesture; it involves, in one of Harry Price's memorable phrases, 'letting the no grow through you'.[26] To abolish metaphor is then, within realism, to marginalize desire, sexuality, fantasy, utopian imagination; these are the necessarily 'lost illusions' of the form, which thereafter become its 'madwomen in the attic', its turbulent Gothic sub-texts.

Up to a point, *Border Country* is sensitive to such exclusions, and even seeks to reverse them. Arriving in Gwenton, Matthew reflects, 'here was the station, by the asylum: both on the outskirts, where the Victorians thought they belonged' – a historical genealogy which implicitly links such repressions to the very form that the book is, paradoxically, trying to re-create. And in the later episode of Harry's shaving Billy Devereaux, the novel insists on the creaturely care which the community extends to its demented members; the moment of Michel Foucault's 'Great Confinement', it seems, is not yet. In point of fact, however, it has already been and gone, with the defeat of the General Strike of 1926. For Morgan Rosser, the structure of that defeat is precisely that of the novel itself, an exiling of 'metaphor' or transformative imagination: 'suddenly the world of power and compromise seemed real, the world of hope and ideas no more than a gloss, a mark in the margin.' Its marginality is both cause and effect of the betrayal of the strike, inhering first in the philistinism of organized labour before it strikes personally into Morgan himself; it is true for the wider movement *before* it is for him that 'we're getting the result of our own denying.' In this sense, *Border Country* is in its form and texture complicit with the political collapse it records. Williams insists, in *Politics and Letters*, on 'seeing whether the realist form is capable of extension and transformation' (*PL*, p. 276); but his own novel demonstrates that it isn't. No wonder, then, that its fundamental energies seem to be directed elsewhere, to pursuing quite different effects: to those strange slippages whereby scenes of the past hover indeterminately between Harry's convalescent and his son's dreaming consciousness ('Matthew woke, suddenly ...'), to Morgan's compulsive, Mephistophelean but also vampiric need to feed off the energy of the Prices, father and son ('Why is it, Ellen? Why I keep coming back here, keep coming and asking ...'), to those uncanny effects of doubling whereby Will almost perceives – what Williams later testified – that Harry and Morgan are one man ('he saw Morgan and his father sitting side by side, looking across at him'), to the eerie dimensions of Will's own researches ('the haunting was perpetual'), to the resonant fragments of Welsh legend which echo Rosser's own political defeat, threatening to invest him with the status of mythic archetype ('the good Gruffydd ap Llewellyn, the head and shield of the Cymri, fell through the treachery of his own men ...'). 'Said I came from a wild place; that I was very superstitious; had thick Celtic blood':[27] this is Will, in bitterness; but all the same there *are* such energies on the loose in the text – which would ultimately be essential to, not a diversion from the political project it adumbrates.

In *Second Generation* realism is 'longitudinal' rather than 'latitudinal', a matter of patiently interlocking social inclusiveness rather than an internal fictional hierarchy of discourses (ametaphorical narrator/Welsh voices). If the chief ideological strategy of the class enemy is, in Harold Owen's view, 'to keep the connections out of sight', then the realist totality will humanely restore them, dissolving class abstractions and separations into the dense network of actual human relationships. But the generous organicism of the form then has the most dubious political consequences; as Kate Owen shrewdly perceives, 'even the thinking that's supposed to be against them is for them.' For if the totality *already* exists, before and beyond the distortions of ideology, then a politics *of* totality, launched in the name of what Arthur Dean at one point terms 'the genuine radicalism of a quite new conception of human life', is at best misguided and at worst threatens wantonly to violate the organic textures of the actually lived – as, in the novel's view, do the relationships of Kate with Arthur and of her son Peter with Rose. At the level of theme, Kate's protest against the drab trade unionism of her husband comes through as passionate and decisive; it is even carried by certain recurrent patterns of imagery, as with that dry, stinging grit in the eyes from which everyone in this book seems to be suffering (and which appropriately crops up elsewhere in Williams's discussions of Orwell). But formally the book enacts Harold Owen's own cautious, step-by-step meliorism. 'All you did', Kate cries to him, at a moment of no longer bearable social and sexual frustration, 'was to stop something happening': 'he patted her shoulder, reassuringly ...'.[28] The pat on the shoulder, registering passion and then moving on, is, however, the novel's own *modus operandi*, as it must be given its ambitions to totality. As J. P. Ward complains, 'time and again in this book the potentially disruptive or critical event, a hint of sexuality, a touch of sudden rearing passionate anger, is then simply eased or withheld, and the community reverts to its thoughtful brooding, its slightly tensed rumination.'[29] If the novel can on occasion focus this process, as in its account of the television programme on the Longston strike in which the militant worker Rathbone is reduced to a 'sense of unreasonableness that was mainly coming through', it for the most part colludes with it. The 'margin', that other recurrent image, which in *Border Country* was the realm of fantasy and the uncanny, is in *Second Generation* the hard-won though still narrow edge of freedom which allows the working-class figures in the book to *compose* their social and sexual conflicts; it is a locus of containment rather than breakthrough. If the more 'Gothic' energies of *Border Country* are not engaged here, that is partly the result of the switch of scene from

Wales to Oxford, a landscape which for Williams seems not to contain the immemorial ancestral potencies that could unleash them, but also because the very categories of fantasy and desire seem to have been captured, as I suggested above, by the stylish modernism of post-war consumerism; they seem now more a resistance than a resource. Peter notes, dubiously, 'this air of fantasy now – in the hairstyles, in the gay dresses, in the glass and bright plastic colours'. In another sense, however, perhaps the more bizarre dimensions of the first novel are not abandoned. For what remains most powerfully in memory is the figure of Kate Owen herself, a 'madwoman in the attic' if ever there was one, whose pain, passion and political imagination brush aside (for this reader at least) the more 'realist', organicist settlement – 'some of us have to live where we are' – that her son finally composes. 'To be humane now, 'Kate insists in the book's closing pages, 'we can't be tolerant.'[30] Nor, it would seem, and by much the same token, can we write realist novels either.

If Williams is Lukács, it has sometimes been argued, then he is at least not 'card-carryingly' so: his instinctual native realism is at least on occasion cut across by strange impulses from European modernism. The truth seems to me rather to be the reverse. The *modernism* that is Williams's almost by instinct is locked in combat, in one phase of his work, with a politico-intellectual decision in favour of a realism that thwarts many of his own deepest political energies. The break back, the return *from* a Lukácsian identity which had only briefly and then always uncomfortably fitted him, comes with *The Fight for Manod* where, for the first time, 'much of it is about projecting and imagining a future' (*PL*, p. 293), and in *The Volunteers,* which uses the popular form of the thriller and is set *in* the future, some ten years ahead of the time of writing. My aim here is not so much to analyse these works as to move from them to a tentative Western Marxist comparison which may hopefully displace the Lukács reference in discussions of Williams, and which has the further benefit of posing the issue of the relation between Williams's early modernist formation and his general social thinking. For if Williams's two most recent novels hinge crucially on the category of the future, so too does the work of Ernst Bloch, Lukács's great antagonist in the Expressionism debates of the 1930s.

Bloch, as it happens, was the son of a railway official – the first in a long series of points of parallel with Williams. His critique of Lukács's generalizing critical methods could be paralleled from a dozen places in Williams's early work, with its sharply 'practical-critical' focus. Bloch's extraordinary style enacts, in its 'recursive modernism', the very devices and energies of the avant-garde practices it celebrates at the level of theme,[31] and so, in a more modest way as I noted above, does Williams's own. His recent wry reference to 'my usual famous qualifying and complicating, my insistence on depths and ambiguities' reads exactly like a roll-call of modernism's most honoured critical terms – as if we were here in the presence of a Marxist Henry James or Robert Musil.[32] I traced above Williams's substantive judgements on Expressionism, which are certainly more Blochian than

Lukácsian; but perhaps the more interesting convergence betwen them here is a theoretical one. One of the reasons Bloch can so nimbly out-manoeuvre Lukács in this debate is the fact that he has *two* languages or codes in which to discuss the Expressionist artefact. It is, simultaneously, unconscious fantasy and active construct, emotional outburst and carefully contrived montage; Bloch, we could perhaps say, holds resourcefully together in his very critical terminology those two dimensions of the movement which Williams is inclined to separate out as individual and social expressionism. But if we then go on to say that, for Bloch, the Expressionist or Surrealist artefact has both a structure *and* a feeling, then Williams's most distinctive theoretical concept may itself come to seem an apt product of the radical, avant-gardiste subculture of his early years.

Does the final chapter of *Towards 2000*, 'Resources for a Journey of Hope', echo the title of Bloch's *magnum opus, The Principle of Hope*? The connections were in fact there to be made, much earlier. As Williams was paying close, hostile attention in the Cambridge of the 1960s to George Steiner's work on the 'death of tragedy', Steiner himself was recommending Bloch in *Language and Silence*: 'a rich share of his achievement concerns the literary critic and student of language'.[33] But not only the literary critic. Martin Jay has written of Bloch that 'his more decentred view of the totality gave him an openness to modern art that Lukács woefully lacked', but can we not reverse the terms of this account, seeing in the fragmentation and discontinuities, the intense formal preoccupations, of modernism the ground of a renewal of a classical Marxism thrown into crisis by the revolutionary failures of 1918-21?[34] Impassioned advocate of Expressionism, Bloch is also the theorist of 'non-synchronicity', of the social formation as a heterogeneous totality composed of manifold differential times not reducible to a single centre or essence. In Bloch's view, Marx had reduced the totality to only one of its elements, production, thus ironically reproducing the very utilitarian impoverishment of reality that he had set out to challenge. This argument, that Marxism was captured by the very categories it opposed, has since been much developed by Williams himself. In this case, too, a fervent youthful admirer of Expressionist and Surrealist film has spent a subsequent lifetime combating the base/superstructure metaphor and developing a specifically *cultural* materialism.

The totality opens both 'vertically' and 'horizontally', synchronically and diachronically. There is admittedly little enough in Williams's work to set beside Bloch's sense of religion as a repository of utopian social hope; only the over-estimate of the transcendentalist drama of Yeats and Eliot at the end of *Drama from Ibsen to Eliot* affords the glimmer of a comparison here. But Bloch's critique of the failure of the German Communist Party in the 1920s to respond to the sexual radicalism of Sex-Pol and the German women's movement is matched by Williams's insistence in *The Long Revolution* on the equal status of the 'system of generation and nurture' with the more traditional Marxist 'levels' of the social formation, and by his recent enthusiasm for the 'new social movements'. Such theoretical commitments are then worked through in powerful renditions of women's oppression in the fiction, which invariably unleash the 'Gothic' dimensions of Williams's imagination: Kate Owen in *Second Generation* and perhaps pre-eminently Gwen Vaughan in *The Fight for Manod*. Both Bloch and Williams eloquently defend the category of fantasy as such against its orthodox Marxist reduction to superstructural echo or precipitate: Bloch repeatedly assailed the impoverished rationalism of the KPD, while in some strange impassioned pages of *Politics and Letters* Williams evokes 'impulses which have not been produced by the known calculus of forces ... these non-traceable, or not immediately traceable, liberating impulses (*PL*, pp. 254–6: the men of 1968 warn that this 'is much too close to the language of mysticism', a charge which Bloch himself often had to face). More decisively still, the totality now opens onto the non-human, towards Nature. It has always been implicitly acknowledged that here we reach the limits of the 'British Lukács' tag; as the theme of Nature in Williams comes into focus in *Politics and Letters*, the point of continental reference becomes the Frankfurt School rather than Lukács himself. But we then simply need to insist that Bloch got there first. As Martin Jay notes, 'Bloch's inclusion of natural subjectivity into the dialectical process of totalization set him apart from the other members of Western Marxism's first generation, although it anticipated some of the concerns of slightly younger figures like Walter Benjamin and Herbert Marcuse.'[35] It still remains true that here, above all, Williams's thought is much 'more effective and materialist' than its European counterparts (*PL*, p. 318). But two points can be added to this. First, that Williams has what we might term a 'modernist' apprehension of Nature, in which experiences of difference, plurality, discontinuity, mobility or what he has called 'the true data of unevenness' (*PL*. p. 433) are paramount. Second, though he would no doubt have little truck with Bloch's Schellingian extravaganzas about a potential subject in nature, his novels do none the less articulate the strange potencies of place: Gwen Vaughan's ride through the ancient burial mound in *The Fight for Manod* immediately precedes the accident in which the tractor crashes down trapping her brother's leg, a familiar castration-motif which is this novel's equivalent of, say, the blinding of Rochester in *Jane Eyre*. Perhaps we now need an account of Nature in Williams based on the concrete enactments of his fiction rather than on his theoretical writing.

But if the 'layers' of the social totality cannot be reduced to each other, nor can they simply be 'reduced' to themselves. Far from being unproblematically self-identical, they are shot through by still active traces of the past and still-to-be-fully-activated anticipations of the future. The Williams triad – residual, dominant, emergent – here catches up two of Ernst Bloch's major themes: the need to 're-baptize the living yesterday' and the 'not yet' as a crucial Marxist category. Williams speaks sombrely in *Politics and Letters* to the very situation that Bloch was struggling to think through in the 1930s, for 'it might even be said that the most prolific generator of modern irrationalism is now a certain kind of urban agglomeration' (*PL*, p. 320). And such dangerous irrationalisms are, for him as for Bloch, a matter of the socialist movement failing to turn to account the utopian potential latent in the 'non-synchronous' contradictions, failing to develop other than a narrowly urban-industrial imagination of modernity, a 'final economic universalism'. Thus he assents to his interviewers' description of *The Country and the City* as 'a criticism of the assumption that the working class could find entirely within capitalist relations of exploitation themselves the necessary strength to overthrow capitalism, as if the severing of that class from its own rural past was not a very damaging blow to its powers of resistance – its capacity to imagine an alternative social order' (*PL*. p. 314). This conjoining of past and future is precise; 'our only utopian critic', as Patrick Parrinder has recently called Williams, pointing to the utopian model of a 'common culture' in the early writings, to the envisaged 'new forms of cooperative effort' which might end the division of labour in *The Country and the City*, and to the attempt to define a 'new socialist order' at the end of *Politics and Letters*.[36] We could add to the list Williams's essays on Rudolf Bahro and 'Utopia and Science Fiction', the effort towards a 'proleptic' analysis in *Towards 2000* and, as an instance of dystopia, *The Volunteers*. The parallels here with Bloch are deep indeed, all the way from *Der Geist der Utopie* onwards, and remain to be worked out in detail – which they will not be if we persist in seeing Williams as the 'British Lukács' (even when he himself counsels us to do so).

My aim here has been more modest, and consists simply in underlining the linkages between these utopian projects and Williams's early formation within a radical modernist or avant-garde student subculture. As with Nature, so with utopia: we can say here too that Williams has a modernist apprehension of the category, stressing complexity and heterogeneity as against earlier socialist projections of a radically simplified 'happy hobbitland'. Here indeed, as Terry Eagleton has argued, is Williams's unique importance in a period of glib post-modernisms: the ability to sustain both a commitment to class struggle *and* a celebration of difference and plurality.[37] More specifically, there seems in Williams to be an inheritance from Futurism itself – though he remains wary of the epithet, which for him denotes an abstract utopianism ungrounded in the actual social tendencies of the present. Only, the Futurist celebration of speed, mobility, power, technology is in him invested, not in the forces or sites of production, nor in their dynamic products (Marinetti's famous racing car bearing down at full speed on the machine gun), but rather in the democratic process itself – in its complex circuits of referral, its speed of recall, its sophisticated communications technology. It is then no accident, surely, that in some of his most recent writings Williams has returned to the founding moment of the European avant-garde. He has found many harsh things to say of specific projects and movements, and yet there has been, beyond the particular judgements, a deep sense of home-coming, of return to those radical modernist subcultures of late 1930s Britain. For it remains as true now as it did then of the European avant-gardes that 'the history and practice of these same general movements, reviewed to disclose in some new ways the profound connections between formations and forms, remain sources of inspiration and of strength.'[38]

Notes

1 Martin Jay, *Marxism and Totality* (Cambridge, 1984), p. 9; Terry Eagleton, *Criticism and Ideology* (London, 1976), p. 24; Raymond Williams, *Politics and Letters: Interviews with New Left Review* (London, 1979), p. 10. References to this ubiquitously necessary text, abbreviated as *PL*, are hereafter given in my text. I dedicate this essay on a fellow-Welshman to the memory of my grandfather, John Vivian Stead (1909–1977), and to his and my relations in Cefn-Coed.

2 Terry Eagleton, *Walter Benjamin, or Towards a Revolutionary Criticism* (London, 1981), pp. 64–8.

3 Raymond Williams, *Culture* (London, 1981), p. 84.

4 Terry Eagleton, 'The end of English', *Textual Practice*, 1, 1, (Spring 1987), pp. 1–9.

5 Raymond Williams, *The English Novel from Dickens to Lawrence* (London, 1970), p. 44.

6 James Klugmann, 'The crisis in the thirties: a view from the left', in Jon Clark et al, *Culture and Crisis in Britain in the Thirties* (London, 1979), p. 18.

7 Cited in Humphrey Carpenter, *W. H. Auden: A Biography* (London, 1981), p. 84.

8 Cited in Breon Mitchell, 'W. H. Auden and Christopher Isherwood: the "German Influence"', *Oxford German Studies*, 1 (1966), p. 167.

9 Raymond Williams, *Drama from Ibsen to Eliot* (London, 1952), pp. 247, 179.

10 R. S. Furness, *Expressionism* (London, 1973), p. 86; Mitchell, 'Auden and Isherwood: the "German Influence"', p. 165.

11 For a more detailed account, see Nicholas Jacobs and Prudence Ohlsen (eds), *Bertolt Brecht in Britain* (London, 1977).

12 Paul C. Ray, *The Surrealist Movement in England* (Ithaca, 1971), p. 240.

13 Perry Anderson, 'Components of the national culture', in Alexander Cockburn and Robin Blackburn (eds), *Student Power: Problems, Diagnoses, Action* (Harmondsworth, 1969), p. 280.

14 Terry Eagleton, *The Function of Criticism: From 'The Spectator' to Post-Structuralism* (London, 1984), p. 112.

15 Ken Worpole, 'Expressionism and working-class fiction', *New Left Review*, 130 (November–December 1981), pp. 83–96.

16 Samuel Hynes, *The Auden Generation: Literature and Politics in England in the 1930s* (London, 1976), p. 280.

17 Ronald Hayman (ed.), *My Cambridge* (London, 1977), p. 60.

18 Eagleton, *Criticism and Ideology*, p. 24; J. P. Ward, *Raymond Williams*, 'Writers of Wales' (Cardiff, 1981), p. 11.

19 Eagleton, *Criticism and Ideology*, p. 23; Ward, *Raymond Williams*, p. 43.

20 Frank Kermode, *The Romantic Image* (London, 1971 edn), p. 168.

21 Williams, *Drama from Ibsen to Eliot*, pp. 184, 95, 118, 179–84.

22 Raymond Williams and Michael Orrom, *Preface to Film* (London, 1954), p. 52.

23 Raymond Williams, *Problems in Materialism and Culture: Selected Essays* (London,

1980), p. 241; Richard Hoggart, *The Uses of Literacy* (Harmondsworth, 1958), pp. 192, 247, 235.

24 Williams, *Culture*, p. 85; *Towards 2000* (Harmondsworth, 1985), pp. 141–3.

25 Williams, *The English Novel*, p. 32.

26 Raymond Williams, *Border Country* (Harmondsworth, 1964), pp. 72–3, 231. On this question of metaphor, see my 'Nineteenth-century studies: as they are and as they might be', *News from Nowhere*, 2 (October 1986), pp. 38–55.

27 Williams, *Border Country*, pp. 13, 147, 276, 66, 244, 239, 273, 163, 272.

28 Raymond Williams, *Second Generation* (London, 1964), pp. 192, 190, 36, 110-12.

29 Ward, *Raymond Williams*, p. 40.

30 Williams, *Second Generation*, pp. 296, 148, 315, 339.

31 'Recursive modernism' is Wayne Hudson's phrase, in his *The Marxist Philosophy of Ernst Bloch* (London, 1982), p. 2.

32 Raymond Williams and Terry Eagleton, 'The practice of possibility: interview', *New Statesman*, 7 August 1987 [reprinted as ch. 10 of the present volume], p. 21.

33 George Steiner, 'The Pythagorean genre', in *Language and Silence: Essays 1958–1966* (Harmondsworth, 1969), p. 115.

34 Jay, *Marxism and Totality,* p. 188. For an attempt at such a 'reversal', see Eugene Lunn, *Marxism and Modernism* (London, 1984).

35 Jay, *Marxism and Totality*, p. 185.

36 Patrick Parrinder, *The Failure of Theory: Essays on Criticism and Contemporary Fiction* (Brighton, 1987), p. 74.

37 Williams and Eagleton, 'The practice of possibility: interview', p. 20.

38 Raymond Williams, 'Language and the avant-garde', in Nigel Fabb et al., *The Linguistics of Writing: Arguments Between Language and Literature* (Manchester, 1987) p. 46. Williams's late essays on this topic are now collected in his *The Politics of Modernism*, ed. Tony Pinkney (London, 1987).

2

RELATING TO WALES

—— Dai Smith ——

'Well, Matthew Price', he said, smiling, 'you're an exile. Perhaps, I don't know, a voluntary exile. So that none of us yet knows your commitment to Wales.'

Matthew leaned forward.

'Enough of a commitment to know the divisions', he said, sharply.

The Fight for Manod

Raymond Williams's emergence as a key figure in the debate about the identity of Britain dates from the publication of *Culture and Society* in 1958. Apart from its dedication to his children – Merryn, Ederyn and Madawc – and a brief biographical note there is nothing in this work, centrally concerned with the interplay of culture–industry–democracy, to suggest that Wales is anything other than a place of origin and a sentimental attachment. Two years later the appearance of his first novel, *Border Country,* indicated the depth of those roots but was, in style and form, very carefully distanced from what had been understood, since the 1930s, as 'Anglo-Welsh' literature. That Williams was Welsh was clear; that the Welsh strands mostly surfaced in his imaginative or fictional writing was convenient for the subsequent divorce between the 'thinker/critic' and 'novelist/artist' which made Williams more readily assimilable inside an oppositional English literary discourse he was doing so much to shape; that his sense of being Welsh was a most intricate question that he was, himself, only then beginning to understand would become, for some, and on both sides of the border, an irritatingly obtuse aspect of his work and personality. Yet in the late 1980s, and able to survey all his work to this point, it is the meaning of that Welsh experience which stands out as the abiding preoccupation of his life.

Certainly, the purely autobiographical note is more and more insistently sounded in the opening and closing pages of critical works but also, as in *The Country and the City* (1973), the wider, encompassing, anglocentric references are often brought up against Irish, Scottish and, more unknown to his readers, Welsh sources of enquiry. By the 1970s he had come to define both his personal/emotional growth and his intellectual/social development by such explicit reference. Within Wales he became a public figure: the recipient of Welsh Arts Council prizes (for *The Fight for Manod* and *Loyalties*), called up to present Honours to distinguished Welsh writers, to address Plaid Cymru summer schools, to lecture to Welsh Labour History societies, to the Welsh Academy, and sought after, constantly, for an imprimatur in word or deed. In 1981 he was the subject of a monograph by J. P. Ward (in the 'Writers of Wales' series)[1] which addressed directly Williams's increasing concern with Wales. Some of this might be taken as a desire for the goodwill, interest or patronage of a major literary figure who had 'made it' outside Wales – except that the Welsh, in this same twenty-year period, had become chary of these induced traits in their own national personality and, more to the point, that Raymond Williams was busily declaring his own deep obsession.

The note was sounded, almost defiantly, in *Politics and Letters* (1979) where, moving beyond the detailed history of an actual Welsh upbringing, he replies to the question – 'what has been the history of your relationship to Wales?' – with the ringing words:

> ... a big change started to happen from the late sixties. There was a continuity in a quite overwhelming feeling about the land of Wales ... But then I began having many more contacts with Welsh writers and intellectuals, all highly political in the best tradition of the culture, and I found this curious effect. Sudenly England, bourgeois England, wasn't my point of reference any more. I was a Welsh European, and both levels felt different ... Through the intricacies of the politics, and they are very intricate indeed, I want the Welsh people – still a radical and cultured people – to defeat, overide or bypass bourgeois England; the alternatives follow from the intricacies. That connects, for me, with the sense in my work that I am now necessarily European ... and my more conscious Welshness is, as I feel it, my way of learning those connections. I mean that over a whole range, from when Welsh-speaking nationalists tell me ... how thoroughly Welsh *Border Country* and the social thinking are ... to when highly cosmopolitan Welsh intellectuals offer recognition of the whole range of my work, which literally none of my English official colleagues has seen a chance of making sense of, then I am in a culture where I can breathe. Or at least take breaths to go back and contend with capitalist Europe, capitalist England and – blast it, but it was there and had to be shown in *Manod* – capitalist Wales.[2]

Despite the qualifying phrases that reduce the overall impact of the statement his intention is clear, almost blunt. This was a challenge directed to his *New Left*

Review interlocutors. The reader waits for them to discuss the implications. They do not. They pass on to another piece of Welsh fiction – *The Volunteers*. Now, Williams's understanding of the complexity of modern Wales is intimately tied in to its precise usefulness for him in his creative work but, in a teasing mode, he also appropriates the general concept of Wales as a metaphor with which to illuminate English darkness. In the early 1980s he hammers out the message in the iciness of Thatcher's Britain over and over; but Wales, unlike Ireland, has never quite caught the English left's ear. It is as if the propinquity and sustained ambiguity of Wales is too much, too close, to grasp for those who can only hear distant trumpets.

> Many of the things that happened, over centuries, to the Welsh are now happening, in decades, to the English. The consequent confusion and struggle for identity, the search for new modes of effective autonomy within a powerfully extended and profoundly interacting para-national political and economic system, are now in many parts of the world the central issues of social consciousness, struggling to come through against still powerful but residual ideas and institutions ... at many levels, from the new communal nationalism and regionalisms to the new militant particularisms of contemporary industrial conflict, the flow of contemporary politics is going beyond the modes of all the incorporated ideologies and institutions. The Welsh, of course, have been inside these cross pressures for much longer than the English. And as a result we have had to learn that we need to solve the real contradictions between nationality and class, and between local well being and the imperatives of a large-scale system. Consequently, we may be further along the road to a relevant if inevitably painful contemporary social consciousness ... What seemed a sectoral problem and impetus, to be dressed or dissolved in mere local colour, is now more and more evidently a focal problem and impetus: not particular to but to a significant extent particularised in Wales.[3]

Naturally there would be a broad range of agreement about such well-tossed notions as 'Labourism', 'post-imperialism', 'corporatism' and 'incorporation', but Williams's insistence on the importance of Wales within such a debate has struck few chords outside Wales. The National Left, a Plaid Cymru grouping, was, down to 1984–5, able to win attention in left-wing Labour circles in England by aligning itself with the potentially disruptive movements of feminism, neutralism, communalism and anti-racism, within a spectrum of left activism. However sympathetic he may be to this as activity beyond the lip-service of local or parliamentary politicking, Raymond Williams shuns the simplistic view that sees a crisis (in victory or defeat) as any resolution of the continuing condition of working-class people.[4] He clings, therefore, along with 'Wales', to the older keywords of his argument – 'culture' and 'community'. This trinity, in which 'Wales' serves to frame the other two, spearheads his attack against the reiterated charges of romanticism and murky nostalgia.[5] The miners' strike of 1984–5, especially inasmuch as the South Wales coalfield came to symbolize an almost unbreakable, communal defiance, gave him the opportunity to re-state, in succinct form, his convictions: for here was a residual, yet recharged, class-solidarity expressing itself still in ways that were inimical to all those who envisaged a more raw transition, free from all such illusions, to the new politics. Williams commented, in the cold winter of that revolt, on a radio report on 'the people of the mining valleys during the present bitter coal strike', and how the presenter had said that the 'three words he kept hearing were "culture", "community" and "jobs"':

> The first two are not the classical words of an industrial proletariat, as universally theorised. Indeed they are words which I have been so whacked for using in England, as if they were my private inventions or deviations, that this reminder of a genuine area of shared discourse was especially welcome. Among some English Marxists this strain has been tagged as 'culturalist'. It is to be hoped that some of them at least will notice that this is the language of what has been, in the worst days so far of the strike, the most solid working class of the British coalfields.[6]

The strength he derives from such connections is undeniable. Yet having sounded these national – cultural – communal notes, scrupulous as ever, he does not hide the sharp divisions within this contemporary Wales where so much has stirred his more conscious Welshness. One or other section might wish his authority to land firmly on their side but, instead, he has urged mutual recognition of common ground against common enemies whether they be internal or external. Thus, any chipping away of Welsh-language rights, inadvertently or otherwise, is insupportable given the present existence of a committed minority (20 per cent) with a genuine centuries-old tradition. On the other hand, a literary/linguistic-based nationality is a piece of mythological manufacturing that must blend with the making of different cultures within that invented Wales in a 'welcoming admission of the latest shift: not as the abandonment of 'Welshness' in some singular and unitary form, but as the positive creation of a still distinctively Welsh, English-speaking working-class culture'.[7] Then, in turn, those radical, largely proletarian societies which have shaped communities of purpose must, he feels, be divested of their particular glamour since 'the authentically differential communalism of the Welsh, product of a specific history rather than of some racial or cultural essence, could become residual if it does not grow ...'[8]

Out of this concern with a future for the Welsh, in despite of the Yookay, he has been at pain, recently, to refine his position on Wales. Without abandoning the significance of 'the remarkable continuity of literature in the Welsh language from ... the 7th century', he digests the 'new' literary, sociological and historical enquiries within Wales and declares (after the rejection of Devolution in the 1979 Referendum, the unparalleled rise of Conservatism in Wales, the concomitant spread of suburbia and, worse, the defeat of the miners in 1985) that a demolition of 'cultural and literary stereotypes of Welshness is not at any point, in my judgement, a move away from Wales. On the contrary it is the accompaniment of a very urgent contemporary concern – for it is, in our time, not only the Welsh who have to discover and affirm an identity by overcoming a selective tradition.'[9]

Once more the challenge is thrown out to his wider (English) audience, though this time affirming all his doubts and queries in the knowledge that the 'non-Welsh reader' has a 'clearer and stronger image of the country and its people than at any earlier time'. The irony being that the Welsh themselves have moved on and away from both the patronizing cliché and even the image possessed by sympathetic outsiders. If the Welsh, or some of them, have learned this through the history, consciously absorbed, of the last quarter century then so, emphatically, has Raymond Williams.

His fusion of personal and public histories is located in that border country which sent Raymond away from Jim (his name at home as a boy) only to force Matthew to rediscover Will (as in *Border Country*). The way out of Wales, as he probed in *Second Generation*, was, for him and so many others, literally through emigration and, maybe, social mobility later. Since 1960 he has been exploring another 'way out of Wales'. This route is circuitous yet not circular. It insists that Wales is rediscovered through understanding the social process of its past. It argues that this is the only real exit from a timeless, mythical Wales which will otherwise suffocate the living Welsh. It embraces change rather than the dynamics of modernism, for it sees change as growth that is rooted, pruned and fostered by communities who strive to make choices for their culture in their own local and national terms. The vehicle for this route is working-class struggle. The map is history.

Looking back, to primary school in Pandy in the 1920s and to grammar school in Abergavenny in the 1930s, he noted how the diet of romantic-nationalist story-telling he was given, in the one, not only led into the British-imperialist narrative he received in the other, but how both versions deprived him of any actual history to which he could relate. There was no kind of intellectual analysis. Hence the long march through the liberation of an intellectualized English culture that did eventually take him home.[10] And when it did, he discovered that such compartmentalization still strove to trivialize what it could not afford to unite. He spotlights the convenience of this for any 'national' culture in his political thriller *The Volunteers* (1978) in which, for a Welsh future, insurrection promises to be the only worthwhile human continuity. The novel contains this disquisition on the actual Welsh Folk Museum:

> It offers to show the history of a people in its material objects; tools, furniture, arms, fabrics, utensils (and) . . . is an active material history of the people of Wales: up to a certain point.

> But . . . this is an active history only of *rural* Wales: of farms and cottages, and of

the early industries of tanning and weaving. All the later history, of the majority of Welsh people, is simply not seen: the mining townships, the quarrymens' villages, the iron and steel works settlements; the pit cage, the picks and shovels, the slate saws, the chisels, the masks of the blast furnacemen, the wrenches, the hoses, the grease-guns. The idea that the museum embodies is of an old Wales, still in part surviving, but with all modern realities left behind in the car park, or brought inside only in the toilets which have replaced the privies. That is why it is called a folk museum. Folk is the past: an alternative to People.[11]

The controlled contempt is of the same kind in *The Country and the City*, that scorned, in contradistinction now, the quite limited validity of Marx and Engels's phrase 'the idiocy of rural life'[12] and would, in *The Fight for Manod*, reject the enforced, outworn separation of industrial/urban from agrarian/rural, since this is the burden of an actual history that has to be transcended. Williams's tingling awareness of this damning fracture (also witnessed by his admired Thomas Hardy) is not just a pious book-learned matter, for such a divide is the principal explanation for the splits (economic – social – political – cultural – linguistic) within his own native country. His projection is, constantly, from localized examples outward because his confident reading of Welsh history underscores their wider application. The shift from agriculture to industry, as two generations of Welsh writers and scholars have proclaimed, was almost as epically melodramatic as the prose frequently employed to describe it. The consequences have been so subversive of traditions and national ideals that it has proved easier to shun them than to comprehend them.[13] This, too, is a Welsh divorce that Williams would see as part of wider separations.

How did 500,000 people in 1800 become 2,500,000 by 1911 and why did over 300,000 Welsh people migrate *internally* in the nineteenth century? The sketch, in narrative or statistical form, of the transformation of a largely pastoral Welsh society whose population was spread evenly across the country into a predominantly urban, cosmopolitan people dependent on industry, and largely concentrated in the southern iron towns, ports and coalfield, becomes fraught with tension only when the concomitant displacements are added: of religion by secularism; of Welsh by English; of radical liberalism by both Labour politics and an industrial militancy once verging on anarcho-syndicalism. By 1914, two out of every three people living in Wales lived in the southern belt which was, by then, the world's greatest coal-exporting basin. More people in Wales were speaking Welsh than ever before and, at the same time, they were becoming a decreasing proportion of the total population. Wales was a vital, regional component of a British imperialism rampant within the Atlantic Economy. Wales, in the early 1920s, was both at the end of a rich period of material success allied to national self-confidence and at the beginning of a half-century of economic decline, population dispersal and fierce contention.[14] In the 1920s, that fragmented people was also united as never before or since by the railway lines which knitted together this 'distended society'.[15]

When Raymond Williams was born in 1921, the pattern of settlement seemed complete. Even the two decades of heavy out-migration and industrial closure did not seriously threaten such received wisdom about Wales. Only in the 1960s did a fresh, bewildering, dislocation of accepted cultures and established communities begin again; and, now, in the mind. Williams's own early life had, in truth, been as tangential to the major thrusts of contemporary Welsh life as his own subsequent career suggested. From the late 1950s, though, his own off-centre apprehension of Wales came to seem more and more like the coming lives of all the Welsh. The re-learning of a connection became the theme of his five Welsh novels to date, but there was, too, the determined conviction that the special story he had to tell derived some of its late resonance by virtue of its early marginality. Fifty years after the General Strike was a good time to elucidate this and, even better, that he was able to do so in the centre of the coalfield before a mass audience of trade unionists and labour historians.

Immediately, in that address,[16] he insisted on the narrow space that separated any time-zone (industry from agriculture) in such a small country as Wales. This made for closeness, but it also heralded the need for 'complex social action' and the 'complex problems of consciousness' which he saw take shape in 1926 in ways that made the development, away from an identifiable centre of working-class solidarity, integral to British working-class history. He offered his listeners only a 'local experience, with a sense of its wider significance', but the latter was shown to be an outcrop of confidence dependent on its being worked through, and understood. When Raymond Williams talks about the General Strike, more so than when he writes delicately about its ramifications, there is a firm note of pride ('Our side'; 'as an adolescent I remember looking at these men ... with a certain resentment – they seemed so absolutely confident. I have never seen such self-confident people since')[17] that is allied to a kind of wistfulness. What had occurred, locally, in 1926 was the mustering of 'a spirit and a perspective' that was dependent on class understanding above and beyond sectional, craft or geographical separation. That victory, within a more general defeat, was not conjured up by any mechanistic determinism. Half a century away from the event he drew the lessons, again, that even such a heavy material presence as that once possessed by the South Wales coalfield ('After all, if it could have been done by talking, Wales could have been a socialist republic in the twenties')[18] was not enough, nor ever could be:

> In 1926 the mining villages were modern communities; our village, even with the railway through it, an older type. Today we have to deal with a social and physical distribution in which mixed communities, not centred on single industries, are much more characteristic. The special struggle for class consciousness has now to be waged on this more open, more socially neutral ground. I still find it impossible, whenever I come to the mining valleys, to understand, at first, why there is not yet socialism in Britain: the need and the spirit have been evidenced so often, in these hard, proud places. But then I remember all the other places, so hard to understand

from this more singular experience, although the actual development of industrial South Wales ... has (since) been in that other direction, with a complex intersection with the older type of community.[19]

The General Strike, especially for those outside the coalfields yet still dependent on them, brought a phase of Welsh history to a climax. A glance at an old Great Western Railway map vividly illustrates the skein of chronological, spatial and personal connections that entwined the Williams family in that process: over the coalfield is a cross-hatching of railway routes, their veins heading to the main arteries that push on outside the region; Abergavenny (the Gwenton of the novels) is at its northern boundary, then comes Llanfihangel, Pandy and Pontrilas with the line moving on, into England and Hereford. The place names and the nationalities are jumbled along this border as they had been, via Romano-British settlements to emergent Welsh tribalism and on through Anglo-Norman lordships to anglicizing gentry, for centuries. The pull – 'There was all the time a certain pressure from the East, as we would say – from England ... In the 20th century there was a big migration to Birmingham, where many of my family had gone'[20] – was increasingly, almost irresistibly, away from Wales. Yet, as Williams stresses, for a time 'modernity' lay to the south-west in the iron and coal townships of Brynmawr, Nantyglo, Ebbw Vale and Tredegar which had dictated the pattern of trade, the movement of population and the transfer of ideas. Raymond Williams's local railwaymen were 'political leaders' because their work put them 'in touch with a much wider social network' than was otherwise available in his region and, in the case of his own father, – a boy-porter on the railways before 1914, conscripted into and radicalized by the army – it was the industrialized world to the west which sealed matters: 'Coming back to the railway (1919), it happened that his first job was right down in the mining valleys (Resolven, near Neath) which were very politicized, with a fairly advanced socialist culture. By the time he moved home to the border again, he had acquired its perspectives.'[21] These same perspectives would serve the son 'in the radically different places where I have since lived and worked. But part of the perspective is the sense of complexity and difficulty, in the differential social and industrial and communal history and geography which was then, and is now, increasingly, our world.'[22]

The meaning of modern Wales, posed to him by this accidental placing and timing of his life, unfolds for him, in demonstrable fashion, as he later enquires into its history. No wonder that Matthew Price in *Border Country* is an economic historian 'working on population movements into the Welsh mining-valleys in the middle decades of the 19th century',[23] for this character, whose concerns are in *The Fight for Manod* so recognizably those of his creator, is by his chosen subject – historical demography – placed at the very heart of the movement from compulsion to choice, and on to consciousness, which signified the history of the Welsh. Except that for Price mere measurement is a betrayal, however sophisticated his techniques, of the 'change of substance' those people must have felt 'when they left their villages'.[24] Later on in the novel Price defines what he *can* do, as an historian, in conversation with the socialist-turned-entrepreneur, Morgan Rosser, yet must add that his ambition (finally realized, years later, we learn in *Manod*) is 'like a fool, to write the history of a whole people being changed'.[25] He sees that the difficulty is that 'the ways of measuring this are not only outside my discipline. They are somewhere else altogether, that I can feel but not handle, touch but not grasp.'[26] The problem, that of representing working-class life without reducing it to an emotive piece of documentary naturalism or abstracting it in other, more distancing ways from its proper context, was an acute concern for novelists too. Wales was not only problematic insofar as its complex history resisted available means of historical analysis; it forced its writers to worry away at issues of form and style or else sink into a second division of genre writing where 'technique' was, quite literally, the way to massage awkward material into shapes devoid of everything except local colour and 'timeless' psychology. The Welsh situation raised, in an extreme form, the dilemma of the 'regional' novelist whose subject-matter automatically tagged the work.[27] By the 1950s there was a readily identifiable Welsh model. Raymond Williams wrote and re-wrote *Border Country*, from 1947 to 1958, in conscious rejection of this type-casting. His spare, descriptive prose and restrained, careful dialogue was a deliberate decision to avoid the rhetorical excess then seen as marking out an 'Anglo-Welsh' school. His ability to fix his characters in relationship to a space and time other than the usual naming of places and dates stood out, however, as the more important conceptual breakthrough. He was aware, of course, of what had already been achieved, and has persistently championed the best writing of Welsh novelists from the 1930s – Jack Jones's *Black Parade* (1937), Gwyn Jones's *Times Like These* (1936), Lewis Jones's *Cwmardy* (1937 and *We Live* (1939) – as serious attempts to write, respectively: the history of a working class in formation, in their 'community class' existence and persistence as families, in their shift from 'family' to 'class' through political and industrial struggle.[28] None of these writers has attracted him more than Gwyn Thomas (1913–1981), whose non-representational narratives, wild hyperbole and black comedy he has depicted as an heroic attempt to find the 'voice of the history' beyond 'either the flattened representations or the applied ideological phrases'. Thomas, he argues, was striving to find 'a composition of voices' to sing 'the larger music of a longer history', and

> 'This is why, in this tradition, Welsh writers cannot accept the English pressure towards a fiction of private lives: not because they do not know privacy, or fail to value the flow of life at those levels that are called individual, but because they know these individuals at what is always the real level, a matter of inevitable human involvement, often disconcerting, which is at once the mode and the release of the deepest humanity of the self. This is a lesson painfully administered by the history of their own people . . .'[29]

It is the same kind of praise he bestowed on Dylan Thomas in 1959 when he wrote of the poet's achievement in discovering, like Joyce, 'a living convention' in which the strange voices, talking at rather than to each other, are so much more real than any flat naturalism: 'The language of dream, of song, of unexpressed feeling is the primary experience, and counterpointed with it is the public language of chorus and rhetoric.'[30]

The acknowledgement of this phase of Welsh literature stops there. No more than admirable Welsh political rhetoric – '... a people who have been united for so long in wanting change, yet in relative isolation, that they think that they have really only to sound the trumpet, and the walls will fall down ... so far aggrieved that there was no need to argue through fundamental questions'[31] – can it be allowed to be the last word. Its logic is closure, his impulse is for development. In the Welsh trilogy, and in *Loyalties* (1985), the lines are kept open. Through his novels he delineates a real integration of Welsh life: into Britain, into Europe, through education, as a result of popular culture, by means of strikes and wars and the manipulation of basic needs. The acceptance of this blending is, then, a conditional one – conditional on thinking through what has happened in order to comprehend it for change. The physical traces of the process are everywhere in his landscapes. The changing shapes of the land interact with a constant presence to summarize the themes with which his novels engage.

The Fight for Manod is directly concerned with the use of land. The new town that may emerge, planned and elaborate, in a countryside aparently natural and primordial, is the future that will come one way or the other. Matthew Price finds himself in dispute with the chicanery of local and international capital that can turn bureaucratic planning their way but, equally, Peter Owen's disdain for anything other than absolute scorn has to be combated for the glib way it translates ideals into illusions ('Your family's like your Wales: an idealist norm. All it does is waste time. The actual history is back there in the bloody centre: the Birmingham – Duseldorf axis, with offices in London, Brussels, Paris, Rome. You ... post-Celts are just revered talking heads.'[32] Matthew, in turn, can only recognize the general truth of Owen's view as another way of reflecting dismissal of the very society, local and rooted, that he wishes to acknowledge and sustain. He argues, therefore, for a 'Welsh policy' of investment suited to the needs of decaying industrial valleys and depopulated hill-country. Transport, new growth towns and light industry may be the reformist crumbs from the Centre's table, but such pragmatism should be taken for tactics in a longer strategy. The Welsh society in *crisis*, that *could* emerge despite constraints, is one that requires attachment to its own past. At the end of the novel Matthew and his wife drive to the Heads of the Valleys road and turn off into the mountains. They look, from here, in all directions 'far into Wales':

Where they were standing, looking out, was on a border in the earth and in history:
to north and west the great expanses of a pastoral country; to south and east, where

the iron and coal had been worked, the crowded valleys, the new industries, now in their turn becoming old. There had been a contrast, once, clearly seen on this border, between an old way of life and a new, as between a father living in his old and known ways and a son living differently, in a new occupation and with a new cast of mind. But what was visible now was that both were old. The pressure for renewal, inside them, had to make its way through a land and through lives that had been deeply shaped, deeply committed by a present that was always moving, inexorably, into the past. And those moments of the present that could connect to a future were then hard to grasp, hard to hold to, hard to bring together to a rhythm, to a movement, to the necessary shape of a quite different life. What could now be heard, momentarily, as this actual movement, had conditions of time, of growth, quite different from the condition of any single life, or of any father and son.[33]

Fathers and sons, Owens and Prices, in the first two novels, are seen in their own limited conditions in the third one; and especially Peter Owen, university son of educated shop steward Harold Owen in *Second Generation*, who is the product of the second Welsh diaspora. The first had moved the balance of population into industry within Wales, and a Harry Price to the railways at Lynmawr. The second, in the inter-war years, had blown out the Owens from the ironworks of Brynllwyd, the other side of Gwenton, to the light industry and car factories of the south-east and Midlands. The population of Wales plummeted. A net loss of almost half a million in twenty years was not recovered until the 1960s. The debate between Owen and Price is not an argument about the validity of their interpretation of that history. It is the constant tension, separately felt in their individual lives and generations, which has been occasioned by that history. Arguably, Williams is less than fair to the Owen personality which, as the *New Left Review* interviewers suggested, is not fully rounded. Williams's view was that he wanted 'a character whose deep internal life is in a way inaccessible to him, though of course all the time he thinks and reasons and acts'.[34] The placing, however sympathetic, stems from a judgement that clearly believes the social uprooting of the 1930s continues as a fracture-line in Owen's incapacity to assess the human values of 'a more integrated kind of life'.[35] Sceptical critics have been quick to suggest there are elements, of a utopian conservative sort, in much of Williams's thinking about his Welsh working-class communities: that these are, at best, atypical and, at worse, falsified models. The charge fits neither the evidence available nor the use he has made of it.

Raymond Williams's Wales could be depicted as a whole community, integrated and cultured, to hold up, as worthy example, against the more rootless life of the university-factory city. There would be enough evidence, from the idyllic evocation of country life in *Border Country*[36] to the patriotic pride in Welsh radical specificities, to bring in the verdict of love-blindness, if it were not that at every juncture he has insistd on revealing the interpenetration of that life by those 'abstract' forces which Peter Owen in the novels rightly identifies as key factors in moulding what passes for the local and the national. This is the tale of

Wales that, for Williams, cannot be gainsaid. It is, indeed, more than any rooted tradition of people or language, the Welsh experience. The culture that he detects is, of course, not given or inherited but, in every real sense, manufactured and created. Like no other Welsh imaginative writer, he has operated in that shadowland between known, ready-for-wear Welsh characteristics and the uncertain identity of all who choose to present themselves, at this late stage, as Welsh. Then, along with that opening out, is the re-affirmation (as by Price against Peter Owen) that those uncertainties can only be managed, controlled eventually, with the help of an ascertainable human experience. Thus, in *Border Country*, Morgan Rosser is at one level right to spell out the inadequacy of industrial action that cannot move readily beyond support for the miners to demand power for a wider working class. He is at the same time wrong not to see that, already in the action of Harry Price and the others in 'standing by' the miners, a more vital form of working-class power has been identified.

The whole rhythm of *Border Country* moves to this conclusion. It is on such disputed ground that, first, Harry Price will act out the part *his* Wales has scripted for him and, then, where his son must affirm the value of cherishing the knowledge, allowing it to be carried forward even in defeat or in flux, that only lived experience provides. It is not, here, the past against the future since that falsifies the issues at stake. It is, instead, the way in which the present is lived that must concern us. Morgan Rosser, for justifiable reasons, moves through the dashed hopes of effecting social transformation by militant class action into a different, partly modernizing future in the grocery wholesale trade. He offers this to Matthew as he earlier proffers partnership to Harry. Neither can accept it. For Matthew the rejection can be viewed, perhaps over-rationalized, by seeing his own academic concerns as another way of attachment to the life he has left. Morgan, in fraught discussion with Matthew (Will) as Harry dies, is more fiercely explicit when Will asks:

'You think he was wrong then? That he missed his chance?'

' . . . He couldn't see life as chances. Everything with him was to settle. He took his own feelings and he built things from them. He lived direct, never by any other standard at all. . . . What we talk about . . . he's lived. It all depends on a mind to it, a society or anything else. And the mind we're making isn't the society we want, though we still say we want it. The mind he's got is to the things we say really matter. We say it, and run off in the opposite direction.'[37]

Neither of them can finish the argument ('It's a lifetime', says Morgan) because it is not a dialectic that can be resolved. The General Strike episode around which this novel revolves only poses the questions which Williams, in the 1950s, wishes us to see afresh. It is the very ordinariness of the railwaymen's solidarity which makes their action truly significant. The inconclusiveness of what occurred in 1926 mirrors the continuity of a working-class condition of being which cannot, by its nature, be transformed into a different state just by reaching some climacteric. Harry, inarticulate and unsure, tries to explain this to Morgan by telling him how useless slogans are for men like Meredith, the one who will continue to work: ' ... "Jack's a funny chap, mind. Don't go talking to him about the working class and power and that." "Why not?" Morgan asked. "He's a worker, isn't he?" Harry hesitated, and looked slowly round the box. "Aye, only it's not the way we talk, so watch him." '[38]

The action that concerns Meredith is less heroic than that taken by the stationmaster, in fact and in the novel, in allying himself with the men against the Company. If less heroic, it is no less a turning point. Meredith discovers his communal solidarity in discovering what he will *not* do, by whom and for what reasons he will *not* be ordered, and the power this gives, though never openly recognized by him, to act out of class loyalty. The subtlety of the episode is contingent upon its being part of a mosaic of contradictory deeds. The understatement confirms the unwanted connections that the General Strike elicits and enforces. The class politics which is seen to be embodied in this community is more profound than the genuine gestures of solidarity that the more advanced, more political, Morgan Rosser can make, briefly, in the miners's cause. His work, in this respect, is a negation of his own unwanted life, whereas Harry acts, always, in affirmation of the life he would wish to see confirmed.

At the beginning of the novel, when Harry goes to Glynmawr to work on the railway, there is a sense of unity in the life. He will earn his wages and maintain his smallholding. He will be fixed yet part of a network stretching beyond the village that he feels to be properly linked to his life:

> The narrow road wound through the valley. The railway, leaving the cutting at the station, ran out north on an embankment, roughly parallel with the road but a quarter mile distant. Between road and railway, in its curving course, ran the Honddu, the black water. On the east of the road ran the grassed embankment of the old tram road ... The directions coincided, and Harry, as he walked, seemed to relax and settle.[39]

The man and wife who feel 'on their faces their own country' possess and are possessed by their own community. Nothing in the lives that they go on to lead boasts this as an introverted self-sufficiency. To argue otherwise because their rural-industrial world is relatively becalmed is to ignore the contextual clues with which Williams surrounds them. Matthew does not 'go back' or 're-discover' or 'imitate'; he locates the stress of their lives to be able to distinguish his own. In *Border Country*, too, he sits on a mountain and meditates by reading off the history of his country in the landscape – the earlier conquerors, the Lords of the March, the later despoilers, the ironmasters to the south – since the 'mountain has this power, to abstract and to clarify, but in the end he could not stay here, he must go back down where he lived':

On the way down the shapes faded and the ordinary identities returned. The voice in his mind faded, and the ordinary voice came back ... History from the Kestrel, where you sit and watch memory move, across the wide valley. That was the sense of it: to watch, to interpret, to try to get clear. Only the wind narrowing your eyes, and so much living in you, deciding what you will see and how you will see it. Never above, watching. You'll find what you're watching is yourself.[40]

Raymond Williams wrote the final version of *Border Country* as a settling of accounts with his father, with himself and with the kind of Wales that had sent him away.[41] As we have seen, the settlement has proved to be of a different kind, and the closer he drew back in memory the more he discovered that his relationship to another Wales was not to have any ending. In particular, he began, quite consciously now, to emphasize its impact in defining relationships. These were to an extent the personal-cum-national notes that many exiles feel compelled to sound, from time to time, when in another country, but the delicacy with which Williams probed undercut any latent chauvinism from whatever direction it came. He argued, too, that work like *Culture and Society*, which redressed an English literary and intellectual balance, derived its insights into culture-industry-democracy from the society which had been shot through with their assumptions and consequences – Wales. The latter term he now saw, in some ways, as a larger synonym for 'community' and a living rebuttal of vacuous universalisms in literature, politics or economics.[42] Without endorsing the wishful thinking of the 'Small is Beautiful' school, Williams began to emphasize the necessity of community breakthroughs and local controls in order to face down both centralized and local power structures. The basic socialist premise was the emphasis on a social and cultural totality and the determining factor of class. The latter still did not mean for him a category differentiated from the places and people that other words, community and culture, also described. What was new in the 1980s was the manner in which the allegedly softer words finally acted to harden his account of a class history in twentieth century Britain.

The gap between Cambridge Communism and the South Welsh working class had not seemed, to so many, to be so unbridgeable. Good faith, ardent teaching and progressive politics could surmount the social divisions of accent, education and expectation. Or so it had appeared to those who did the defining. Williams, on the contrary, felt that this extended patronage was still a marginalization of the working-class experience with which it had sought a relationship. More, that it was in essence a betrayal because it preferred its surrogate conceptualization, with all its consequences of deceit and hypocrisy, to any actual engagement, in equality, with those who had offered their unmediated comradeship. Worse, that those so betrayed were the key part of that intense socialist culture in South Wales. Could a socialist republic really have come about in Wales in the 1920s if it could have been done by talking? It was still stirring to think so and the increasingly uncovered history of the coalfield struggles from the 1930s gave some credence to the claim.[43] What Williams was uniquely equipped to juxtapose to this history, though, was another history of socialist commitments, the one that weighted the dialogue, detested the compromise it felt paramount in working-class behaviour and theorized the reality with which it was confronted out of any tangible existence. He told this bitter version of events in a cold anger unlike the tone of anything else he had ever written. Wales was, again, centre stage in this narrative of indictment. The accused were sections and attitudes of the intellectual class in whose circles he had uneasily moved since the late 1930s.[44] In *Loyalties*, Raymond Williams's labyrinthine novel of events, places and people involved in left-wing activism from the Spanish Civil War to the 1984 Miners' Strike, he pulls threads together with such a vengeance that their tautness serves as a noose for hanging.

> ... this basic anger had seemed to be left behind when he had left home. It was not beliefs or positions he had then left behind; these could be packed and taken. It was the thing itself; the active alignment. Without that, in the world in which he had come to move, the beliefs and positions were matters for explanation, argument, even qualification, and he had always defended this, even against Dic, as being necessary for entry into a wider, more diverse ... world: the fight for the high ground, as he had once incautiously said, and been jeered at by Dic 'while we're still bloody underground'.
>
> It was not that he was now renouncing his new ways of seeing and arguing. It was that bursting out under them was this long repressed class anger ... At one level this could rejoin the open beliefs and positions: the settled critique of a hard ... capitalist state. But also, in more complicated ways, it was coming through, as he had put it, against people in that other and hated class who in terms of beliefs and positions were already on his side 'our side', as he had without thinking put it.
>
> Yet the Braoses were often quicker than his own people to talk the hard general language of class. Where Bert or Dic would say 'our people' or 'our community', the Braoses would say, with a broader lucidity, 'the organised working class', even still 'the proletariat' and 'the masses' ... he had been told, kindly enough, that the shift to generality was necessary. What could otherwise happen was an arrest or a relapse to merely tribal feeling. And he had wanted even then to object: 'But I am of my tribe' ...[45]

The prologue and end of the novel deal with the closed answers television wishes to present and the decision, by some, to keep the questions open. In between, decisions to act, and how to act, in the service of 'proletarian internationalism' are traced through all their intricacy. The actors are from the university at Cambridge and the mining communities in Wales. The novel begins in Williams's familiar border country, 'on the edge of the mining valleys', with a summer school, to organize 'as a base for political work'. The direction of the relationships so formed will eventually question the role of leaders and led and pose intelligence against intellectuality. This is a novel which, in no uncertain terms, despite its subtle appreciation of motives, chooses sides. We are given a hint of this early when Emma, well-meaning sister of Norman Braose, lectures Jim, miner and brother to Nesta, on the sweep of fascism across Europe. It is Bert Lewis – the miner, who will fight in Spain and in Normandy before marrying Nesta, and thereby serving as father to her child (Gwyn Lewis) by Braose – who quickly tells her that Jim is not uncertain about the need for opposition, only its direction – 'What Jim ... means is not whether we fight it but where'.[46]

Williams does not hold up one set of characters against others in a phoney chess game of decisions. His narrative indicates the restraints under which all manner of choice, personal and political, is made. Those who pass information, as scientists and civil servants, to the Soviet Union are not without good cause in their politics. What is awry is their failure to comprehend both the limited rationale of their actions and the destructive consequences of it for the continuing integrity of native socialist politics beyond either reformism or adventurism. The novel's discourse is, therefore, unusually reliant, even for a Williams's novel, on the full details of a more general, ascertainable record. To be convincing it has to be able to invoke the history of a people which, more than any individual story or episodic crisis, can be known to have achieved a density of community life that made for a vital working-class culture and politics. He conceives these Welsh working-class characters, then, and for the first time, directly inside the 'places where the direct causes, the central actions and the long consequences ... are so ... evident'.[47] The citation of the Welsh Valleys' history in *Loyalties* is abrupt in order to match the dramatic events of fifty years, from Spain to Suez and from 1968 to 1984, with which it directly connects. It is as if all of *Border Country* was written from the crisis point of 1926. The very power of those 'events' is what unites, momentarily, these disparate characters but what occurs, in the longer rhythms of social being between those points, declares a tragic separation. South Wales really does become in this novel a world to hold up, in measurement, against other worlds. It is the reality of that achieved history, experienced not completed, which must spurn the patronage of passing fashions – 'on the landing Gwyn noticed that Nesta's green heads of miners had disappeared. Where it had been hanging there was an embroidered African landscape'[48] – whose only interest is parasitic. The events – moments of defeat or of victory – serve only as signposts for a packaged and delivered history. Conscious understanding through survival is mostly unwritten but its traces are articulated through those common lives.

Gwyn Lewis, another son in quest of his origins, will remain in an uncertain state of mind at the novel's end because he cannot float free of the attachments, 'personal and political', that have deprived him of simple certainties. In one basically important sense he cannot be free of his father, Norman Braose. He can, nonetheless, be instructed by his other 'father', Bert Lewis who, dying in Danycapel in 1968, shows Gwyn a pick handle used against the police horses in 1910–1911 and given him, though for the having not the use of it, in the union struggle against blacklegs in 1936–7:

'So why did he give it to you?'
'He didn't say. He just give it me'.
'So you could use it?'
'No, no, we had plenty of picks'.
'What did you think, then?'
'I didn't. At that age you don't'

He rolled again on the pillows.

'You'll know better than me', he said, with his eyes closed,
'but I don't reckon much to this memory they call history'.
'Why's that?'
'History, I don't know. Your aunt Emma's always saying it. Only what I've
noticed is you get this story, this record, this account they call it. And of course
you can soon take it in. Aye that was Tonypandy. That was Bettws. That was
Spain. That was Normandie. You know it all, you know what I mean?'
'Aye'.
'And you know nothing. Like a birth certificate, or a diary.
Accurate granted . . .'
'Not always even that.'
'Aye, but still when it is you know what it means you to know. And it still isn't
none of it what it was. That was why old Vanny gave me the pick handle.'
'To feel it? Through the actual thing?
. . . And did you?'

Bert opened his eyes.
'No. Not then.'[49]

Nor, in 1984, will Gwyn understand immediately why his mother will scream
out, at his appreciation of the beauty he detects as 'truth' in her shocking portrait
of Bert's war-mutilated face. Nesta insists it is ugly and that Gwyn has still
understood nothing after all he has been told. Nesta's drawings and paintings are
at once directly accessible and shadowily removed from mere representation,
counterposed to the driving tendency to reduce the independent tonality of their
lives to the one note of imposed summation – 'In particular perspectives, and
always in its unexpected contrasts, the valley could be seen as dramatically
beautiful: "the view from outside", he had once said to Nesta, but she had shaken
her head and said it was always there to be seen, to show it to others was the
problem, getting past what was already in their heads. "But, Mam, you're not
saying that really it's beautiful?" "I'm saying what can be seen", she had
answered, reluctantly, 'but it's different what happens."'[50]
    Loyalties rejects the idea of one-dimensional portraiture. In it Raymond
Williams affirms the universal interest of what happened on his native grounds.
Clearly, he believes, and for reasons interrelated in the intellectual as well as the

political life of the left in Britain, that the advanced nature of that Welsh experience has been little appreciated. Yet here once was a paradigm case. To assert that is to argue against the *idea* of centres, whether in existence geographically or in the mind as mythology: 'There are many profound questions in the changing relations between the identity and rootedness of certain kinds of art and the mobilities and extended learning of a more consciously international scope. Such questions are not to be settled by old kinds of labelling.' And these relations apply and affect us across all the borders of our lives, sometimes distorting our perceptions: 'But always one way of approaching them is to see what is happening where you are. Sometimes, when you do this you find that the most local is also the most general.'[51]

Raymond Williams relates to Wales by making what has been local to him and his people a general condition of culture, community and class. Wales is related by the work of Raymond Williams in a way that does not wrench the significance of that history apart from the lives of the people who made it. If there remain divisions, there continues the commitment necessary to end them.

Notes

1 J. P. Ward, *Raymond Williams* 'Writers of Wales', (Cardiff, 1981). And see Jeremy Hooker, 'A dream of a country: the Raymond Williams trilogy', *Planet*, 49/50 (1980).

2 Raymond Williams, *Politics and Letters: Interviews with New Left Review* (London, 1979), pp. 295–6.

3 Raymond Williams, 'Wales and England', in John Osmond (ed.), *The National Question Again: Welsh Political Identity in the 1980s* (Llandysul, 1985), pp. 29–30.

4 Interview with Raymond Williams, 26 August 1986.

5 See, for example, Francis Mulhern's 'Towards 2000, or news from you-know-where' in *New Left Review*, 148 (November-December 1984) [reprinted as cl. 4 of the present volume]: 'As Williams himself has observed, no one speaks of "community" with critical intent, and this fact alone betrays its ideological function. "Community" is not an integral social entity, past, present or possible, but a fetish that disavows the reality in which its sponsors are so deeply engaged: the politico-cultural clash of collective identification. It would be wrong to undervalue the kinds of collective identification that Williams insists upon. But it is wrong also to consecrate them as "community" and to suppose that they can or should be generalised.' (pp. 24–5).

6 *London Review of Books*, 24 January 1985.

7 Ibid.

8 Osmond *The National Question Again*, p. 30.

9 *New Society*, 4 July 1986.

10 Raymond Williams sets this out in *Politics and Letters*, pp. 28–9, where he talks, too, of his rejection of the smug hypocrisy he found in Welsh noncomformity in the 1930s. And see his *The Country and the City* (St Albans, 1975), p. 368.

11 *The Volunteers* (London, 1978), p. 28.

12 *The Country and the City*, p. 364.
13 See Prys Morgan, 'From a death to a view: the hunt for the Welsh past in the Romantic period', in E. Hobsbawm and Ranger (eds), *The Invention of Tradition* (1983), and, for the consequences, Dai Smith, *Wales! Wales?* (1984).
14 Consult Kenneth O. Morgan, *Re-birth of a Nation: Wales 1880–1980* (1981) and Gwyn A. Williams, *When Was Wales?* (1985).
15 The phrase is the one Robert Wiebe used in his brilliant analysis of the USA in the same period, *The Search For Order, 1877–1920* (1967).
16 'The social significance of 1926', *Llafur: The Journal of the Welsh Labour History and Society*, 1977.
17 *Politics and Letters*, p. 35.
18 Ibid., p. 369.
19 *Llafur*, 1977.
20 *Politics and Letters*, pp. 21, 23.
21 Ibid., p. 24, pp. 26–7.
22 *Llafur*, 1977.
23 *Border Country* (Harmondsworth 1964), p. 9.
24 Ibid., p. 10
25 Ibid., p. 273.
26 Ibid., p. 10.
27 See Raymond Williams, 'Working-class, proletarian, socialist: problems in some Welsh novels', in H. Gustav Klaus (ed.) *The Socialist Novel in Britain* (Brighton, 1982) and 'Region and class in the novel', in his *Writing in Society* (London, 1984).
28 He discussed these matters in the inaugural Gwyn Jones Lecture, *The Welsh Industrial Novel* (Cardiff, 1978).
29 Introduction to Gwyn Thomas's 1949 historical novel about an insurrection in the 1830s, *All Things Betray Thee* (rep. 1986), pp. vi–vii.
30 Raymond Williams, 'Dylan Thomas's play for voices', in C. B. Cox (ed.) *Dylan Thomas: Critical Essays* (1966), p. 98.
31 *Politics and Letters*, p. 369.
32 *The Fight for Manod* (London, 1979), p. 136.
33 Ibid., pp. 206–7
34 *Politics and Letters*, p. 293.
35 Ibid., p. 287.
36 Rather oddly, but perhaps significantly, described as 'the evocation of a rural way of life in the years between the World Wars' in Meic Stephens (ed.), *The Oxford Companion to the Literature of Wales* (1986), p. 49.
37 *Border Country*, pp. 275–6.
38 Ibid., p. 83.
39 Ibid., p. 32.
40 Ibid., p. 281.
41 Raymond Williams, 'The tenses of imagination' in *Writing in Society*.
42 'Unconsciously my Welsh experience was operating in the strategy of the book [i.e. *Culture and Society*] ... The way I used the term community actually rested on my memories of Wales ... Even a Keynesian economist could tell me ... that the sooner the sheep farmers of Wales give up ... leaving those hills, presumably as an empty recreation area, for the discovery of nature. When I hear that kind of final economic

universalism ...' Quoted together in Ward, *Raymond Williams*, pp. 72–3.

43 John Stevenson's admirably non-anglocentric survey *British Society 1914–45* (1984) in the Pelican series refers, in a slightly bemused fashion to 'South Wales in the 1930s ... as a kind of hot-bed of militancy' and 'perhaps the most militant area in Britain during this period' (p. 292, p. 478). Which perhaps makes it inessential if 'the essential flavour of British society' was indeed 'one of moderation and consensus.'

44 Interview with Raymond Williams, August 1986.

45 *Loyalties* (London 1985), pp. 292–3.

46 Ibid., p. 26.

47 *Llafur*, 1977.

48 *Loyalties* p. 307.

49 Ibid., pp. 253–4.

50 Ibid., p. 329.

51 Raymond Williams, 'Introduction' to Meic Stephens (ed.), *The Arts in Wales 1950–75* (Cardiff, 1979), p. 4.

This essay was completed in 1986 before Williams's death and appears here in its original form.

3

POLITICS AND LETTERS

—— *Stuart Hall* ——

This is a somewhat unusual essay – more a commentary on some of the major themes and issues posed by this long and intense interrogation of Raymond Williams's work *Politics and Letters: Interviews with New Left Review* (1979) than, in any strict sense, a critical review of the book. There are several reasons for adopting this approach. First, the form of the book invites it. It is in the form of a series of extended interviews conducted with him by Perry Anderson, Anthony Barnett and Francis Mulhern on behalf of the *New Left Review* editorial board. I comment on the success of this form below. But here I simply note that the interrogative form, when well done, invites the reader to become involved in what is in any case a dialogue – with Raymond Williams, but even more importantly, with his work. The second reason is that my own work in cultural studies has so often followed, and in many instances been guided by, those key points which mark out Williams's own development, that I feel the strictly objective and external critical eye would be inappropriate here. The third reason is closely related to that. It is simply the fact that, apart from the influences which have naturally arisen in the course of working in closely cognate areas, there are several strategic points at which our careers have intersected. At very significant points in my own intellectual and political life, we have found ourselves shaping up to the same issues, or crises: and shaping up, if by no means in identical ways, then certainly from the same directions. I read an early essay of his, 'The Idea of Culture', which enunciated some of the themes of *Culture and Society*, in *Essays in Criticism* at exactly that moment when I had decided, on other grounds, that my intermittent interests in questions about 'culture' had to assume something of the nature of a more committed project. The essays of his which we were privileged to publish in *Universities and Left Review* were amongst those from external contributors which most closely resonated with the internal project of that venture. His dispassionate wisdom and support sustained me through some of the rougher passages of the early *New Left Review*. In the depths of the recoil from the manifest taming and political defeat of the 1964–66 Labour government, we found ourselves in the same room again, working on the draft of the statement which eventually became the *May Day Manifesto*. And so on. I put this somewhat too weakly and hesitantly. The fact is that in a broader, intellectual sense, I have often had the uncanny experience of beginning a line of thought or inquiry, only to find that, apparently coincidentally, he had not only been travelling much the same road but had given the issues a clearer, more forceful and clarifying formulation. *Politics and Letters*, the first, long overdue, attempt at a 'retrospective' seemed to call for something other than the usual balancing of accounts.

I have mentioned the form of *Politics and Letters*. I am not over-fond of the extensive interview form. It tends, on the whole, to a looseness of formulation: extensiveness at the expense of depth and penetration. However, on this occasion, I think the form has been deployed with extraordinary success. There are three reasons for this. First, it isn't a set of interviews in the usual sense at all, subsequently transcribed for publication. It is an extended conversation. The *New Left Review* editors have entered into the dialogue as full partners to the conversation. They have interpreted their brief as not merely to interview well, but to probe; to expand their questions into statements which are worth considering in their own right. They have formulated critical remarks and alternative positions, to which Williams has had to react positively. On many occasions I find myself disagreeing either with the form in which a criticism is made or with the direction in which the dialogue is turned. Often, I have felt myself gaining an unexpected insight into the collective mind of the *New Left Review* editorial team as much, if not more, than I am learning something about the development of Williams's work. But that is a minor point. The degree to which they have made themselves partners to the exchange has paid off. Second, their ability to become part of the dialogue in this way is clearly the result of extremely conscientious and careful preparation. They know Williams's work in all its detail. They have a comprehensive grasp of the turning points, the main lines of development. They have done their homework. The results show up in the text.

But the principal reason for the success of the form is undoubtedly the manner in which Williams has responded to the challenge. The self-reflexivity which the form demands suits him well. He has seized the opportunity to meditate and reflect. He has a remarkable ability to treat himself and his own work dispassionately, from the outside, as it were, without losing his line or his characteristic 'voice'. His capacity to respond affirmatively to criticism offers a most positive contrast with the intellectual defensiveness and the polemic search for an impossible retrospective consistency which characterizes so many of his contemporaries. And this is due, in the last resort, to a virtue which is to be found, not only in these interviews but in all his work – especially, perhaps his most recent work. I mean his capacity simply *to go on thinking*, to go on developing and changing in response to new intellectual challenges. In *Politics and Letters* he gives a quite exemplary demonstration of this dialogic quality of mind.

Biography

The Book is divided into six sections: Boyhood, Cambridge; then the major intellectual themes – Culture, Drama, Literature; finally, Politics. Readers will know more of Williams's personal background and boyhood than they would with comparable intellectual figures because he has written of them in fictional form in his 'Welsh Trilogy', *Border Country, Second Generation* and *The Fight for Manod*. His father was a railway signalman, but he lived in a village where more than half the population were small farmers. He comments here on the unusual way in which the rural pattern of small farmeres interlocked with the unionized and waged world of the railway. The strong and rooted sense of community – a concept which has taken on a peculiarly resonant meaning in all of Williams's writing – and his double attachment to countryside and the world of the railway workers are strands in his early formation which have been continuously reworked as themes in his later work. But for me the first arresting exchange in the book occurs at the beginning of chapter 2 – 'Cambridge' – where, in response to the question as to what the impact of Cambridge was like on the young, bright, already politically committed young man from the Welsh valleys, Williams simply responds: 'I was wholly unprepared for it. I knew nothing about it.'

Though I myself came from a very different background, to Oxford not Cambridge, and a decade later – beginning of the 1950s rather than the 1940s – those stark sentences carried enormous reverberations for me. I still feel a strong sympathy for that way in which the bright young lad from the 'periphery', coming to Oxbridge as the idealized pinnacle of an *intellectual* path, first experiences the actual *social* shock of discovering that Oxbridge is not only the apex of official English intellectual culture, but the cultural centre of the class system. I know at once what Williams means by remarking, in his usual understated way, that 'the class stamp of Trinity was not difficult to spot'; and also that inevitable path which led, in the search for some kind of refuge, to the discovery of the Socialist Club – 'a home from home'. In the Oxford Socialist Club of a decade and a half later, there was also a moment when the Welsh, Scots and other 'colonials' took a look around the room and came to the startling conclusion that 'There is not an Englishman among us.' Williams arrived in Cambridge at the end of the 1930s as the bright 'scholarship boy' from the valleys. He records with feeling how that brash, radical certainty was constantly broken against the effortless assumption of superiority of the system: the sense, as he put it, that any critical statement he made could be immediately beached by a knowing reference to a comparative text he had not read; the sense of being 'continually found out in ignorance'; and being forced to look at himself, increasingly, with radical doubt. I still experience that indefinable sense of being absolutely placed and put down even today, whenever I cross the threshold between Oxford railway station and Broad Street, gateway to the 'dreaming spires'. In the light of these pages, I now know just what is meant by thinking of this as a 'colonial' experience. Williams, being made of sterner stuff, has remained his own man through very long sojourns in both places.

By the time Williams returned to Cambridge at the end of the War, the 'break' had already occurred. In 1939–40 his project had seemed 'confident and unproblematic'. By 1945–6, it had become 'incredibly problematic'. It is difficult, even in the light of these pages, to distinguish between the elements of the personal, the political and the intellectual within this break. But, not surprisingly, for Williams (as for many of us a generation or two later), this 'sense of the complexity of things' was, in its own complex way, intertwined with the impact of Leavis. It is difficult now to convey to those who only know the conservative after-glow of Leavis and the *Scrutiny* tradition, the paradoxical nature of the influence of what Williams quite rightly calls Leavis's 'cultural radicalism'. For those who were part of the privileged Downing-*Scrutiny* circle, things were always different. They were committed, not only to the culturally conservative programme, but to following every twist and turn of the Great Man's idiosyncratic critical judgements, to imitating his ascetic, non-conformist ethic and to a mimicry of that highly distinctive style of writing, with its peculiar involutions. But why on earth should such a formation have had so powerful an impact on others of a more radical political temper, committed to an egalitarian educational practice? Williams cites in explanation Leavis's attack on the metropolitan literary and commercial cultural scene, the excitement of the discovery of practical criticism and the *Scrutiny* emphasis on education. But I wonder if these things didn't resonate more because of the immediately dominant ethos of Oxbridge itself? Certainly, in the 1950s, *Scrutiny's* 'seriousness' about serious issues contrasted favourably with the dilettantism of the Oxford approach to literary and cultural questions. Practical criticism seemed to offer some sort of discipline with which to combat the effortless exercise of 'good taste' which passes for the critical enterprise. Leavis discussed cultural issues as if they mattered. Finally – to repeat a point which Williams made with force in *Culture and Society* and which he makes again here, at a later point in the argument: If your field happened to be literary and cultural questions, *Scrutiny* offered a recognition of 'complexity' much more adequate to the complexity of the forms one had to deal with than anything which at the time passed for a 'native' Marxist literary or cultural criticism or theory. Practical criticism was the practice which condensed this value in its most available form. Williams is right, both in identifying its weakness (its evasion of the problems of structure, ideology and belief) and in acknowledging its persistent hold on those who were trained in it. Somewhere in there the commitment to 'a new cultural politics' was born.

But the break was also a political one. The sense of the loss of impetus in the
1945 Labour government, coupled with the impossibility of rejoining the
Communist party (which he had joined within a month or two of arriving at
Cambridge), left Williams, objectively, in what later we would have called a 'new
left' position – if any such thing had existed. 'You are a Communist, not a
member of the Party, but still a Communist,' people said to him, 'I did not know
what to reply. Neither no nor yes was the right answer.' But, of course, there was
no such political space then between the intolerables. And the collapse of his first
venture into active cultural politics – the break-up of the group around the
short-lived *Politics and Letters* – Williams appears to have experienced as a
personal crisis. 'I pulled back to do my own work. For the next ten years I wrote
in nearly complete isolation.' *Culture and Society* was, in part, the fruit of this
'retreat'. But, as others have suggested, the isolation took its toll, as certain notes
and tones in *Culture and Society* itself attest.

The *New Left Review* interrogators do not hesitate at this point to pose the
awkward political questions. Why didn't *Politics and Letters* nail its socialist
colours to the mast? Why didn't it go for a more direct intellectual-political form
of engagement? Williams does not duck the issue here. He bravely identifies the
costs of a prolonged sorting-out of the 'emerging terms of the collaboration
between left politics and "Leavisite" criticism.' This is true, and honest of him to
say so – as anyone who has gone through that painful 'sorting-out' will testify.
Yet, from a different point of view, the question is too *politicized*. There was
radically important work to do, precisely in the space which *Horizon* then and
Encounter a decade later occupied so effectively; a contest in the struggle for
intellectual hegemony over the liberal intelligensia in the polarizing climate of the
Cold War. It was a task which the Communist party should have filled but could
not. The historians clearly could and did for a time win some space within the
orbit of the Party for a different and telling kind of intellectual project:
accordingly, amongst those who, between 1946 and 1956, did stop and fight
inside the Party for a separate position, the most significant formation was the
historians, tutored and sustained by the elusive Dona Torr. But, as Williams
frankly and correctly puts it, 'The Party had absolutely no implantation of a kind
I could respect in any of the fields of work I was involved in.' Start of a new
chapter . . .

Culture and Society

The 'new chapter' was, of course, *Culture and Society* – which Williams shows
here to have been a genuine voyage of intellectual discovery, not a mere reworking
of an old Cambridge 'Moralists' course. It was an oppositional enterprise,
attempting to redress the appropriation of a long line of thought about 'culture'
to reactionary positions. In short, another episode in the engagement with the

Leavisite inheritance: that is why the reassessment of Arnold, though still too muted for my taste, is one of the main pivots of the book. Yet *Culture and Society* is profoundly marked by the imprint of the tradition to which it was counterposed: and nowhere so much as in its *method*. I am thinking of the preference for text over general argument or theory; the procedure by way of the 'local instance' and particularity: 'I shall try to do this by examining, not a series of abstracted problems but a series of statements by individuals.' This is the long shadow of 'practical criticism'. There is also the obliqueness of the approach to political questions – via, so to speak, the displacement of 'culture'; and the privileging of 'complexity of response' over position. If one asks what constitutes the unity of this 'tradition' it is certainly not a unity of positions adopted by the writers who compose it. Rather, it is the unity of an *idiom* – posing of the right, qualitative question; the priority given to the complexity of an articulated response to experience ('politics saturated with thought').

Of course, Williams is not wrong to have identified this underlying commitment, amongst writers who would have sharply disagreed with each other, to a particularizing, empirical-moral, anti-generalizing idiom of discourse about culture and society. The problem is that its presence in the book is over-determined from at least three directions: the force of the idiom itself amongst 'culture and society' writers; the preferring of this idiom in the qualitative side of the Leavisite appropriation of them; its underpinning in the method of analysis which Williams adopted – which carried the idiom, so to speak, in its very bloodstream, but as a *methodological* rather than a substantive imperative. It is this, I believe, which gives the book, ultimately, its undertow towards a certain 'inadvertent conservatism', despite the many other tendencies in it. The difficulty is that, since Williams's method underpinned the idiom it was analysing, the book itself offered no rallying point outside this empirico-moral discourse from which its limitations (as well as its strengths) might have been identified. Actually, of course, this was not a only a *cultural* question: in the English context, it was precisely the manner in which a particular set of political and social values had sedimented into a habitual inflection of language and thought. This book does not and could not place this because it remains, in some ways, methodologically trapped inside the discourse.

Something of this comes across in Williams's forthrightly self-critical response to a question from the *New Left Review* team, when he identifies in the book what he calls the way it is 'negatively marked by elements of a disgusted withdrawal ... from all immediate forms of collaboration.' Perhaps this goes too far, now, in the other direction: for, as he also insists, this very 'drawing back' allowed him to reintroduce themes and issues which have since become crucial, politically, but which were 'absent from what I knew then and often know now as politics'. Still, I think Williams has put his finger on a sensitive point in the *Culture and Society* project, though he has attributed it to too personal a cause.

His interlocutors take him to task, undoubtedly, for the 'absent traditions' and influences in the book; no French Revolution, or popular radicalism, or sociology; the lack of an international perspective and of Marx. Finding what *Culture and Society* left out has become, over the years, something of an intellectual game. Including them all would have required a book four times the length of the existing one. Perhaps it is a measure of the book's achieved stature that its critics expected it to be comprehensive. Yet these *are* convenient ways of trying to isolate some of the weaknesses of the book, even recognizing its properly limited scope. A comprehensive account of the French Revolution was certainly not on the cards. But its absence as a precipitating intellectual force within the corpus of English ideas means that not only is there little indication of the radical character, the growth and challenge, of popular radicalism, and the quite striking non-intellectual culture which sustained it; but also, the book lacks, as a dramatic episode, the sharp ruptures in the very liberal-intellectual climate of thought which Jacobinism provoked which *is* the centre of the book's concerns. The absence of 'sociology' is less surprising. Not only did it not manifest itself at the time when *Culture and Society* was being written as a comparable intellectual formation. Those who knew of its existence barely understood that the issues arising from 'the twin revolutions' were actually what the 'science of society' addressed. (This was the hey-day of American structural-functionalist gobbledygook.) As a result, the book could literally not address the questions as to why what, in Germany, was sustained in a historico-philosophical mode, and in France a 'positive social science' one, should have been sustained in England in so pre-eminently a *literary-moral* mode of discourse. But I confess that my own candidate of omission is none of these – though I do think the failure to recognize the non-literary culture of popular radicalism is both a product of *Culture and Society's* literary centredness and contributes to the book's over-literariness. What I have always regretted most in *Culture and Society* is the absence of any developed reference to the *dominant* intellectual formations of the time – political economy, political individualism, liberalism, empiricism – against which the 'culture and society' tradition was pitched. It is the ideas which formed the great heartland of the 'English ideology', and a sense of the profound sedimentation of these ideas into the habits and idioms of everyday life – the weight of English 'common sense' and its roots in the thought of the previous century and a half (Hobbes, Locke, Adam Smith and Bentham, to cite a few key names almost at random) – which needed at least to be sketched in, if we are to understand the force, within the culture-and-society tradition, of the conservative critique of utilitarian possessive-individualism (to coin a phrase). This would have given us a better sense of the somewhat 'exceptional' character of the literary-moral social critics, and placed them, as a formation, more appropriately, socially and historically. Williams makes a small gesture in this direction towards the end of this discussion in *Politics and Letters* where he regrets not yet having written up his early lectures on Hobbes. But it is a line I wish the *New Left Review* interviewers had pressed harder. Its relation to what the book is actually about is more organic: hence, in my view, its presence in the book only as an eloquent absence (what everybody in 'the tradition' was, implicitly, *against*) is rather more damaging.

The Long Revolution

The exchange achieves a particular pitch of intensity in the debate about *The Long Revolution* – and rightly so since its project was so thoroughly innovatory: a difficult, not always successful, but in its way *heroic* attempt to break, finally, with the idiom and method of *Culture and Society*: and, on the back of a mode of discourse militantly hostile to the very idea of generalization, to begin to construct a cultural *theory*. In a radical sense, *The Long Revolution* is a 'settling of accounts' – a text of the break. Its notorious 'difficulty' stems, I believe, precisely from the ambitiousness of its project. Often, the attainment of a genuinely sustained mode of theorizing falters, and the argument falls back on a sort of abstract generalizing. But the pressure to formulate was exemplary.

The main controversial themes are all touched on here. The tendency towards too evolutionary a notion of 'culture' – 'way of life' – which provoked E. P. Thompson's famous and strategic response – 'way of struggle' – is openly acknowledged. (The polemical manner in which this revision was advanced is noted, in a characteristically understated aside.) This leads Williams to a reformulation, expanding the difference between the permanent and inevitable presence of 'class conflict' – endemic in a capitalist social order, and those moments of 'conscious and mutual contention, an overt engagement of forces' – class struggle – which may not always be to the forefront. Actually, I would myself prefer to reverse Williams' proposed usage: using the more classic term, 'class struggle', to identify the general process, and 'class conflict' for those moments of more sustained and open contention. But this may be just a quibble. Thompson was undoubtedly correct to force the absolute centrality of these dimensions for any socialist definition of 'culture' to the forefront. Nevertheless, Williams here does rescue an important qualification, while conceding the general argument. He notes that the stress on 'struggle', appropriate for heroic periods of class conflict in history, may be less satisfactory for dealing with 'unheroic decades'. In the context of the 1950s, and later – indeed, perhaps from the 1920s onwards – not only do we have to confront 'unheroic periods'; but the nature and causes of their 'unheroic' character constitutes *the* absolutely key and prior issue for socialist analysis. In fact the problem of 'reformism' and containment is inadequately addressed by either an heroic emphasis on 'struggle' or Williams's more evolutionary 'way of life'.

Then there are the two characteristic stresses in *The Long Revolution*, for which Williams, despite his openness to the critical comments which his interviewers address, provides a tougher defence. The first is the stress, in the

Long Revolution, on the impossibility of separating out the different lived systems and according one any prior determinacy, the theoretical basis of the radically interactionist conception of the social totality which the book advanced. The second is the complementary stress on 'experience' as the authenticating test of cultural analysis, as well as the privileged object which it attempted to 'produce in thought'. Williams receives a strong challenge on both questions from the *New Left Review* team. On both he has conceded something – especially with respect to the first; making a sort of return, in more recent work, to a stronger sense of 'determinacy' than the 'interaction of all practices on one another' which marked his position in the *Long Revolution*. Nevertheless, I see a striking continuity of basic position on these issues even in his more acceptable recent formulations. Both a marked disparity between different systems and a temporal unevenness in social formations are now more openly acknowledged. But Williams continues to resist any attempt at the analytic separation of different structures and practices. He acknowledges that his earlier 'appeal to experience' as a way of grounding this unity of structures was unsatisfactory. But he stands by the reformulation of this position which achieved its clearest statement in *Marxism and Literature*: 'indissoluble elements of a continuous social-material process'.

This is an area where I continue to take issue with him. I do think that the indissolubility of practices in the ways in which they are experienced and 'lived', in any real historical situation, does not in any way pre-empt the *analytic* separations of them, when one is attempting to theorize their different effects. The ways in which everything appears to interconnect in 'experience' can only be a starting point for analysis. One has to 'produce the concrete in thought' – that is, show, by a series of analytic approximations through abstraction, the concrete historical experience as the 'product of many determinations'. Analysis must deconstruct the 'lived wholeness' in order to be able to think its determinate conditions. I believe this necessary use of abstraction in thought is quite mistakenly confused, in current debates, with a sort of 'fetishization of theory' (theoreticism, of course, exists, and is a plague on all our houses: but so is empiricism). And I do think that this confusion, which persists even in Williams's later work, is predicated on an uninspected notion of 'experience' which, in the earlier work, produced the quite unsatisfactory concept of 'a structure of feeling' and which continues to have disabling theoretical effects. However one attempts to displace the plenitude which the term 'experience' confers, and however much one allows for 'marked disparities' and 'temporal unevenesses', so long as 'experience' continues to play this all-embracing role, there will be an inevitable theoretical pull towards reading all structures as if they expressively correlated with one another: simultaneous in effect and determinancy because they are simultaneous in our experience. Here I find myself in agreement with the *New Left Review* questioners: 'structures can be temporally simultaneous, but they need not thereby be causally equal.' The more recent emphasis on 'indissoluble socio-material practice' does, of course, go a great deal of the way towards a more materialist theory of cultural practice. But what I think, without being unfair, we can call the 'experiential' paradigm does continue to cause some theoretical fluctuations in Williams's work around such key problems as determination, social totality and ideology. Williams is admirably clear on these questions in this section, and always open to critical argument. But he does not concede much ground.

Literature

In the hot-house climate of theoretical sectarianism through which we have recently passed, it has often been assumed that a theory which *tends* towards the correspondence between different practices (or the dissolution of them all in 'material praxis', which is a variant of the same position) would necessarily produce a corresponding problem when applied to more local instances. But this is to deploy the theory of 'symptomatic reading' in a hopelessly theoreticist way – reducing all of every text to its 'problematic'. In fact, when we come to Williams on literature, there has never been any simple parallelism of this kind. Indeed, as we move from the discussion of literature and society in the 1840s, in *The Long Revolution*, through *The English Novel from Dickens to Lawrence to The Country and the City* – one of his finest but most neglected works – we move further and further from any such correspondences. In part this is because of a rich, deeply organic but non-formalist conception of 'form' – a theme, first enunciated in rather organicist terms in *The Long Revolution*, which has undergone progressive transformations since.

I wish I had more space to devote to the passages in *Politics and Letters* which deal with literature, literary theory and drama, because they are among the richest in the volume. In the early 'Cambridge' section, it comes as something of a shock to find that the literary intellectuals in the Communist party at the time were regarded by their comrades as 'aesthetes' because of their commitment to the project of a modernist literature (Williams cites Joyce in particular here). For much of his work in this area, the common view would be that which notes his strong attachment to and vigorous defence of the *realist* tradition. He means 'realism' in the Brechtian sense. And his critique of the absolutist manner in which the debate about realism has been conducted (the worst excesses have been in film theory) and his gentle reproof of the a-historical way in which an immovable correspondence has been assumed between modernist aesthetics and revolutionary socialism is well made, and timely. But, his reflexive remarks on *Dickens to Lawrence* – apart from many illuminating asides – are important primarily because of the manner in which the term 'form' is deployed. The distinction between an attention to the 'form' of the work (for example, the contrast between the reproduction of 'known forms' in Trollope, and the 'formally disturbed novels' of George Eliot and Hardy) and a formalist criticism, is a highly relevant one for contemporary debates in aesthetics. It has not, I think, been sufficiently noticed how systematically, in these more 'traditional' works of literary criticsm, Williams has tried to fight his way – not always successfully – out of the pull towards the 'practical critical' approach towards a different kind of critical practice.

My own view is that this break is not fully made until *The Country and the City*. The difference here consists, primarily, of two elements. First, the formalized and conventional nature of much 'pastoral' literature has *forced* a more sustained attention to displacements and disjunctures, which earlier work on more 'naturalistic' and 'realist' forms did not. But the more significant element is the sustained and detailed historical work, and its integration into the thematic of the book, which radically and irretrievably interrupts any residual pull towards 'practical criticism'. The *New Left Review* interviewers put their finger on this point very precisely when they note how prolonged and how full of subtle reformulations have been Williams's efforts to define what constitutes the literary text. In *Reading and Criticism* the documentary aspect was still paramount: the text was 'a record of human experience'. *Culture and Society* added a more active element: there it is both 'record' and 'response'. The 'response' side is developed in *The Long Revolution* in theoretical terms: literature provides the most intense kind of 'response' to cultural change; but it is also placed as a 'special kind of communication' and therefore part of a more general 'creative' process. *The English Novel* describes literary texts as a 'dramatization of values' – 'an action'. We can see the movement here from the characteristically Leavisite inflexion – record-response-expression – to a more 'Brechtian' conception of literary production. But it is only in *The Country and the City* that these two warring conceptions are brought into direct confrontation: and what produces this is the fact that 'for the first time literature is distanced and contrasted against a history that is systematically and separately analysed'. Williams's response to this point is very direct. The project was 'to show simultaneously the literary conventions and the historical relations to which they were a response . . . to see together the means of production and the conditions of the means of production'. This remains the most challenging of Williams's efforts in this field to put to use his own specialized notion of what is involved in seeing literary forms *historically*. Interestingly, then, the discussion in this section does not remain at the 'literary' level, but is obliged to engage very central historical and theoretical questions: the relationship of classical Marxism to 'city' and 'country', and the vexed issue of whether or not one can speak of 'progressive' literary forms. The question of rural and urban is one of the 'lost' themes in Marx. Williams's approach to this question – informed as it is by his own background and experience – is one of his most creative moments.

It is nevertheless the case that, theoretically at least, *Marxism and Literature* takes the notion of 'literary production' several stages on even from the positions adopted in *The Country and the City*. The former is one of the clearest statements we have of Williams's current position – a masterpiece of condensed formulation. It takes his earlier conception of the 'continuum of creative practices of communication' several steps further than the earlier volume; and it produces some challenging theses, mainly grouped around a new, provisional definition of his own project as that of clarifying and developing 'a cultural materialism'. The first thesis evokes from the *New Left Review* team a somewhat outraged and scandalized defence of 'the received idea of literature' – a piquant moment for *New Left Review* watchers, this. But the second leads to one of the most provocative exchanges in the book – around the 'cultural materialism' thesis. The exchange deserves to be read in full. The important point seems to me to be the fact that Williams is still on surer ground when he identifies negatively the positions against which 'cultural materialism' is defined ('a totally spiritualized cultural production' on the one hand; on the other, its 'relegation to a secondary status') than he is in clarifying the positive content of his thesis. Clearly the challenge of recent debates around 'material practice' have stimulated him to a whole new phase of thinking – a welcome sign of the continuing vigour and freshness of his mind, even if one could have wished that *Marxism and Literature* fingered its opponents in a more open way. The question of determination continues to be the theoretical thorn in his side. Only those who have not suffered from this continuing irritant could afford to be cavalier with the problem, even if they also recognize that the definition of 'determinacy' as 'limits and pressures' is nothing more than a holding operation.

Politics

The *conscience collective* bristles again at what they somewhere describe, with alarm, as a 'veering towards a radicalism of the ultra-left' in Williams's current position. The actual course of the closing discussion on 'Politics' must be reassuring in at least this respect. The emphases are characteristic: the break with 'Labourism' (which leaves open the question of strategies towards the Labour party), the need to by-pass received models of socialism, the question of self-management. If this is 'ultra-leftism' it is only in the mildest of doses – and a thoroughly necessary tonic. In fact, alerted as we are by the ruffling of *New Left Review* feathers, what surprises us most about this concluding section is the steady and persistent way in which Williams sticks to his guns: I mean, responding to the more overtly 'political' issues by having at his disposal all the complex themes of his particular preoccupations with broadly 'cultural' questions. In others this may have appeared as an evasion. In this instance it provides a sort of demonstration that, properly understood, the distinction politics/culture is, for him, an irrelevant one. To sustain *that* point while facing up to questions *inter alia* about the Labour party, the tender issues surrounding the transfer of power between the 'New Left' Marks I and II, the 'October Revolution' and the future of socialism, is a remarkable testimony to his single-mindedness, his absolute singularity of tone and address.

I return, in closing, to my original starting point. Both in form and content, *Politics and Letters* does not ask for, and should not get, blanket affirmation. This would be a hopeless exercise, since the book is instinct with revaluations, reformulations, taking criticisms, opening new lines of thought. There is no 'position' here to subscribe to. It is not a book for the religious. What is consistent is a *project*: the project of working through some of the most difficult and thorny problems in Marxist cultural theory. What the book is evidence of and for is the capacity to sustain a project at full intellectual strength: or, more simply, what I called his determination simply *to go on thinking*. On this matter, *Politics and Letters* is simply an exemplary performance.

4

TOWARDS 2000, OR NEWS FROM YOU-KNOW-WHERE

────── *Francis Mulhern* ──────

Calendars are never innocent, but in recent times they have become positively lurid. Even the soberest temporal reckoning is open to the suggestions of political numerology, which fascinates by its very lack of reason. The year now ended [1984] was for a generation the deadline for the most widely propagated of latterday political forebodings, George Orwell's vision of 'Ingsoc'; and, as if that had not been distraction enough, 1984 found us exactly mid-way between 1968 and the millennium, 2000. Such thoughts are whimsical, but whimsy is not random. It is a sign of anxiety, in this case a political anxiety whose real grounds are evident. The stronger probabilities of the years ahead appear dispiriting and dangerous, and, more gravely, it is increasingly widely feared that the reservoir of historical possibility is in fact a mirage. Contemporary culture is pervaded by what Raymond Williams has come to call 'the sense of the loss of the future'[1] – the future not as a continuation of recognizable forms of social existence but as a locus of realizable alternatives. It is ironic that capitalism should at length have 'advanced' to this. Familiar as the most dynamic mode of production in history, capitalist culture valorized the attainable earthly future as no prior culture could have done. The theme of 'modernity' was and is just this: an endless serial presentation (*making present*) of the future. The ambition was not empty: capitalism has remade and continues to remake the earth and its populations. But the accumulation of tomorrows is self-depleting. The physical landscapes of advanced capitalism are now littered with stalled and abandoned futures, things and people alike, much metropolitan culture is an aimless circulation of retro-chic, and apocalypse itself is just the last word.

But socialism too has seen its futures come and go. Capitalism has survived longer, and with far greater material and social successes, than most nineteenth-century socialists would have forecast. Social democracy, in spite of governmental opportunities extending over as much as half a century, has nowhere prevailed against the rule of capital, and in many cases is unable even to sustain its limited achievements. The Communist tradition has been much more successful, abolishing capitalism across one-third of the planet; but, for all their social gains, the bureaucratic regimes of the East have one after another dissipated their original power of example and attraction for socialists elsewhere; and the Communist parties in the West are caught in a political latitude whose climate varies only between Stalinist freeze-up and the treacherous thaw of social democracy. Revolutionary tendencies – including, indeed, state practices – continue to reassert themselves against this virtual system of political frustration, but none has yet summoned the force necessary to break through its cyclical present into a hopeful socialist future.

This is the context in which to retrace the fortunes of 'projective' and 'prospective' discourse on the left. The rhetoric of social dissent has traditionally included projections of the desired alternative. However important the main critical modes of analysis and polemic, there was obvious, perhaps even special, utility in the attempt to give body to the values that animated them. This was the work of the 'utopia' (and the closely related 'romance'), a fictional mode in which the optative assumes the forms of the indicative, the goals of the struggle appearing as if already fully and securely achieved. The utopia was a powerful inspirational device, and was valued as such in the diverse radical culture of the nineteenth century. But its defining operation was wish-fulfilment; it dealt in idealities whose earthly home was, admittedly, 'nowhere'. By the end of the century this fiction, together with other forms of discourse to which the generic term 'utopian' was now applied, had been depreciated, as a radically different conception of intellectual priorities won hegemony over the socialist movement.

The theory inaugurated by Marx and Engels was distinctively 'scientific'. Communism was possible because of the real movement of material history, and would come about not through the redemptive human incarnation of an ideal scheme but by the overthrow of capitalism at the hands of its own social creation, the proletariat. Utopianism was now obsolete. The primary responsibilities of 'scientific socialism' were the analysis of capitalism and the states that defended it, and the development of organizations and programmes capable of mobilizing the working class against them. The projection of desirable futures now gave way to the analysis of historical prospects. Utopian and romantic writing did not wholly disappear from Marxist culture: William Morris produced the classic *News From Nowhere*; Engels's *Dialectics of Nature* veered at times towards a kind of evolutionary romance; revolutionary Russia stimulated Kollontai's fiction and the rhapsodic finale of Trotsky's *Literature and Revolution*; and 'socialist realism' bore a heavy charge of official romance. But the main prospective mode was the strategic forecast. Works such as Trotsky's *Results and Prospects*, Luxemburg's *Accumulation of Capital* and Lenin's *Imperialism* addressed themselves to the existing systemic trends of capital and its political and military apparatuses. Their analyses were in one sense bleak, predicting the impossibility of 'normal' political development in Russia, an inbuilt capitalist drive towards barbarism, a century of inter-imperialist warfare. Yet they were motivated by a powerful historical optimism. They prepared for the worst because only in that way could they prepare to forestall it, turning the contradictions of capitalist development to revolutionary account. The socialist future was not in doubt, but it depended on the strategy and tactics of the socialist revolution.

This definition of priorities remains valid, but it no longer possesses a monopoly of realism. 'Socialism' is official fact for the hundreds of millions who live in the post-revolutionary bureaucracies of Europe, Asia and the Caribbean. The ambiguous record of these states, interlocking with the history of social-democratic management of capital, has deformed and discredited socialist politics throughout the world. In such conditions, some kinds of projection are no longer idle, and 'strategy' risks abandonment as the last utopia.

Anything but novel, considerations of this kind have already run to practical results in the politics and culture of the left, both East and West. Rudolf Bahro's agenda for renewed advance in the post-revolutionary societies united social analysis and Communist moral affirmation in a remarkable 'concrete utopia', his *Alternative.* In the West, the putative instrumentalism of traditional strategic thought is now widely challenged by an expressive, 'prefigurative' politics whose key references are feminism and ecology. The cultural capacity of 'the new social movements' is widely acclaimed – and is nowhere more telling than in its rediscovery of the fictional modes of romance (Alice Walker's *The Color Purple*) and utopia (Ursula Le Guin's *The Dispossessed,* Marge Piercy's *Woman on the Edge of Time*). There is no need to accept developments like these at their own assessment, but it must be recognized that they signal a deep and probably permanent change in the conditions of socialist strategic thinking.

Towards 2000

This recognition has long been a force in the work of Raymond Williams. It has governed the development of his central concept of 'culture', which, while gaining in specificity as an object of materialist analysis, has remained a criterion of moral judgement; and it has supported his steady criticism of any too-peremptory dismissal of romanticism. His writings have repeatedly questioned the meanings of 'nature' in bourgeois (and, by inheritance, socialist) culture. He has written valuable essays on Bahro and on Morris and Le Guin, and has made his own contribution to the fiction of the future in his 'hypothetical' novel, *The Volunteers.*[2] At the same time, Williams's work has always been distinctive for the radically historical, anti-essentialist stress of its analyses, and its tough-minded wariness in political response. He has never accepted the analytic and the moral, the indicative and the optative, as truly sustainable alternatives. Constructive, if tense, argument between them is a necessary condition for the creation of an informed, authoritative and capable socialist movement.

All such positions must find their support in the evidence of the past; but their point concerns the future. In *Towards 2000*, Williams turns forward in time, to assess the probabilities of the remaining years of the century.[3] The title of the book is an argument in itself. Invoking old and non-rational traditions of discourse on the future, it signifies the decision to venture beyond strategic minimalism into the possible reality of a socialist order – and this as a condition of renewing social 'hope'. But Williams is equally concerned to avoid the typical prolepses of utopianism. His objective is to understand the future *historically*, in a 'prospective analysis' that seeks to interpret 'the underlying problems, forces and ideas' of capitalism and its probable future, and to 'indicate some possible ways through them' towards a decidedly non-millenarian socialism.

Towards 2000 is a difficult book to write about, in the first place because of its form, which emerges from the special circumstances of Williams's own work. It is written as a review and extension of an earlier 'prospective analysis' entitled 'Britain in the Sixties' and first published as that decade opened, in *The Long Revolution*.[4] Williams reprints his analysis here, and resumes its discussions of economic, cultural and political structures and ideologies, and of the labour movement; then takes his argument into new territories, with chapters on 'the culture of nations', the world economic and political order, and the arms race; and finally moves to a reflection on the available theoretical and political 'resources for a journey of hope'. Demanding in range, the book is also variable in analytic focus, moving from the abstract (capitalist production as such) to the concrete (the international economic system), the general (bourgeois-democratic representative practices) to the particular (the British Labour Party), sometimes without notice. *Towards 2000* is then 'open' in a sense that is not merely polite: it is amenable to several quite distinct kinds of assessment, and demands not summary but elaborated responses. The scope, proportion and nuance of Williams's analyses will not be represented adequately, much less emulated, in what follows here: a clipped account of his main theses, and some thoughts on their theoretical and political implications.

Williams's argument is centrally a critical analysis of the dominant culture in its most practical, even 'functional', aspect. The real objects of this culture (economic, political and, of course, cultural too) are discussed directly, but in a selective mode whose priorities are dictated by a strategy of ideological displacement and counter-formulation. The field of analysis is Britain and its international relations, in the perspective of a reachable and sustainable socialism.

Analysing the mystifications of 'consumer' capitalism on the eve of the 1960s, Williams queried the expectation of 'a steadily rising standard of living in this economically exposed and crowded island. Both the rapid rate of economic growth elsewhere, and the certainty of steady industrialization of many areas now undeveloped, seem ominous signs for a country so dependent on trade and in fact given its prosperity by its early industrial start (now being overtaken) and its empire (now either disappearing or changing its character).'[5] The signs were not deceptive, and now the balance of Williams's attention shifts towards production, to the fateful realities invoked in such terms as 'post-industrialism', 'de-industrialization' and 'employment'. Arguing through and against the assumptions clustered around these words, Williams maintains that the current crisis must be understood and tackled as that of the *international capitalist social order*. The closures and redundancies of the past decade are attributable not to a new phase of technical innovation *per se*, but to technologies designed and deployed in accordance with the ordinary logic of capitalist production and marketing. To construe the present restructuring of manufacturing capital as 'de-industrialization' is to misrecognize capitalism, which is now a synthetically international system, and industry itself, which will continue its uneven transformation of economic activity well into the future. In the face of this reality, the policy nostrums of reflation and protection are utterly inadequate. They fail to confront the social implications of continuing technical development and assume an impossible national autarky; they preserve the socially null value of aggregate production and – the ultimate economic irrationality – remain trapped in the bourgeois fantasy of 'infinite production' in a 'finite world'.

Yet more ominously, the crisis has begun to dissociate a trinity whose substantial unity has long been a tenet of capitalist faith and of Labour's alternative accountancy: that of 'work', 'employment' and 'income'. In effect, Williams argues, capitalism can understand 'work' only as industrialized wage-labour. This can be seen in the conventional tripartition of economic activity, which models all social labour as a factory process, and is then obliged to classify most of it in the absurd category of 'services'; in a classification of 'skill' that bears no relation to any rational assessment of expertise; in the occlusion of household labour and the devaluation of its socialized extensions and equivalents. The economic crisis is, among other, more familiar things, a crisis of this world view. For given the probable course of world demand for manufactured goods and the technical transformation of production processes, unemployment can be ended only by a major development of the labour-intensive activities of 'nurture and care' – kinds of work that attract low (or no) income because they do not, and cannot, reward capitalist investment. 'Welfare capitalism' has always been a contradiction in terms, Williams argues. Only if 'welfare' is generalized as the shaping principle of all economic activity can technical innovation become 'labour-saving' in a positive sense. But this entails the institution of a planned and socialized economy, and, as a necessary practical and moral corollary, a break with capitalism's accounting of labour and income, in conditions that will demand the sharing of abundance but also of want. To propose less or to promise more is merely to echo 'the death-cry of an old social democracy'.[6]

The imagined and real bearings of 'technology' are again to the fore in

Williams's discussion of contemporary *culture*. Here too a new phase of technical innovation has begun, and, with it, a new round of controversy. Cultural conservatives resist cable and satellite broadcasting systems, discerning in them (as in so many earlier developments) the final onset of barbarism. They are joined in their opposition by many on the left, who see the new systems as the instruments of an increasingly powerful apparatus of cultural domination. This reaction is understandable but dangerous, for 'all that follows from so undeveloped a position is a series of disparaging remarks and defensive campaigns, leading in so many cases to tacit alliance with the defenders of old privileged and paternalist institutions, or, worse, with the fading ideas of the old cultural argument: a high culture to be preserved and by education and access extended to a whole people.'[7]

Williams's response is to analyse the actual significance of contemporary developments in communications, and to assess the position of that 'old cultural argument' and its defenders. Again he insists on the fundamental distinction between *techniques* and their variable social elaborations in specific *technologies*: the former are subject to physical necessity but the latter are crucially shaped by economic, political and cultural forces. The new technologies are menacing because they are being deployed in the service of a very few 'paranational' corporations and metropolitan power-centres; the culture they relay is correspondingly homogenized, and will tend to weaken and marginalize significant alternative practice. The traditional 'minority culture' cannot resist this trend, for the simple reason that it has already succumbed. The evolution of its means of support furnishes material evidence of its loss of independence, passing from private patronage through state subsidy to commercial sponsorship – from Harriet Weaver to the Arts Council to Booker-McConnell. Where this culture survives, it is increasingly given over to a stylish, fey nostalgia financed by the 'paranational godfathers' and diffused world-wide by grace of their technologies. Modernism has meanwhile adapted itself to the conditions of commodity-exchange, its 'originally precarious and often desperate images' now routinized as a bleak social ontology whose assumptions and idioms not only persist in minority art but have entered much 'popular' culture. This convergence, impossible according to the axioms of modernist ideology, was in fact programmed by the historical conditions of modernist practice. For the processes that brought modernism into being – the new concentrations of economic and political power, the remaking of old societies and cultures – also created new systems of production and distribution, which have taken over the 'once liberating' alienations of that art and projected them as the truth of a human condition. 'The monopolizing corporations and the elite metropolitan intellectuals', apparently timeless antagonists, were in fact accomplices. 'One practised the homogenization, the other theorized it ... The real forces which produced both, not only in culture but in the widest areas of social, economic and political life, belonged to the dominant capitalist order in its paranational phase.'[8]

'The new technologies' have of course been the instruments of this development, and much 'popular taste' has been shaped by them. But the realities to which these stereotypes are fastened retain the potential of a quite different culture. Outside the dominant order, though never safe from incorporation in it, there exist oppositional, intentionally 'popular' forms and practices; and more widely and fundamentally, there are forms of comedy, music and even 'popular "domestic" drama and fiction' that are simply irrepressible. An alternative deployment of the emerging technical systems could sustain and develop this now subordinate culture, just as it could decisively alter the conditions of many economic, social and political processes. These systems, Williams declares, are the 'indispensable means of a new social order'.

The *political forms* of a new social order are the subject of Williams's chapter on 'democracy old and new'. In *The Long Revolution*, Williams highlighted the autocratic strain in British parliamentary government and its reductive, 'liberal' version of democracy, and stressed that even a fully democratized parliament was not a sufficient condition of a self-determining society. *Towards 2000* renews this analysis and extends it to query prevailing norms of 'representation' and the current political conceptions of the Labour left. 'Parliamentary democracy as we know it' is plainly not fully democratic: sovereignty resides not with the people but with 'the Crown in Parliament', a threefold entity of which only one component is elected – irregularly, according to the limited but effective discretion of the prime minister, and by means of a voting system that actively misproportions the recorded distribution of electoral options. A further limitation is the prevailing notion and practice of 'representation', which condenses two crucially distinct senses: 'making present' and 'symbolization'. The first is the democratic sense, and, fully understood, entails the principles of delegation, mandate and revocability. The second, a pre-democratic conception derived from the metaphor of 'the body politic', describes current practice. It provides ideological support for political careerism – for the presumption that an individual can be a 'representative' by vocation, in advance of (and often in defiance of) any specific warrant of democratic acceptability. It is part of a system of values that betrays the existence within 'parliamentary democracy as we know it' of an effective counter-ideology and counter-polity: 'the institution of a temporarily absolutist body within the carefully preserved contradictions of the electoral process and the monarchical state.'[9] Even after reform of all these undemocratic structures, Westminster's claim to embody democratic government would remain spurious. Parliamentary decisions are taken in an environment dominated by the social powers of capital: the finance houses, industry and the press. An internally reformed Westminster system would therefore remain *bourgeois*-democratic, its effective powers subject to the overarching will of capital.

Socialists project a 'higher' or 'fuller' democracy, Williams continues, but have yet to clarify its necessary and feasible forms. The familiar principles of 'a left government and self-management' are not self-evidently compatible, especially when the former is construed as in the present arguments of the Labour left. Here, democracy is invoked above all in demands for the accountability of the parliamentary fraction to the party. But the party itself is not fully democratic, and cannot become so while conference decisions are reached by the non-proportioned and often non-accountable votes of trade-union and constituency delegates; and the left's proposals for reform of the polity run no further than abolition of the House of Lords. It appears, if only by default, that the existing apparatuses are to be used to implement radical change but not to undergo it themselves. This is a commandist prospectus, Williams argues, and the appeal to the countervailing effects of self-management in particular social processes is 'a pious hope' or 'a pathetic delusion'. The tension between 'fully adequate general powers' and 'deeply organized and participating popular forces' must be regulated through suitably designed democratic institutions. The critique of 'representation' must extend to individuals and forums alike, 'all-purpose' mandates and assemblies giving way to decision-making processes of 'specific and varying' scale. And all such processes, including the most general and central, must be governed by 'the distinctive principle of *maximum self-management*, paired only with considerations of economic viability and reasonable equity between communities'.[10] The elaboration of such socialist-democratic perspectives is now 'our central historic challenge'.

Communities, Societies and States

The economy and culture of capitalism have never readily yielded to any existing boundary, traditional or revolutionary. Structurally 'paranational' in their advanced forms, they work against all local resistances, coordinating social relations – *societies*, in the effective sense – ever more widely across the earth. Yet the bourgeois polity is entrenched in the nation-state, and its dominant ideology reserves a correspondingly prominent place for the values of nationality and patriotism. This political form is not an inert 'survival', Williams argues. Persisting against universalist ideals and amid the real universalizing tendencies of contemporary economic and military systems, it is centrally functional to capitalism, and an obstacle to the elaboration of a socialist alternative.

Offical 'communities' such as 'the Yookay' (Williams's derisive acronym for the United Kingdom) have been raised over the bones and ashes of the human settlements whose forms they now impersonate.

> Both in its initial creation of a domestic market and in its later organization of a global market, the capitalist mode of production has always moved in on resources and then, necessarily, on people, without respect for the forms and boundaries of existing social organizations. Whole communities with settled domestic forms of

production . . . were simply overridden by more developed and more centralized and concentrated capitalist and capitalist-industrial forms. Communities which at simpler levels had relatively balanced forms of livelihood found themselves, often without notice, penetrated or made marginal, to the point where many of their own people became 'redundant' and were available for transfer to new centres of production. Capitalist textile production, ironmaking, grain production and a host of other industrial processes set in train immigrations and emigrations, aggregations and depopulations, on a vast scale. Typically, moreover, people were moved in and out on short-run calculations of profit and convenience, to be left stranded later, in worked-out mining valleys or abandoned textile towns, in old dockyard and shipbuilding areas, in the inner cities themselves, as trade and production moved on in their own interests.[11]

The image of capitalist progress so familiar from *The Communist Manifesto* is here set against the damning evidence of its negative. However, the image and the negative are seldom brought together in ordinary experience. The same accumulation process is felt here as catastrophe but there as prosperity, and in the era of consumer capitalism there are usually just enough means of temporary escape for just enough people just enough of the time. 'Mobile privatization' is Williams's name for this everyday culture: 'at most active social levels people are increasingly living as private, small-family units, or, disrupting even that, as private and deliberately self-enclosed individuals, while at the same time there is a quite unprecedented mobility of such restricted privacies.'[12] Such atomism is serviceable to capital, economically and also politically. Yet the processes that generate it are vulnerable to social attack. 'Thus "law and order"; armed forces called a "defence" force even when some of their weapons are obviously aggressive: these, unambiguously, are the real functions of a state.'[13] This state seeks legitimation, then, not in actual communities but by organizing identification with a larger entity hospitable to the necessary mobility of capital yet capable of miming the values of kinship and settlement: the nation. And so 'the circle is squared' and an 'artificial order' unsurps the authority of 'natural communities' even as it sanctions their destruction.[14]

The nation-state is the most functional of capitalist 'contradictions', Williams argues; the left must think and plan beyond it. Social democrats, with their characteristic shuttle between 'patriotism' and what they call 'internationalism', simply demonstrate their own political and cultural subordination; and socialists who try to muster support for radical-nationalist economic schemes are engaged in a hopeless contest that the right alone can win. The fact is that 'the nation-state, in its classical European forms, is at once too large and too small for the range of real social purposes.'[15] States like Britain are too small and weak to be equal to the crises of the international economic and military order. Alternative economic strategies and old-style unilateralism alike are deficient in that they misread the paranational realities of the world and grossly overestimate the independent efficacy of any independent British state, including a socialist one.

Such states are at the same time too large, too 'artificial' and distant to sustain 'full social identities', to attract and hold the kind of popular commitment on which a 'substantial' socialism must depend. Social relations are now 'variable' in extent, from one level to another: the spatial conditions of 'effective self-government' cannot be specified once for all. A 'substantial socialism' must therefore be a 'variable socialism', dispensing not only with 'all-purpose' assemblies and representatives but also with 'all-purpose' *societies*, discovering a flexibility of institutional reach adapted equally to intercontinental networks and to local communities.

Plan X or Socialism? The Labour Movement

The commanding political formula of this paranational order Williams terms 'Plan X'. As a deliberate attempt to scan and shape the future, this formula is indeed a strategy – *a plan*. But it differs from familiar kinds of strategic thinking in that it is ultimately goalless: its object is, precisely, X. Plan X consists in the systematic pursuit of temporary advantage in an admittedly insoluble crisis. It is recognizably the creature of capitalism, its overall thrust and effects determined blindly by the assertion of self-validating particular interests, and as such, Williams argues, it finds adherents in every kind of social situation. But, crucially, it is the now dominant practice of capitalist ruling classes and their operational elites. Plan X thinking is visible domestically in the Thatcher government's drive to break the power and will of the working class, even at the expense of existing local capitalist interests. Internationally, it has motivated the West's ceaseless efforts to penetrate and effectively reclaim the post-capitalist economies, and, most vividly and dangerously, the new arms race. The prospect it offers is one of increasingly authoritarian bourgeois regimes devoted to policing social distress at home and to reckless military confrontations abroad. Plan X is the long counter-revolution.[16]

Plan X *will prevail*, Williams believes, unless it is cut short by socialism. But 'it is impossible, ... in Western Europe, to conceive of any important socialist movement which is not largely based on the industrial working class, including its most traditional formations.'[17] Attempts to estimate the chances of socialism must therefore centre on the condition and prospects of the labour movement.

Williams's discussion of the British labour movement opens with a critical response to current arguments concerning the supposed weakening of the relationship between the working class and socialist politics, of 'the dissolution or the classical proletariat'. Williams accepts much of the evidence adduced in favour of such theses – the changing occupational and gender composition of the wage-earning population, the decline in the Labour party's electoral strength, the pressure of sectionalist tendencies in the unions – but is sceptical of the conclusions drawn from it. First, he points out, there is no single, politically decisive demarcation of 'the working class'; second, all the available sociological indices suggest that the class – politics relation has never actually known the unison now supposedly lost; and finally, the fortunes of Labour, historically 'an all-purpose radical party', are by plain definition not the same thing as the fortunes of socialist politics. The general voting pattern in Britain remains substantially class-differential; the real failure, more visible now that the post-war phase of two-party electoral competition has ended, is that of the received formula of 'the labour movement'.

The *movement* existed as a coherent and authoritative reality only in so far as workplace and political struggles were united in the pursuit of a 'general interest'. The main ground of this interest was the fact of avoidable primary hardship and want; another was the Marxist proposition that the capitalist mode of production is intrinsically exploitative and anarchic, and therefore incompatible with any general interest. The former supported the struggles of the labour movement in its most impressive phase, but now, and largely thanks to those struggles, is much less generally relevant in advanced capitalist societies; the latter has remained a minority conviction. Now lacking any forceful version of a general interest, the 'movement' has lost coherence. The party's dominant tendency, its right and left variants alike, in government or in opposition, claims to speak for 'the national interest' as such. The unions, while retaining a strong organizational hold and some political influence on the party, have increasingly been reduced to piecemeal bargaining over wages and conditions, to the serial assertion of particular interests. This negative, 'particularist' tendency is aggravated by shortcomings in the inherited self-definition of the unions. The bonds of kinship and settlement have at times been indispensable supports to those of generic 'class' in the labour movement, sustaining its struggles and its non-particularist values. But in conducting themselves purely as organizations of wage-labourers, who are then typically figured as male breadwinners, the unions abstract themselves from the complex reality of their social relations, both 'external' and 'internal'. This abstraction weakens and deforms them, encouraging practical adaptation to the rationality of the capitalist market and to its perfected strategic formula, Plan X.

Socialism is the only concrete alternative to Plan X. But if its necessary historical agency, the organized working class, succumbs to the politics of temporary advantage, then socialism will be reduced to a hopeless sectarian passion. This is the bleakest of Williams's anticipations. But, he insists, it is better to say such things 'than to go on acquiescing in the limited perspectives and the outdated assumptions which now govern the movement, and above all in its now sickening self-congratulatory sense of a taken-for-granted tradition and constituency. The real struggle has broadened so much, the decisive issues have been so radically changed, that only a new kind of socialist movement, fully contemporary in its ideas and methods, bringing a wide range of needs and interests together in a new definition of the general interest, has any real future.'[18]

Towards the Present

Williams has written the agenda for a long and difficult discussion, in which
openness – that is, both a calm attention to criticism and a candid offering of it –
will furnish our best chance of collective self-enlightenment. Some will seek to
match the range of Williams's analysis; others will bring more intensively
developed specialisms to bear on the general debate. *Towards 2000* outlines the
space of an argument, not the format of individual contributions to it. My own
list of differences or queries would include the following. Williams's qualitative
analysis of the world capitalist *economy* disposes of many reformist illusions, but
it is not a sufficient ground on which to base a truly realistic socialist alternative.
His prospect of the paranational future takes too little account of the quantifiable
cycles of capitalist accumulation, and of the course of inter-imperialist rivalries in
the period ahead. Again, welfare and capitalism are indeed contradictory in the
way he describes, yet welfare capitalism is a substantial reality in nearly all the
OECD countries and seems likely to remain so, in part because of working-class
resistance to cuts in social provision but in part also because Plan X accountancy
may reckon it an unavoidable political expense. And if world capitalism comes
through the present recessionary wave without a major war or a serious
revolutionary defeat and enters a new long boom, then all socialist expectations
of the year 2000 will have to be rewritten. Williams's account of bourgeois
politics include a sketch of the now-dominant strategic formula of capital and a
radical critique of prevailing norms of 'representation'. But it may be asked, on a
point of method, whether a fully concrete prospective analysis should not attend
more closely to the discernible trends of bourgeois *party competition*, especially
where, as in Britain, this has entered an important phase of regroupment; and, on
a point of substance, why there should still be a need for bicameralism in a
consistently democratic order enshrining the right of recall. Williams's
interpretation of contemporary *culture* is one of the most powerful and arresting
passages in his book; no serious partisan of neo-modernism can make light of it.
But he follows Lukács in homogenizing the artistic departures of the early
twentieth century and in reducing them to an indifferently degraded (or
degradable) 'ontology'. On this count, his theses are open to historical objection
and also to the counter-arguments of theorists and practitioners who approach
modernism not as a seamless text of revelation but as a heterogeneous array of
artistic possibilities always at least partly amenable to new assessments and
usages.

But even this shortlist is too long. My intention here is to concentrate on the
summarizing theoretical and political themes of *Towards 2000*, on the 'resources'
that Williams deems necessary for a socialist 'journey of hope'.

Materialism, 'Technology' and 'Production'

Towards 2000 embodies what Williams describes as 'the outlines of a unified alternative social theory'. His central proposition, as set out in the closing chapter, is that economic reason must be integrated at every level with ecology, as a necessary condition of all fruitful socialist thought and planning.[19] Capitalism (including its social-democratic subaltern) assumes a possible infinity of production in a physical world whose elements are discrete and inert, Williams maintains, and this is a fantasy that no rational socialism dare entertain. There simply cannot be infinite production in a materially finite world, and the so-called 'by-products' of modern industrial economies are so many unsightly, noisome or downright lethal reminders of the earth's physical reality as a 'dynamic' and 'interactive' *system* of 'life forms and land forms'. The study of these limitations and counter-finalities is the special province of ecology. Socialists need not accept any of the currently influential quantitative forecasts issued in the name of ecology; nor should they indulge those who call for the suspension or reversal of industrializing processes – Williams is sharply critical of these. But equally, they need more than a chastened (or tactical) awareness of 'environmental issues'. What must be recognized is that no economy shaped and run in ignorance of its own ultimate conditions of possibility can be, in a fully rational sense, *planned*. Moreover, Williams maintains, the distinctively capitalist drive to mastery over nature is the real foundation of a dominative tendency that has come to pervade all social relations, from labour to sexuality, in direct contravention of any project of human emancipation. An ecologically blind socialism is in effect utopian.

This general case is supported by two arguments bearing directly on Marxist theory. The first of these animates Williams's repeated attacks on 'technological determinism', that is, the thesis that the history of technology obeys an autonomous, 'natural' logic and is, at bottom, intractable in its social functions and effects. This assumption is active in much contemporary cultural argument, where it leads the left to an implicitly reactionary pessimism, and in debates over the arms race, where it supports the politically confusing notions of 'the military industrial complex' and 'exterminism'. Against this trend in theory and analysis, Williams insists on the constitutional inseparability of the forces and relations of production, and on the economic, political and cultural determinations of all social instruments. The second argument moves from 'forces and relations' to 'production' itself. Marx's concept of 'mode of production' was misconceived, Williams believes, in so far as it generalized the specifically capitalist value of 'production' as the basic drive of all societies. In effect, Marx relayed the material triumphalism of the Victorian bourgeoisie – its commitment to natural intervention as such – as a central value of the communist future. This is the real reason for Marxism's weak projective capacity, Williams suggests: the new mode of production – the collective appropriation of the ever-developing productive forces – would essentially *be* the new society, and there was little that could or need be added. A full and consistent historical materialism must advance from the idea of a 'mode of production' to the guiding concept and value of *Towards 2000*, the 'mode of *liveihood'*.

The case for a unification of economics and ecology, as Williams states it, is surely cogent. The prospect he outlines is a difficult one: quite apart from the formidable intellectual difficulties of the enterprise, ecological thinking is open to more than one kind of cultural and political elaboration; genuinely scientific analyses will be permanently vulnerable to the lure of reborn ideologies of 'nature', and the local successes of green movements will do as much to re-style the postures of bourgeois politics as to develop the programmes of the socialist left. However, these considerations cannot turn the point of Williams's argument. Increasing control of the physical world remains the only conceivable basis of a socialist 'realm of freedom'. But control presupposes power *and* knowledge. An ecologically blind economic policy is in any long historical view incapable of such control; it is a programme of main force, which no amount of stamina and ingenuity will save from ultimate frustration.

'Technological determinism' can only confuse ecologically informed analysis and projection, as it also confuses so much cultural and political argument, and Williams is right to reaffirm the constructive power of the relations of production. But caution is necessary here. Arguments against 'technological determinism' (of which there has been no shortage in recent years) quite commonly end in the opposite error, asserting the *primacy* of the relations over the forces of production. This kind of reductionism (symptomatically, it lacks a label) is idealist, relativizing all knowledge and denying physical necessity, and voluntarist, rediscovering always and everywhere the banal nostrum of 'struggle'. Williams's assertion must therefore be read as a twofold corrective, and indeed his own concrete analyses suggest this: the value of his distinction between 'technology' and 'technique' is that it illuminates the truly social formation of the one while respecting the specificity of the other. But the balance of the distinction is crucial: if 'technique' is tacitly marginalized in the interests of a historicist conception of 'technology', then the real physical necessities of social life are denied, and – among other things– the case for ecology is undermined.

The argument concerning 'production' and ' livelihood' is more problematic. It would be foolish to claim that Marx's writings were – or could have been – proof against the bourgeois culture of his day. But it is questionable to assert that specifically capitalist values seeped into the core of his theory. Marx did indeed assert that any society was determined in the last instance by its prevailing mode of production; his grounds for this were in effect anthropological, pertaining to the human species as such. But he expressly rejected the imputation that this thesis enshrined economic production as the ruling *value* of all societies. In current theoretical terminology, he distinguished between the order of social 'determination', in which the role of the economic was constant, and that of social 'dominance', which was recomposed from one mode of production to the next.[20] The capitalist mode of production was not typical but *distinctive* in assigning dominance to the economic. The outstanding feature of this dominance of the economic was the impersonally dictated social objective of capital: not 'production' as such, but profitable production – *accumulation*.[21] The communist mode of production, Marx argued, would inscribe a different objective: not profit but 'use', the freely determined correlation of 'ability' and 'need' – or simply 'livelihood'. Williams's argument against Marx is misconceived. 'Livelihood' cannot be opposed to 'production', which is, unalterably, its fundamental means. The real opposition is between a mode of production governed by the logic of accumulation, all else making shift, and one in which production is organized in the service of an optimum common livelihood. Marx underestimated the havoc of capitalist progress; Williams, surveying the evidence of a century and more, is not inclined to dwell on its achievements. But on this decisive issue – the qualitative distinction between capitalist and socialist economies – they concur.

Class and Social Movements

This theoretical reorientation will find some of its strongest practical supports in the new movements of recent decades and in actually existing or potential 'effective communities', Williams believes. Of the first he writes: 'All significant social *movements* of the last thirty years have started outside the organized class interests and institutions. The peace movement, the ecology movement, the women's movement, solidarity with the third world, human rights agencies, campaigns against poverty and homelessness, campaigns against cultural poverty and distortion: all . . . sprang from needs and perceptions which the interest-based organizations had no room or time for, or which they simply failed to notice. This is the reality which is often misinterpreted as "getting beyond class politics".' The local judgement on the narrowness of the major interest groups is just. But there is not one of these issues which, followed through, fails to lead us into the central systems of the industrial-capitalist mode of production and among others into its system of classes. These movements and the needs and feelings which nourish them are now our major positive resources, but their whole problem is how they relate or can relate to the apparently more important institutions which derive from the isolation of employment and wage-labour. At the margins of those institutions, in fact, there have been significant developments which make new kinds of linkage possible – plans for workers control and for socially useful production, to name two. None of these 'has yet come to command the substantial support of the labour movement as a whole, yet they show that the possible resources are there'.[22]

This argument is at once contentious and not contentious enough. Addressed to the labour movement generally, it is pertinent and largely just. If the record of support for such campaigns and initiatives has been more varied than Williams's generalization allows, the partial advances of recent years have not redeemed a history of neglect and worse. But as an intervention in current socialist opinion, it runs the risk of being accepted on the nod. Not that it comes too late: the agenda it implies has scarcely been broached. But one of the sharpest ironies of left culture at the present time is that the 'new social movements', and above all women's movements, are increasingly drawn into a ceremony of approval that inhibits, and is sometimes meant to inhibit, serious political and intellectual engagement. Purposeful discussion of the 'new social movements' must begin by disaggregating the category itself, which is a spurious one. Nothing unites them except their organizational separation from the labour movement. It is true, as Williams writes, that their demands press ultimately against the very order of capital, but too much can be made of this: the same might be said of the British strike movements of 1972–4 and 1978–9, which are definitionally excluded from his inventory. Some – the peace and ecology movements for example – are essentially elaborations of single-issue campaigns, contingent in their social bases; the awesome scale of the issues in question does not alter this fact. They are therefore structurally distinct from movements based on objective social categories – nationalities or ethnic minorities, not mentioned by Williams, or women – which test socialist current politics in a different way. The few remarks that follow will be confined to feminism and the women's movement, not because this is a typical case – there is no wholly typical 'movement' – but because it is a salient one.

Williams is right to argue that women's liberation is a necessary goal of any consistent socialist politics today. 'Necessity', here, does not mean 'happy fatality': the historical record shows the real variability of class-gender relations in socialist revolution, and illustrates the antagonisms that may arise as mutually discrepant interests are pressed in difficult situations. But the new feminist upsurge of the past fifteen years has confronted traditional socialism (and above all socialist men) with a political and moral challenge that will not be withdrawn and cannot be turned aside. It is not enough for socialists merely to endorse, as if externally, women's autonomous fight against their oppression. Marxists see proletarian revolution as the means to a general human emancipation, but the temporality implied in this thesis is misleading. For the strategic prerequisite of the revolution, optimum unification of the working class in political opposition to capital, itself implies a struggle against any oppression that jeopardizes the cohesion and morale of the class, irrespective of its kind and provenance. In other words, socialism scouts even its own self-defined class duties if it does not take up the cause of all the oppressed as its own. This is the full implication of Marx and Engels's declaration that their movement had 'no interests separate and apart from those of the proletariat *as a whole*.'[23] Thus, a socialism that does not address the specific oppressions of women workers (who constitute a significant and now rapidly growing proportion of all wage-earners) is in its own terms incompetent. And it cannot hope to understand these unless it commits itself to the fight against gender oppression as such, becoming in that generic sense feminist.

However, there is nothing 'generic' about the reality of contemporary women's movements. There is no pan-feminist programme that socialism can simply adopt. By definition, the women's movement is, or aspires to be, inter-class in composition, and its social horizons are correspondingly uncertain. These necessary indeterminacies are among the main material causes of the deepening divisions in the movement. Class, ethnic and other social or cultural antagonisms have asserted themselves within it, in the form of rival ideological and political – or apolitical – tendencies, some of which are theoretically and practically imcompatible with, or expressly hostile to, socialism. (Indeed the very term 'the women's movement' is somewhat misleading, suggesting a singular and continuous phenomenon, where the apparent reality is an irregular sequence of heterogeneous coalitions or fronts.) In such conditions, even the most sincere avowals of 'feminist' commitment are abstract, and even self-defeating. The fight for a feminized socialism must be linked with an active struggle for socialist feminism within women's movements.

The main obstacle facing this twofold effort is close at hand. Women's oppression is organized at every level of the capitalist order, which benefits from it in obvious ways. But its main beneficiaries are men, as a category and as individuals, male workers and male socialists not excepted. The existing assumptions and practices of the socialist and labour movements do not merely 'neglect' women; they subordinate and marginalize them, often to the advantage of their 'brothers' and male comrades. A genuine commitment to women's liberation will not, then, merely supplement these assumptions and practices with 'women's issues'; it will extensively revise them. This work of revision need not always follow the rules of a zero-sum equation (in wage-bargaining against capital, for example, that could only be damaging). But in many instances it will, and should. Demands for positive discrimination, for example, whether posed in capitalist workplaces or in trade-union and socialist institutions, are aimed against male privilege, and where they succeed, individual men will be the losers, in the short run at least. Williams is rightly critical of those who imagine that 'growth' will amortize the costs of economic reconstruction; there is no painless road to women's liberation either, and only a lucid and determined socialism will prove equal to its social and psychic stresses.

'Our Major Positive Resource'

What does it mean to say that the social movements 'are now our major positive resource'? I have already suggested that the term 'resource' is too comfortable a summary of the necessities, opportunities and difficulties that agitate relations between socialism and feminism. There is a second, more general and fundamental objection. To speak of all or any of these movements as our *major* resource is to yield precious ground to those who now dismiss the labour movement as an effective socialist agency. Williams expressly rejects this position but does not state his reasons for doing so, with the result that a generally negative verdict on the existing labour movement unites with a positive judgement on the social movements to create the contrary appearance. The working class is revolutionary, Marxists have maintained, because of its historically constituted nature as the exploited collective producer within the capitalist mode of production. As the *exploited* class, it is caught in a systematic clash with capital, which cannot generally and permanently satisfy its needs. As the main *producing* class, it has the power to halt – and within limits redirect – the economic apparatus of capitalism, in pursuit of its goals. And as the *collective* producer it has the objective capacity to found a new, non-exploitative mode of production. This combination of interest, power and creative capacity distinguishes the working class from every other social or political force in capitalist society, and qualifies it as the indispensable agency of socialism. To reaffirm this proposition is not to claim that socialism is assured – it is not – or that the labour movement alone is likely to achieve it. What has to be said is that 'our major positive resource' can never be other than the organized working class, and that if it cannot regenerate itself, no outside intervention can do so. If that resource should, in some calamitous historical eventuality, be dispersed or neutralized, then socialism really will be reduced to a sectarian utopia beyond the reach of even the most inspired and combative social movement.

In fact, the structural trends of late capitalism continue to corroborate Marx's fundamental thesis. The paranational economic order itself, which appears in *Towards 2000* only in its destructive aspect, as the anarchic private appropriation of whole continents, is evidence of the reality of the 'collective labourer'. The internal development of particular economies points in the same direction. High-technology industries are remaking the relationship between 'mental' and 'manual' labour in ways that facilitate newly 'organic' kinds of programmatic thinking: the Lucas Aerospace workers' plan, to which Williams rightly pays tribute, is a pioneering instance of the new kinds of struggle that such objective developments make possible. The quasi-industrialization of social reproduction has also encouraged developments in the forms and scope of working-class struggle. For the 'goods' produced by workers in welfare, education and other public services are not particular commodities but commonly valued services; and their conditions of work and remuneration are decisively shaped by government policy. The logic of their workplace struggles is therefore intrinsically anti-particularist. Even the narrowest dispute over wages and conditions contains a political judgement on capitalist and social priorities; and mere tactical common sense, if nothing more, impels strikers in, say, the health services towards initiatives in workers control, in response to the unignorable social demand for minimum emergency cover. Williams has himself emphasized the social creativity of working-class struggle, in an essay on the South Wales railways in the 1926 general strike.[24] The scope of working-class creativity has widened since then, and will become still wider as we approach the year 2000. Creativity is a potential, not an achievement – true enough. But the potential itself is not determined by the moral and political vicissitudes of the labour movement. It is fostered by the ordinary contradictions of capitalism, whose processes of expanded reproduction have brought forth a structurally collective economic and social order and, willy-nilly, the conditions and agencies of a real 'general interest'.

Williams would probably be critical of these suggestions, arguing that they rely on abstract class determinations and fail to appreciate the importance of the other social bonds that, for good or for ill, shape all human allegiances. One of the most insistent themes of *Towards 2000* is that socialism must commit itself to 'lived and formed identities', actual or possible, to the struggle for 'full social identities' and 'effective communities'.[25]

'Community' is a difficult and elusive idea. Its role in the historical romances and political polemics of conservative social thought is well known, not least to Williams and any reader of his work. Yet it is also a part of the cultural bequest of popular and working-class struggle, and Williams remains convinced that it must be kept and developed in this sense, as a key 'resource' for the future. What, then, is the meaning of 'community' here? Most simply, it is associated with what Williams defends as 'the principle of maximum self-management'. In a socialist democracy, decision-making powers should as far as possible be exercised by those directly affected, in their own enterprises and localities. 'Community' is thus a necessary counter-value to the bureaucratic gigantism of Stalinist and social-democratic traditions. However, it refers also to social relationships of a certain type and quality, distinguished from those of class and official nationality by their concrete 'fullness'. The instance to which Williams returns is that where class or specific occupational allegiances are reinforced by bonds of kinship and settlement – as in the mining villages of Yorkshire and South Wales. In its first sense, this stress on 'community' is persuasive; but its second gives cause for worry.

There can be no doubt of the potency of communal allegiances as supports of class struggle. But equally there is no room to doubt the force of the familiar objection that 'community' can act very powerfully against the interests of workers – or women or oppressed minorities. Against the villages of Britain's coalfields must be set the small towns of Northern Ireland and the embattled immigrant hostels of the Parisian red belt. Kinship obligations can sustain strikes but they can break them too; and they can also enforce arranged marriages and silence battered women. Continuity of settlement can be a powerful bond, but it is merely a provocation where, as in Cyprus, the land itself is in question.

The real experience of 'community' is always mixed, and the attempt to abstract a stable general value from it must be correspondingly fraught. Indeed, Williams's own arguments suggest a further inadequacy in the appeal to 'community'. The 'variable socialism' envisaged in *Towards 2000* presupposes not only more local but also more extensive decision-making systems than any now existing. But how, in Williams's terms, can there be 'community' across oceans? He is wary of 'abstract' internationalism, but what other 'bond' can define and order the necessary interrelationships of peoples or movements a hemisphere apart?

In fact, there can be 'community' across oceans, as the history of the great world religions attests; and considerations of this kind prompt closer theoretical examination of the concept itself. The meaning of 'community', in *Towards 2000*, is evoked in such phrases as 'lived and formed identities' or 'full social identities'. These are sympathetic ideas, but the distinctions they imply are dubious. How could an identity be *un*lived or *un*formed, or – for quantitative metaphors are inappropriate here – be anything other than 'full'? 'Identity' is a universal necessity of human existence.[26] To be human at all is, among other things, to be 'identified', by oneself and others. 'Community' is likewise universal, representing one major form of 'identity'. It is best understood as the effect of any identification that positions individuals as members of a group of comparables or counterparts; it is the work of a process of collective identification. As a singular, identity is an abstraction, for any person or group possesses more than one. Concrete human beings are a complex of such identities, which need not be harmonious or coextensive and are very often mutually contradictory. Identities of class, ethnicity, gender, religion, generation and so on coexist in all social aggregations (households, towns, trade unions, countries alike), implying different and often conflicting rights, duties, capacities and positions for their members. If 'communities' are notoriously hard to find, it is because they are everywhere – not *places* but *practices* of collective identification whose variable order largely defines the culture of any social formation. Prevailing ideological usage denies this, spuriously actualizing 'identity' as empirical individuality and 'community' as a certain kind of social formation. The appeal to 'community' is normally a conservative attempt to represent one collective identification (the family, the nation) as the real substance of social relations. This is certainly not Williams's purpose: 'community', as he invokes it, distinguishes a kind of social formation in which the most salient identifications are mutually supporting, for progressive ends. But inevitably it signifies much more. As Williams himself has observed, no one speaks of 'community' with critical intent, and this fact alone betrays its ideological function.[27] 'Community' is not an integral social entity, past, present or possible, but a fetish that disavows the reality in which its sponsors are so deeply engaged: the politico-cultural clash of collective identifications. It would be wrong to undervalue the kinds of collective identification that Williams insists upon. But it is wrong also to consecrate them as 'community' and to suppose that they can or should be generalized. Some of these identifications are crucial: a politics that addresses the working class only as producers is stupidly self-limiting. But other, such as the very potent community of white male privilege, are reactionary and must be attacked, whatever the offence to customary loyalties. Furthermore, the struggle of collective identifications is not wholly autonomous: it is subject in the last instance to the structural (and therefore strategic) determinations of class, and to evade this is to give credence to a dangerous and now widespread opportunism. Here, as in relation to the social movements, the 'major positive resource' of socialism can only be its own principled theory and practice.

The National Community

The most powerful of all non-class collective identifications in modern history is nationality. Williams's analysis of 'the culture of nations' is his most important extension of 'Britain in the Sixties' and includes a great deal that is cogent and timely. But it is precisely here that his appeal to 'community' lets him down. No one has done more than Williams to educate the left in a properly historical and critical understanding of the 'vocabulary of culture and society' (the subtitle of his *Keywords*).[28] It is disturbing, then, to see him rest his analysis on a distinction between '*natural* communities' and the '*artificial* order' of the nation-state. While there is nothing 'natural' about nations and the states that enclose them, there is much that is 'artificial' in all 'communities', and Williams concedes this. But the issue is not merely one of balance. The romantically derived opposition between 'natural' and 'artificial' conditions of society can only obstruct historical understanding and mislead political judgement. If official nationalism were no more than a misappropriation of 'real', more local affections, much of modern political history– in the metropolises and also in the ex-colonial world – would be incomprehensible. The nations that capitalism has everywhere fostered at the expense of smaller and larger entities are more than flag-bedecked marketplaces. They are collective identifications with strong supports in economic, cultural and political histories; they are, as much as any competing formation, 'communities'. To deny this is not to rout official nationalism, merely to misjudge its very potent everyday manifestations and weaken oneself in the face of them.

Racism is a case in point. Williams rejects the ideology of a timeless and exclusive 'English' or 'British' identity, and affirms the right of black people to defend themselves by all necessary means. But his distinction between 'natural community' and the 'artificial' state undermines the balance of his analysis of racism in Britain. He writes:

The real working of ideology, both ways, can be seen in that most significant of current exchanges, when an English working man (English in terms of the sustained modern integration) protests at the arrival of 'foreigners' or 'aliens', and now goes on to specify them as 'blacks', to be met by the standard liberal reply that 'they are as British as you are '. Many people notice the ideological components of the protest: the rapid movement, where no other terms are available, from the resentment of unfamiliar neighbours to the ideological specifications of 'race' and 'superiority'. But what of the ideology of the reply?[29]

Williams's point, correct in itself, is that appeals to abstract legal rights (and facile and patronizing ideas of 'assimilation') are unequal to the social strains of Britain's changing ethnic composition. But he seriously underestimates the critical value of such appeals for the people who actually suffer the strains: the ethnic minorities themselves. The Northern Irish civil rights campaign of the late 1960s, in which the traditionally nationalist Catholic minority massed under the banner of 'British standards of justice', shows just how explosive the appeal to bourgeois right may be in the struggle against communal oppression. Moreover, he neglects to consider that the British state is itself racist, with its battery of immigration laws whose leading function is to isolate and harass black people already living here (nearly half of them from birth), and a police force to match. And in neglecting this, he mistakes the character of popular racism, which is not merely the xenophobia of settled neighbourhoods but part of the politico-cultural inheritance of the British *'national community'*. This combination of terms may be offensive to Williams (and for good reasons) but its referent is no less real for that. The racism of 'the English working man' actually pre-exists the arrival of black neighbours or workmates, who merely trigger the chauvinist presumptions of the common 'national' history of empire. This is the second misrepresentation of Williams's small parable, and it complements his occlusion of official racism. Disputing the claims of 'artificial' state nationalism, he unwittingly makes light of its real potency; at the same time upholding the settled solidarities of 'natural communities', he flinches from the necessary judgement on their negative expressions. In the resulting confusion, it is as if Bebel's famous dictum were inverted, and not popular racism but liberal anti-racism is exposed as 'the socialism of fools'. The lesson to be learned from this political misjudgement bears on the idea of 'community'. Not an actual social reality but a polemical attribution (or 'interpellation'), 'community' is an untrustworthy category. It obscures the real object of socialist analysis, which is the existing order of collective identifications, and can seriously confuse the corresponding task of socialist politics; the effort, which may be supportive but will at least as often be antagonistic, to create a 'community' of anti-capitalist interest.

There is a further, more general difficulty in Williams's evaluation of the nation-state. The economy, he writes at one point, is where most of the people are, most of the time, and for that reason alone economic policy must be central in any socialist programme. That is well said. But the nation-state is where *all* of us are *all* of the time – now and for the directly relevant future. Williams is right to insist that the most important unities of a socialist society will be either smaller or larger than the nation-state. But to read this future back into the capitalist present is to effect a wishful *fuite en avant*, a truly utopian dissolution of politics. The arguments of *Towards 2000* press consistently in this direction. The very structure of the book dissociates the category of politics. Parliament, the military apparatus, official nationalist culture, the general game-plan of capital: all these are discussed, but separately. Nowhere is there a unified analysis of the bourgeois political order as a whole: the state and the party system organized around it. The consequence of this dispersal of attention – for, in a book so passionate and determined, that is what occurs – is an unsteady sense of the counter-order of political struggle. The concluding chapter of *Towards 2000* offers an estimate of 'resources', not a *strategy*. Some key elements of a strategy are present, however. Williams argues convincingly that the imperative task of the years ahead is the elaboration of a new 'general interest', a socialist programme, and the struggle to win active popular forces to it. He identifies the main principles of the former and the main agencies among the latter, along with the organized working class, the social movements and the campaigns of people united in their localities. But this prospectus remains abstract in one crucial respect. A political capable anti-capitalist bloc cannot be mustered by simple addition: there is no spontaneous harmony of the oppressed and therefore no spontaneous convergence in their struggles. The formulation of a socialist 'general interest' requires a continuing process of synthesis, and this – the critique of 'all-purpose' political formations notwithstanding – is the distinctive and abiding rationale of a party. Of course 'we' already have a party, and that is the foremost strategic issue now confronting the left in Britain. Just as no struggle for socialism can evade the state, with its monopoly of legitimate sanction over social relations, so no struggle for socialist politics can evade the monopolist of left and working-class political representation, the Labour party.

Williams is right to argue against general abstention from the Labour party and its electoral campaigns. Socialist attempts to displace Labour through ordinary processes of political competition – in unions, broad campaigns and elections – have little chance of success. The experiences of the Communist party since the 1920s, the New Left in the 1950s and 1960s, the revolutionary left in the 1970s all suggest this. One common reason for these successive frustrations is inscribed in the existing order of party competition, which simultaneously exposes Labour to the right and strengthens it against the left. Campaigning as the capable steward of 'the national interest', the Labour Party must submit its record and manifesto to comparison with that of the right, and may then gain or lose a significant share of the popular vote. But defending itself against the criticisms and urgings of the left, the party faces no equivalent test. It need only appeal to the historically accomplished fact of its monopoly, which, merely by existing, undermines the authority of any who contest it. This reality has led many socialists into deflated reconciliation with the party, and, at the extreme, to the masochistic cult of defeat that is the dead centre of labourist ideology. But Williams is equally emphatic in his rejection of this course. There can be no principled general accommodation with Labour's politics, and the reason is simple. It is not that Labour socialism is too resigned to 'the inevitability of gradualness', it is that the Labour party as such is not socialist at all.

Williams has addressed this issue directly in his article, 'Splits, Pacts and Coalitions'[30]. The occasion of the article was the continuing debate over proposals for a coalition of the non-Conservative parties at the next general election – whose sponsors now range from the Communist party right to the Liberal peerage. Williams rejects these proposals, but in a way that casts decisive new light on the real terms of the controversy. The proffered choice is between a Labour-Alliance pact designed to unseat the Thatcher government and an independent Labour intervention in a three-cornered fight; the suggested criterion of judgement is electoral plausibility. But there is another, more testing criterion, Williams argues, which reduces these competing options to their due proportions. The controversy is actually over the relative merits of *two* coalitions, the 'larger' including the SDP–Liberal Alliance, the 'smaller' being the existing coalition of socialists and social democrats that is the Labour party. Neither one – the first by definition, the second as it stands – is an option for socialism. The Labour party is the necessary political setting for the development of a 'fully contemporary argument for socialism', Williams believes, but the demands of commitment to this task must be understood. 'We can sustain the Smaller Coalition without any real work on policies, or reach out for the Larger Coalition, adapting ahead of its formal arrangements by trimming or underplaying those innovative socialist policies which are known to be incompatible with it' – or, refusing these two variants of a single, familiar and now devalued option, we can resolve to 'draw a clear line, to our mutual advantage, between socialists and coalitionists. We can begin to see where we really are, and what we have to change.'[31]

Towards Socialist Politics

Towards 2000 says clearly 'where we really are': 'what really failed [in 1983] was the concept of an all-purpose radical party, nominally but always ambiguously socialist, which temporarily succeeded within a two-party system but then fell back within a multi-party system.' And 'what we have to change', he maintains, is *policy*, an area in which the left has much to learn and unlearn. That is true, but as a political assessment it is somewhat intellectualist. For what is going on in the Labour party is not only an 'argument' but a test of forces including those forces to which Williams looks for a renewal of the labour movement and of a socialist 'general interest'. The fight against institutional racism and sexism in the party is an elementary condition of any general programmatic advance in relation to non-class movements of the oppressed; and in the cities and boroughs controlled by left Labour councils, this fight has already assumed the forms of social policy. In these places too, the unresolved, often antagonistic relations between party, unions and community, between bureaucratic administration and 'local democracy' are now inescapable priorities in general debate and in concrete policy-making. These councils were created in the face of the militant cynicism and plain hostility of Labour's dominant centre-right; and only tepid support can be expected from that quarter as the Conservative government moves to usurp their powers of initiative, through financial control or outright abolition. Their record has been mixed and often troubling; but the experience itself, fully analysed and assessed, will be an invaluable programmatic gain for the entire left.

Here, then, are some intimations of a new 'general interest' in the existing practice of Labour's left. They find indispensable support in the allegedly 'narrow' or 'abstract' contentions of the inner-party struggle itself. For the greatest obstacle to the elaboration of a socialist 'general interest' is not the spontaneously particularist trend of wage-bargaining in capitalist conditions, but the *existing generality* to which Labour has traditionally subscribed: the 'national interest' of British capital and its state. The expressions of this interest are as numerous as the mummeries, markets and missiles that embody it, but they all converge on the politico-ideological institution of *parliamentary sovereignty*. Here is the sticking point of even the most garrulous Labour opportunist, for to question the capacities and prerogatives of parliament is to question the idea of a paramount national interest and thus the historic political formula of the labour movement, party and unions alike. And this is precisely what the left has done. The struggle within the party has centred on the left's demand for an accountable parliamentary fraction, and that, it may be said, need not be decisive: even the most disciplined representatives are no better than the manifesto they defend; it is policy that counts. But the ulterior logic of the struggle is not at all formalistic. The unfinished campaign to democratize the party constitution is, in embryo, a challenge to the authority of its more venerable namesake, the British Constitution. It is widely feared and resisted as such; it should be defended in an answering spirit and pursued to an unambiguous conclusion. For that challenge is the necessary beginning of the intellectual and political effort to forge a truly oppositional, socialist 'general interest' and a party willing and able to assert it.

But what about 'party unity' and its overriding purpose, 'victory at the next election'? This objection is not only inadequate in principle, for the general reason so clearly stated by Williams; it is also idle. No lucid observer can pretend that the party is united. The political peace of autumn 1983 was a half-tactical, half-naive armistice, and the steady weakening of its symbolic guardian suggests that it may not hold for long. The inadequacy of the Kinnock leadership – outgunned in parliament and abjectly 'statesmanlike' in the face of the class struggle in the coalfields – betrays the real disunity in its rear. Electoral calls to order will no doubt exert unifying pressure, but their effect will be neither decisive nor long-lasting. The manifesto – necessarily the centrepiece of the electoral campaign – is itself a matter of contention. And beyond the campaign itself, it is hard to imagine any electoral outcome that will not sooner or later lead to a new inner-party struggle. Meanwhile, the party's organizational link with the unions – a crucial support of centre-right hegemony in both – is now under legislative attack from the government, and in any case may not survive the vicissitudes of the next electoral round. In short, the historically formed set of relationships and expectations that we know as Labourism is now being shaken apart, victim of a capitalist crisis to which it has no cogent response and of a vengeful Conservative government bent on shifting the terms of class struggle to the strategic advantage of capital and the right. The post-war 'settlement' is nearing extinction, and with it the rolling five-year plan that has been the beginning and the end of stategic wisdom among Labour's electoralist unitarians. To cling to it now is not to practise 'realism' but to succumb to that most hapless of all political indispositions: opportunism without opportunities.

There are real opportunities ahead, as well as dangers. Like most real opportunities, they are not easy options. But what Williams says of our general historical situation applies also to the party through which most socialists in Britain have attempted to act upon it: 'It is not some unavoidable real world . . . that is blocking us. It is a set of identifiable processes . . . of nameable agencies . . . all these interlocking with the embedded short-term pressures and the interwoven subordinations of adaptive common sense. It is not in staring at these blocks that there is any chance of movement past them. They have been named so often that they are not even, for most people, news. The dynamic movement is elsewhere, in the difficult business of gaining confidence in *our own* energies and capacities . . . It is only in a shared belief and insistence that there are practical alternatives that the balance of forces and chances begins to alter. Once the inevitabilities are challenged, we begin gathering our resources for a journey of hope. If there are no easy answers there are still available and discoverable hard answers, and it is these that we can now learn to make and share.' Turning now towards 2000 – the less illusioned for what Williams obliges us to reconsider or to reaffirm – we cannot ask for more but dare not settle for less.

Postscript

This essay was not written for eternity, and I cannot reconstruct it now. It was a markedly occasional text, and in one decisive personal respect, its moment has passed forever. But otherwise, its anachronisms appear to me circumstantial. The political and theoretical problems the essay tried to address have not been substantially eased or recast by the events of the past four years, and, writing now in the early weeks of 1988, I wish to make only one correction, in the spirit of what I originally wrote. Looking forward from the midpoint of the miners' strike towards a general election now past, I did not foresee just how much sustenance the present Leader of Her Majesty's Opposition would draw from the defeat of working-class and socialist struggles, how he would exploit them to further his normalizing campaign in the Labour Party – and how many on the left of the party, succumbing to the logic of electoralism, would fall in with his designs. In short, I failed to think through my own claims about the stubbornly conservative nature of British labourism. That culture and politics are incapable of achieving any kind of 'socialism', let alone the qualitative social transformation outlined in *Towards 2000*.

Notes

1 Raymond Williams, *Modern Tragedy*, (2nd, rev. edn, London, 1979), p. 208.
2 See respectively 'Ideas of nature', 'Social Darwinism', 'Beyond actually existing socialism', and 'Utopia and science fiction', all in *Problems in Materialism and Culture* (London, 1980); *The Volunteers* (London, 1978).
3 Raymond Williams, *Towards 2000* (London, 1983).
4 Raymond Williams, *The Long Revolution* (London, 1961).
5 Raymond Williams, *Towards 2000*, p. 26.
6 Ibid., p. 100.
7 Ibid., p. 129.
8 Ibid., p. 143.
9 Ibid., p. 118.
10 Ibid., p. 125.
11 Ibid., p. 184–5.
12 Ibid., p. 188; cf. Williams's 'Problems of the coming period', *New Left Review*, 140 (July–August 1983), pp. 7–18.
13 *Towards 2000*, pp. 190–1.
14 Ibid., p. 184.
15 Ibid., p. 197.
16 Ibid., pp. 243–8.
17 Ibid., p. 170.
18 Ibid., pp. 173–4.
19 Ibid., pp. 260–7.
20 Karl Marx, *Capital Volume 1*, (London, 1976), pp. 175–6n.
21 Ibid., p. 711, and part 7 generally.
22 *Towards 2000*, pp. 172–3.
23 'Manifesto of the Communist Party', *Selected Works*, (London, 1970), p. 46.
24 Raymond Williams, 'The social significance of 1926', *Llafur: The Journal of the Welsh Labour History Society*, 1977.
25 *Towards 2000*, pp. 196–7.
26 This passage owes much to the stimulus of Göran Therborn, *The Ideology of Power and the Power of Ideology* (London, 1980), and Benedict Anderson, *Imagined Communities* (London, 1983).

27 Raymond Williams, *Politics and Letters: Interviews with New Left Review*, (London, 1979), pp. 119–20.
28 Raymond Williams, *Keywords: A Vocabulary of Culture and Society*, (London 1976: 2nd expanded edn, 1983).
29 *Towards 2000*, p. 195.
30 *New Socialist*, 16 (March–April 1984).
31 Ibid., p. 35.

5

RAYMOND WILLIAMS AND THE ITALIAN LEFT

—— *Fernando Ferrara* ——

Cultural experiences cannot be communicated unless the knowledge of the terrain on which they grow is shared. Since much of what I am going to say in this first part has its roots in the 'Orientale', I intend to devote a few paragraphs to the identification of the ground where Raymond Williams and I first met.

The 'Orientale' – originally a Jesuit college for the instruction of missionaries bound to the East and Africa, later a half-élite, half-popular smaller State University of Eastern (with about 200 'upper caste' students) and European (with about 4,000 'lower caste' students) linguistic, literary, and political studies – is set in the very core of the most ancient district of Naples, huddled just at the back of the harbour. A network of densely populated alleys and lanes clings to the late seventeenth-century, four-storied baroque palace, once the seat of a powerful aristocratic family, which now houses this unconventional university whose body of students mirrors the composition of society in the south of Italy.

The fourth floor, where the English Department has its offices, classrooms and lecture halls, is always packed with hundreds of students of mixed social extraction coming both from the lower middle- and working-class quarters of the city, and from the heterogeneous social groups of the agrarian districts of Campania and Southern Italy. There is also a thin sprinkling of upper middle-class and even aristocratic young men and women.

In order to make itself heard, the lecturer's voice has to force its way through a thick texture of sounds flowing in at the windows. Traditional street-cries half shouted, half sung by barely surviving vendors only partly conscious of what they are pronouncing, merge with the roar of low-flying jets getting ready to land at the city airport or screaming past after taking off from the deck of the US Navy carrier lying at anchor in the bay. High-pitched, trailing voices of over-protective mothers calling out to their prodigiously noisy children at play in bustling little squares mix with the petulant clamour of horns from the queues of motionless cars trapped in the tortuous narrow lanes. This continuum of sounds and voices is a choral feedback which reminds the speaker of the extraordinarily complex cultural system he or she is addressing. After 1968, this sonorous texture coming from below was interwoven with new yarns of sound: traditional revolutionary anthems rose from the nearby Communist party branch; new political chants came out of the loud-speakers of the Marxist-Leninist association which had its seat in the square right at the back of the 'Orientale'; residual Fascist songs grew fainter and fainter, while Maoist passwords and rigmaroles became louder and louder. When Raymond Williams first came to Naples from the secluded green bowers of Cambridge, he had to face all this, and did face it masterfully, realizing what it all meant at the first impact, quickly discerning the various strains in that noisy output of hegemonic, residual and emergent elements.

He was, to us all, students and staff, the ideologue. He had come to discuss culture as a 'structure of feeling', to point out the political implications of his concept of 'cultural production' as opposed to the traditional Marxist view of culture as superstructure, to stress the strategic role communications played in social and political life. He argued his points with the dispassionate objectivity of the cultural theorist who refused to abandon the ideological foundations of his theory and practice. I remember, for instance, his careful, discriminating approach to the problem of 'power and the media': he advocated a new system of communications which would break up the large-scale strategies of national and international power through the diffusion of local broadcasting, which he saw as a promising beginning of a new democratic-participatory system of communications.

He fought bravely against Adorno's view (which was and is my own) of manipulative communication. He ceaselessly argued, gently and somewhat wearily, against the Marxist-Leninist 'base/superstructure' orthodoxy and tried to show with punctilious meticulousness how Britishness had peculiarities of its own which only tradition could account for and no general theory could explain. He urged how changes could be brought about, in the radical-liberal tradition, from within the system. He was attacked as a belated Fabianist but still refused to accept the summary views of the 'dominance of the economic base' and of the 'ubiquitous plot of power', insisting instead on the democratic-participatory principle of multiple access to communication.

He argued his case bravely and calmly and taught much to our students and us. With his exemplary attitude he taught the power of poise and balance in political debate; in his theorizing, he showed how to argue with a philosophical and political belief without dogmatism. In his analyses, he taught the uses of subtlety and discrimination, the honesty of examining each problem within its own limits with instruments especially designed to respond to its peculiarities.

He had come amongst us, a distinguished Cambridge professor of drama, and the overheated atmosphere of the 'Orientale', where the students' movement was still raging, had brought him back to the kind of political and ideological debate he had just left and was probably trying to forget. You could feel his weariness: he continually remembered – you could see this – his strifes and discussions of the previous ten years: the New Left, the 'New' New Left, the *May Day Manifesto*; all this had cost him much and after all had not completely succeeded. He was wearied by the hard thinking, the pitiless arguments across a generational gap, the fatigue of coming back to the same point again and again. But he forgot all that. Our discussion groups would go on until late hours and continue in the street, on his way home.

He was the ideologue: and many students who spoke then for revolution and are now full-grown men content in their conventional, settled middle-class lives, still flare up with enthusiasm when they remember his masterful mixture of painstaking analyses of the present and of sweeping foreviews of the future. Raymond Williams had come to cooperate in a project we had designed to support the introduction of cultural studies into the English curriculum of our university (as a second step, in all the curricula of Southern universities; and, as a last step, in the curricula of Italian universities at large)[1]. Our research and teaching had had a new start after 1968: we had openly assumed a theoretical basis which founded our research on Marxism and structuralism, and we wanted to break up the dominance of Crocian, neo-idealist attitudes still rampant in the academy, especially in literary studies. Our new approach implied a re-reading of English as a facet of British culture; we realized that cultural studies in England were born through a similar process, and we were sure that the support of the recently started British cultural theory movement was essential for our survival and progress. We were then facing a strong conservative reaction, which reached its peak in a rough witch-hunting campaign ending in a faculty meeting which was suddenly turned into a sort of improvised trial, during which I was indicted for transforming my classes into left-wing propaganda sessions. The students eventually came to my rescue and dispersed the meeting by sheer force. So the reactionaries realized their hegemony was over and resorted to more subtle forms of obstruction.

Our idea was to have with us – in the first three years – the 'fathers' of cultural studies; each of them, in turn, would give a series of lectures to our students, and hold discussion sessions with them and with the staff. This opportunity would further our project by defining methods, theories, and analytic tools, and by mapping out the area and scope of cultural studies. I had come into touch with Richard Hoggart – who was then Director of the newly constituted Centre for Contemporary Cultural Studies – through Lidia Curti (a brilliant member of our staff who is now one of the leading figures of the field in Italy)[2]; she was then doing research at the Centre in Birmingham, and had also met there, among others, Stuart Hall.

Richard Hoggart's impact on our students and staff was striking, though perhaps somewhat superficial: we were caught by his working-class manners and linguistic turns (this was before his long stay in Paris at UNESCO). He would sit on the desk or straddle a chair while talking to the students, he would drink his soup out of his dish right in front of a stunned, covertly indignant British Council local representative; he would say he liked me because I was 'bloody-minded' and did not beat about the bush when I talked to him or anybody else. Though it was rather obvious he acted it a bit, to us he was the incarnate working-class intellectual and we sometimes looked upon him as an improved version of the Gramscian archetype of the 'organic intellectual' with working-class credentials to boot. From him we learned that cultural studies were meant to give a voice to the working-classes and other subaltern sections of society.

Stuart Hall was more complex, more subtle and intriguing. When he first came to Naples we knew him, above all, as the 'media man' (because of his book *The Popular Arts* written with Paddy Whannell and his familiarity with rock music), but we soon discovered his complexity: a peculiar mixture of international, up-to-date structural and cultural theory and of discriminating pre-Althusserian Marxism. His Jamaican origin gave him the advantage of a distanced outlook on British culture, and his Oxford education a penetrating insight into British society: he expressed his views with a soft, polite voice and with restrained, accurately controlled manners, veined but resentful innuendos smothered in apparently artless tones and statements. His love for paradoxical fun, in private conversation, reminded me of my Sicilian ancestors. To us he was a new, unlooked-for face of cultural studies, connected with race, the Empire, the voice of minorities, and a theoretical attitude more akin to the Italian and European temper. In Richard and Stuart we had found our 'elder brothers' in the struggle for the development of cultural studies in Italy. They both had suggested, of course, that Raymond Williams should come. When he did we found in him the 'father' of cultural studies.

Political militant, ideologue, and historian, he had battled and thought through the social and cultural changes which had swept over England from the 1930s onward and had abstracted rules and definitions of the cultural process, laying out the bases for a theory of culture. As a historian of culture he had traced the roots of contemporary cultural struggles through two centuries from the middle of the eighteenth century, through the 'Condition of England' debate, down to D.H. Lawrence and George Orwell. These aspects – the political militancy, the ideological debate and the construction of a new historical perspective – were present in all he had written between 1955 and 1970. This complex system, with its strong theoretical and historical foundations, was essential for the grafting of cultural studies on to the Italian tradition of humanities and social sciences – a tradition which is neither empiricist nor pragmatic, and therefore cannot consider a new field without sound theoretical, philosophical, and historical foundations.

Williams was also the man of letters: 'This is my training and interest', he stated in an interview.[3] A playwright and a novelist; though imbued with the Great Tradition he had found in himself the strength and capacity of renewal, to go from Leavis to Lucien Goldmann and beyond. A man of the written word who was not content in the world of written words: 'I started this work on films and about television in the 50's and the late 60's and probably I've written more about television than about literature,' he said during the same interview.

I had planned a course for our students on 'The origin and development of the modern concept of literature: 1750–1900'.[4] It was meant as a revision of the assumption that literature had its own autonomous status completely disengaged from other cultural practices. I had come to the conclusion that the concept of literature, as we have it nowadays, has been historically determined and was linked to the rise of the bourgeoisie and the idea of nationhood. Literature has been shaped through four main operations: the establishment of literary theory, the institution and practice of criticism (the selection of the literary from the non-literary, based on the criteria of theory), the constitution of the canonical corpuses of literary works (the result of such selection), and the development of literary history (the foundation of literary tradition, going back to the beginnings of national languages). By these observations and by the study of the rise of the teaching of English in the universities, Laura Di Michele (then a promising lecturer of our group who was working with me on this course) and I knew we could show how literature was one of the practices of cultural production which had been selected as a privileged channel of communication destined to convey the substantial core of a middle-class culture during the period of that class's dominance.

I was then following a track which was similar to Raymond Williams's and, though we never discussed the subject at length, it was clear, when first *Keywords* and then *Marxism and Literature* appeared, that we had come to the same conclusions which allowed him to describe literature – with certain qualifications – as 'a formulation of bourgeois culture at a definite period of its development from the mid-eighteenth to the mid-nineteenth century.' I then thought of how deeply such theoretical ideas were embedded in his mind. After all, here he was, a man of letters – writer of plays and a novelist – directly involved in examining the myth of literary creation and therefore more subject to the idea of the separateness or unity of the literary experience. And yet, though he had spent six to twelve years in writing and rewriting each of his novels, or maybe just for this reason, he was so clear-minded as to see that the mode of writing, the art form he was making, was historically determined; he saw lucidly that the novel was originally 'shaped by the bourgeois world' and that he did not have 'social forms available to him for development',[5] which was a sort of curse for his own writing. So in the end his being a creative writer, a man of letters, not only did not hinder him from seeing the truth about literature, but helped him to find that truth through the difficulties he had never really overcome in his own search for a proper form of fictional writing.

We studied Williams's novels (I never enjoyed very much his tragedy, *Koba*) and some of our best students wrote dissertations on them, examining them as working-class fiction, as documentary fiction, as post-Hardian fiction, as socialist fiction, as autobiographic fiction, as Welsh fiction, as ideological fiction. I always saw them as a sort of matrix, a projection of his pre-mental activity: the dramatized expression of the structure of feeling to which he belonged. To me they stand to the other aspects of his writing in the same relationship as the first part of the fourth tempo of Beethoven's *Ninth* stands to the rest of the symphony. They contain the shaping forces and the molten materials of all his books from *Culture and Society* to *Towards 2000*.

The man of letters helped us very much in finding our way to the sources of British culture and to the inner reasons and deep structures of cultural studies. Williams's 'progess' to cultural studies had been in fact very similar to ours: after the first two books, wholly dedicated to literary studies, he had started his 'personal revolution' by writing two more books on literary problems which mediated between literature and culture. In *Communications* he finally broke from literature, producing 'an exemplary model for socialist cultural politics . . . something very rare in the programmatic texts of the revolutionary left'.[6] Many of our group were going through the same itinerary, and I myself was still in the culture-through-literature phase. The parallel of experiences and phases was crucial in reassuring us. We were not going the wrong way, since Williams had gone the same way.

We kept meeting, though quite rarely, in Italy or in England. We met in Cambridge several times both at his cottage near Saffron Walden and at the University. Once I was there at a conference of professors of English from European universities organized by the British Council and Cambridge University. I had been unwise enough to sketch out the literature-within-culture programme we were developing in Naples. From that moment I was singled out as the black sheep. The whole flock of priggish professors – whose only aim was to look and sound more conservative than the worst of their Oxbridge hosts – had gathered again in the afternoon at a welcoming party organized by the Cambridge authorities. After a short time Raymond Williams entered the hall to greet the continental guests; as soon as he saw me he realized I had been singled out and 'banned' and came to my rescue, embraced me like a brother, and never moved from my side for the whole afternoon. He would not speak a word to anybody but me, simply turning his shoulders to those who came up to chat with him. That was the occasion on which I discovered the proletarian self and the Welsh self of Raymond Williams: of course it was all done with finesse, with casual, well-bred politeness, even with perfect poise and affected absent-mindedness. But underneath it you could feel the tough core of the border-country working-class man, and the flaring rage, warm-hearted solidarity and emotional commitment of the proletarian. In the evening we went out together and discussed the hardships one has to face if perchance one has the idea that something has to be changed in the established tradition in order to respond to new demands that come from a changing cultural situation. He told me about the difficulties he had to face and the obstacles he continually found in his way. It was clear that he was more concerned with my problems than with his own.

Jesus College Cambridge and the 'Orientale' are of course very different, as I think I have shown. However, there must be a structural similarity in both our cases. A similarity which then was to be found in the relation each of us had to his institution. I had this feeling on that occasion and had it again when, during another visit to Cambridge, Raymond Williams invited me to dinner at his College. A few members of the staff were there and as he sat at the head of the table he had to 'say Grace', that being the custom there. He did so, candidly explaining to me that in his position he could not ignore what everybody's expectations were. He was gently ironical and significantly summary in the execution of this ritual task. His colleagues hesitated, then officiously smiled in affected compliance with his irony. There was a moment's uneasiness; something nasty hovered over us. He seemed not to notice it and in fact nonchalantly drove away all unpleasant feelings, displaying his high-mindedness, his well-meaning kindness and sympathy to all, his refined detachment from trivialities. On that occasion I recognized Williams's most unique characteristic: his being the pure aristocrat,[7] in the Lawrencian sense of the word, of being one who 'is with the sun'. This gives him the possibility of ignoring meanness and of forgetting vulgarities through his belief in humanity, in his 'democratic practice, determined humanity, and active critical intelligence'. Yet just for this, I knew, there was danger for him. I do not know why my mind went back, on that occasion, to the risk I had run in 1968, in that faculty meeting which had been suddenly turned into a summary trial against me. And I regretted that there was no student movement at the time either in Cambridge or anywhere else.

Only five of Williams's books are available in Italian translations;[8] his influence on Italian culture has therefore been delayed by various misunderstandings due to the partial diffusion of his works; moreover, until about 1968 the Italian cultural system was particularly impervious to British influences, especially in the areas of the humanities and politics. Of course all his books are known, in their original form, to Italian specialists in the field of English studies, and they are continually referred to and quoted from by them and, less frequently, by scholars in other fields (especially cultural anthropologists, sociologists, and political scientists) who find it rather difficult to interpret with accuracy the author's complex, terse writing style.

Ever since the foundation of the concept of 'literature', literary studies have been based on the presumption that literature finds its justification in itself. This belief has survived in different forms for more than two centuries. In Italy, it has given rise to the widespread conviction of the autonomous status of literature and of the secondary importance of social and historical determinations. After the Second World War, a rapidly growing trend of Marxist criticism challenged the traditional hegemony of Crocian neo-idealists and of Catholic spiritualists, and began to secure some key positions in the world of letters with the support of the increasing political power of the Communist party. Most of the new left-wing literary scholars were persuaded by the support of the party to accept the orthodox Marxist view of literature as a super-structural phenomenon determined by 'structural' socio-economic causes. Many of those scholars, however, who had been formed in the Crocian tradition, could not accept a culturalist view of literature as part of the larger system of culture.

Culture and Society collided with both these attitudes: on the one hand it transgressed the base/superstructure orthodoxy; on the other hand it conflicted with the notion of the separate status of literature. It took ten years to convince an Italian publisher to publish a translation, and when it appeared it was seen as an unconventional specimen of the sociology of literature. *The Long Revolution*, though included in a series called 'Cultura e società' (which I need not translate) was in its turn misinterpreted and reviewed as a further essay in the sociology of literature (a sort of institutionalized no man's land which the 'letterati' refused and the sociologists considered an annexed area for second-rate, 'non-scientific' sociologists). Nobody seemed to be aware of the fact that those two books constituted the corner-stones of a dynamic, rapidly developing area of study and research, in spite of the clear identifications of the significance of Williams's contribution to the history of English culture and to the general theory of cultural studies. 'Culture, society, communication, class, revolution are the most significant terms through which the intentions of Williams's production as a whole can be defined.'[9] Italian left-wing literary scholars were not ready to accept the new frame of mind from which the idea of a long (and slow, and very complex) *cultural* revolution sprang. Italian Marxists were also rather unwilling to accept radical changes either in Marxist doctrine or in the theory of literary studies. The 'period of active development' characterized by 'openness and flexibility of theoretical development'[10] which Williams later considered to be under way, had only just started in Italy when *Marxismo e letteratura* appeared in Italian translation.

Leaving aside *The English Novel from Dickens to Hardy* – whose polemical attitude towards the 'Great Tradition' was not even noticed in Italy – and the booklet on *George Orwell* (which was considered either too respectful, by Communists, or too disrespectful, by social-democratic intellectuals), the almost complete failure of Italian literary scholarship to grasp the novelty of Williams's insights into literature is shown by the absence (with rare exceptions) of reviews of his greatest book, *The Country and the City*, which had not yet been translated into Italian. 'Italian scholars have not yet even come into touch with Raymond Williams; in Italy he still is a half-clandestine author who was known too late by unsympathetic critics living in a world which is impervious to his problematics.'[11] This, perhaps too ominous statement, written by G. Corsini in 1983, may be taken as an indicator of the cultural lag which has hampered the diffusion of

Williams's literary theories, characterized by their cultural concerns and by his peculiar brand of unorthodox, democratic Marxism. Times and discourses are now changing: the crisis of Marxist orthodoxy, and a new approach to Gramsci (promoted in part by the spreading of Louis Althusser's theories) have partly deleted the boundary between base and superstructure; the influence of the French *Annales* school and of some post-structuralist and post-Freudian critics have contributed much to the development of studies of 'mentalities', structures of feeling and the sociology of culture. These new trends, and the growing impact of cultural approaches to literature, are now setting Williams's literary studies in a more congenial framework which will rapidly abolish the misunderstandings that have limited their influence on Italian scholarship.

After the Second World War, the Italian Communist party (PCI) acquired an outstanding position on the Italian left. The PCI was the largest mass party of the European left and from its foundation had developed a crucial theoretical debate which had its most striking culmination in Gramsci's *Quaderni*. These conditions gave the PCI a privileged status among Western Communist parties. Italian communist and Marxist intellectuals looked down on their English comrades with the half-sceptical, half-patronizing attitude of the full-grown man towards the unripe youngster. Even the Italian New Left formations which flourished at the end of the 1960s had a similar attitude towards the English left, and observed with mixed feelings their odd insular blend of 'reformism', non-violent radicalism, and half-hearted Marxism.

The *May-Day Manifesto* was one of the culminating points of the political experience of the English New Left. Its complex analyses and political proposals were the work of Williams, E.P. Thompson, Stuart Hall and some of the contributors to *New Left Review*. It failed to rouse any keen interest in the Italian left; in fact it was blandly discussed, if not dismissed, as 'a re-proposal of the ancient attempt to rally old and new left-wing movements in order to change the character of Labourism from within and oppose Wilson and Wilsonism'. Williams's share was approximately defined as 'cultural socialism ... in the Morrisian tradition',[12] by unorthodox Marxists, while Communist intellectuals did not hide their disapproval of his theories.[13] It is true that only a few of Williams's writings can be styled as technically political; it is also true that *all* his essays, articles, novels and plays are fundamentally political in the sense that they are concerned with the most basic issues of society, and that their aim is to determine a better future for existing societies. Probably the most overtly political of his books is (in spite of its title) *Communications*,[14] and it is significant that in reflecting on this aspect of social life, he realized how complex and many-sided the way to a new society must be. Later, he issued one of his most pregnant political statements on this point:

It is only in very complex ways that we can truly understand where we are. It is also in very complex ways, and by moving confidently towards very complex societies, that we can defeat imperialism and capitalism and begin the construction of the many socialisms which will liberate and draw upon our real and now threatened energies.[15]

In the light of this statement we can understand the deep political meaning of all his work. He never thought that the liberated energy of the oppressed proletariat could in one stroke put an end to the flexible, self-adjusting system that centuries of capitalist dominance have accurately built and strengthened.

Looking back on the 'culture and society' of the industrial revolution, he sensed that to counteract that hegemony a 'long revolution' was needed, a complex revolution which was to be first of all a cultural revolution permeating the whole system of 'communication'. 'Marxism', after exploring the ancient realm of the written word, where the debate between 'country and city' had been expressed, had now to explore the new realm of audio-visual communication, where the new forms of culture were being shaped. And since, at this point, an exact and detailed definition of the new socialist order which is still to come must be produced, he drew up a complete description of the structuring elements of 'culture'. His recent essay on *Culture* is another fundamental step in his 'long revolution', necessary as a premise for the shaping of new structures of society based on socialist criteria, which cannot be achieved without detailed knowledge and a complex approach.

The Italian left, which down to the end of the 1970s has failed to recognize the cogency of Williams's ideas, is now beginning to sense it. As a matter of fact the proposals of Eurocommunism, dating back to the middle of the 1970s, which Williams applauded and in which he recognized some of his own lines of thought, were sometimes akin to his approach. And the recent Communist search for a 'third way to socialism', together with some of the best work of Italian dissident left-wing thinkers and philosophers are, in their turn, following the route he is so laboriously and painstakingly trying to chart.

The centrality of cultural studies in Raymond Williams's thought is strictly linked to the complexity of his view of society and politics. In order to grasp the complexity of all the practices, institutions, forces and discourses which make up that many-sided whole we now call 'civil society', in order to 'see where we are' and also to work out a model capable of transforming our whereabouts by abolishing the negative forces and by 'liberating ... our real ... energies', a deep comprehension of what culture actually is and an accurate description of the forms of consciousness, of the institutions, and of the practices which make up its complex whole is necessary. This centrality of culture implies that it is a system mediating (not merely reflecting but also partly determining) the essential forces and movements of the structural base. Williams's view of the meaning and function of culture is both the cause and the effect of his peculiar type of

Marxism. Only the English tradition can explain it, in spite of the fact that it derives features and attitudes from Italian, French and, more generally, Western and Eastern unorthodox Marxisms. These adoptions are of course important, and they are accepted with deep consciousness and real conviction. But they may be seen as ways of solving problems, rather than as autonomous theoretical propositions – ways of solving those problems which arise from the internalized structures of feeling generated by the English tradition.

It seems to me that Williams is wholly aware of there being two foundations to his political thought: Marxism and the British tradition. The second element can be expressed, in generalizing terms, as national culture. It is for this basic reason, I think, that he deliberately speaks of 'many socialisms'; socialisms being, I think, as many as there are national cultures. This explains why he has found so many interesting promptings in Gramsci's writings, Gramsci's whole theoretical effort being an attempt to mediate between Marxian doctrines and Italian national culture. Williams's concept of culture as a 'structure of feeling' and Gramsci's conception of 'hegemony' are plainly akin.

> Gramsci's emphasis on the creation of an alternative hegemony, by the practical connection of many different forms of struggle including those not easily recognizable as and indeed not primarily 'political' and 'economic' thus leads to a much more profound and more active sense of revolutionary activity in a highly developed society . . . [16]

Two things at this point can be said. The first is that about 1975 Williams realized he had been unconsciously working along Gramscian lines when – in *Culture and Society* and in *The Long Revolution* – he had proposed a cultural approach to social (and socialist) change: in a highly developed society, a long revolution which would gradually permeate the national culture till it gained the control of hegemony was the only modern way to socialism. The second is that Gramsci's doctrine made it clear to him that the process of hegemonization of culture and society involves the dynamic, ever-changing permeation of all lived experience of individuals and groups (of their 'common sense', of their extra-conscious way of understanding the world) by an interpretation of reality rising from the structure of the national culture and society and from the coherent forces of Marxian doctrines. Hegemonization was the longest revolution; it is in fact a never-ending revolution. This doctrine at once authenticated and added new drive to his own ideas. If Gramsci can be considered an authority in the field of cultural studies, then this is what Italian cultural studies have contributed to Raymond Williams as a cultural thinker. Perhaps it is not accidental that when he wrote *Problems in Materialism and Culture* (1980) and *Culture* (1981) his books were promptly translated into Italian and acknowledged as participating in an international discussion that went back to Tocqueville, Marx and Weber and extended to Gramsci, Lukács, Brecht and Goldmann. The Italian scene reacted, on this occasion, quickly and properly, showing that there was a more mature consciousness and a real sympathetic attention of Williams's thought. And while, in the now expanding world of Italian cultural studies, new intellectual fashions come and go, and just because of this ever-changing scenario, every new adept who wants seriously to find his or her way in this field of intellectual commitment knows that he or she cannot do without Raymond Williams's faultless example and his masterly works, which for so many years have decisively contributed to the foundation of that area of research, and today still are an unstinted source of energy guiding cultural studies 'towards 2000'.

Notes

1 The project has not been completed yet. However, Cultural Studies are nowadays strongly represented at every yearly Conference of the Association of Italian Anglicists (AIA) with a workshop dedicated to Italian Studies in the field, and in 1989 formal degree courses in English Cultural Studies will be run both in Naples (at the Orientale) and in Pescara.

2 Lidia Curti translated and wrote a preface to the Italian edition of R. Hoggart's *The Uses of Literacy*; among other writings, she has published 'Cultural Studies: the contours of a problematic', *Anglistica*, 21, 3 (Naples, 1978); 'The "Unity" of Current Affairs television' (with S. Hall and I. Connell), in *Popular Television and Film* (London, 1981); 'Silent Frontiers: an Italian debate on the "Crisis of Reason"' (with I. Chambers), *Screen Education*, 41 (1981); 'A volatile alliance: culture, popular culture and the Italian left' (with I. Chambers), in *Formations of Nation and People*, (London, 1984); 'Popular broadcasting in Britain and Italy' (with I. Connell), in *Television in Translation*, (London, 1986).

3 The interview was conducted by Paola Splendore (an active member of our group) and published, with the proceedings of our first Conference, in *Anglistica*, 21 (Naples, 1978); see p. 235.

4 Some conclusions of this research were presented in a paper I read at the First National Conference of Sociology of Literature in 1974 and later published as 'The origin of the modern concept of literature', in *Sociologia della letteratura*, ed. F. Ferrara, A. Abruzzese, M. Rak and R. Runcini (Rome, 1978), pp. 140–57.

5 Raymond Williams, *Politics and Letters: Interviews with New Left Review* (London, 1981), p. 272.

6 Cf. *ibid*, p. 370.

7 I know that Raymond Williams will probably object both to this definition and to D.H. Lawrence's quotation, yet I think that in this case he should rely on the more objective view of his personality that comes from an external observer and acknowledge, beyond all ideological biases, his deep sympathy with the author of *Sons and Lovers*.

8 Both the dates and the variations in titles are meaningful. The list runs as follows: *Culture and Society* (as *Cultura e rivoluzione industriale*, Turin, 1968), *The Long Revolution* (as *La lunga rivoluzione*, Rome, 1979), *Marxism and Literature* (as

Marxismo e letteratura, Bari, 1979), *Problems in Materialism and Culture* (as *Materialismo e cultura*, Naples, 1983) and *Culture* (as *Sociologia della cultura*, Bologna, 1983).

9 P. Splendore, 'Introduzione' to *La lunga rivoluzione* (Rome, 1979), p. 11.

10 Raymond Williams, *Marxism and Literature* (Oxford, 1977), p. 1.

11 G. Corsini, 'La sociologia della letteratura: dieci anni dopo', *La critica sociologica*, 68 (Rome 1983), p. 35.

12 M. Teodori, *Storia delle nuove sinistre in Europa* (Bologna, 1976), p. 113.

13 Cf. M. Fugazza, 'P. Anderson, la 'New Left' e il marxismo inglese', in *Critica marxista*, 3 (Rome 1977), p. 124.

14 See n.7 above.

15 See *Politics and Letters*, p. 437.

16 *Ibid.*, p. 101.

Raymond Williams:
a photographic sketch
Compiled by Robin Gable

Raymond Williams, aged five, with his father, Pandy, 1926

County scholarship pupils, Pandy, 1932

Raymond Williams's father, Henry Joseph Williams

With his mother, Esther Gwendolene Williams, Teignmouth, 1930

Pandy, 1934

Switzerland, 1937

Pandy, 1938

Editor of *Cambridge University Journal*, Spring 1941

Below: Raymond Williams and Joy Dalling, Trinity College, Cambridge, 1940 (photograph: Michael Orrom)

Call-up photograph Royal Corps of Signals (Raymond Williams:
back row, second from left), Prestatyn, North Wales, 1941

Wedding photograph, Salisbury, June 1942

Scarborough, Lieutenant, Royal Artillery
Instructors' Course, Winter 1943

Editor of *Twentyone*, journal of
the 21st Anti-tank Regiment,
Germany, 1945

...ord, Summer 1949

Promotional photographs for *Drama from Ibsen to Eliot* (Chatto & Windus), 1951

Joy and Raymond Williams at WEA conference reception, Hastings, 1956 (photograph: Gifford Boyd)

...mond, Joy, Ederyn, Merryn and Madawc Williams, WEA summer school, Oxford 1954

Left: Receiving an honorary doctoral degree from Lord Gardiner awarded by the Open University, Cardiff, 1974

Below left: Acceptance speech degree ceremony, Cardiff, 197

Below right: Signing copies of Welsh trilogy novels at Oriel, Welsh Arts Council Bookshop, 1979 (photograph: Welsh Arts Council)

Below: Lecturing in Cambridge, 1982

Right: With Frank Kermode, Cambridge, 1981, during the 'McCabe Affair' (photograph: Times Newspapers Ltd)

ow: In discussion at eting during the 'McCabe air' (photograph: Times wspapers Ltd)

Proposal speech at the same conference (photograph: Andrew Wiard, *Report*, London)

Below: At the founding conference of the Socialist Society, London, 23 January 1982

Above: Pandy signal box, Gwent (photograph: Mike Dibb)

Below: Saffron Walden 1986 (photograph: Mark Gers

ron Walden 1986 (photograph: Mark Gerson/Camera Press)

Raymond Williams, 'You're a Marxist Aren't You?' in *Resources of Hope*
(Verso, London 1989), pp. 75–6 (photograph: Hardwick; photographer: Lutfi Ozkok)

If I am asked finally to define my own position, I would say this. I believe in the necessary economic struggle of the organised working class. I believe that this is still the most creative activity in our society, as I indicated years ago in calling the great working-class institutions creative cultural achievements, as well as the indispensable first means of political struggle. I believe that it is not necessary to abandon a parliamentary perspective as a matter of principle, but as a matter of practice I am quite sure that we have to begin to look beyond it . . . I think that no foreseeable parliamentary majority will inaugurate socialism unless there is a quite different kind of political activity supporting it . . . involv[ing] the most active elements of community politics, local campaigning, specialised interest campaigning . . . I believe that the system of meanings and values which a capitalist society has generated has to be defeated in general and in detail by the most sustained kinds of intellectual and educational work. This is a cultural process which I called 'the long revolution' . . . a genuine struggle which was part of the necessary battles of democracy and of economic victory for the organised working class. People change, it is true, in struggle and by action. Anything as deep as a dominant structure of feeling is only changed by active new experience. But this does not mean that change can be remitted to action otherwise conceived. On the contrary the task of a successful socialist movement will be one of feeling and imagination quite as much as one of fact and organisation.

6

HOMAGE TO ORWELL:
The Dream of a Common Culture, and Other Minefields

—— *Lisa Jardine and Julia Swindells* ——

In the Britain of the fifties, along every road that you moved, the figure of Orwell seemed to be waiting. If you tried to develop a new kind of popular cultural analysis, there was Orwell; if you engaged in any kind of socialist argument, there was an enormously inflated statue of Orwell warning you to go back. Down to the late sixties political editorials in newspapers would regularly admonish younger socialists to read their Orwell and see where all that led to.

Raymond Williams, 'Orwell', *Politics and Letters*

The first question that arose in my mind was: what have I to do with Orwell?

Bea Campbell, *Wigan Pier Revisited*

This essay[1] is inspired by Bea Campbell's question, as it is, in the end, by her whole book – her (as the jacket blurb tells us) 'devastating record of what [she] saw and heard in towns and cities ravaged by poverty and unemployment', as she travelled in the footsteps of Orwell's *The Road to Wigan Pier*. We, socialists and feminists, found ourselves driven by our delight at her posing that question, on which the book hangs (what, indeed, have any of us to do with Orwell?), to want to explore it further. At this point, at the outset, she answers: 'Only a point of departure. Though nearly fifty years later I have followed a similar route to

Orwell's, his book is all that we share.'[2] But when she asks the question again, at the end of the book, after she has struggled to put the reality (and that's a crucial matter) of urban poverty before the reader, she answers: 'The question isn't simply academic – George Orwell is part of our political vocabulary, he changed the very language we speak, and he is a prize in the contest for our culture between the Right and the Left.'[3] We seek here to build on both these answers to that original question, because we believe that they focus a crucial area of difficulty in any encounter between feminists and men on the left, concerning culture, and socialism, in a tradition which we shall argue is shared by Orwell and Raymond Williams, as they cast their long, overlapping shadows over debates on the left.

One left reviewer called Campbell's book 'a flawed but in parts brilliant piece of reportage depicting a journey through the depressed towns of the North and the Midlands, written from a feminist and socialist perspective.'[4] And he went on (let's leave the 'flawed' for a moment): 'Her chapter on the 'Landscape', a graphic evocation of the physical environment of jerry built high rise council estates, with their sweating walls, uninsulated rooms and concrete flaking off like snow ... deserves to stand comparison with the most memorable of English journeys from Cobbett onwards, and if only for this reason should be read by anybody concerned about Britain today.'[5] So there is a pretty positive response of the male left to *Wigan Pier Revisited* too ... apart from that 'flawed'. The flaw is in relation to Williams (whose *Towards 2000* is the subject of the same review). 'Williams [suggests] a new form of socialism which might be built around the ecology movement, the feminist movement and the peace movement. Such a change might occur "when we have replaced the concept of society as production with the broader concept of a form of human relationships within a physical world: in the full sense a way of life"'.[6] Campbell apparently fails in this enterprise: 'What Bea Campbell's book highlights is how much more difficult it will be to achieve a new form of alliance between socialism and feminism – let alone between men and women who aspire to be socialist and feminist – than is evoked by Raymond Williams'.[7]

We shall argue here that the tension between this version of Williams and Campbell's enterprise (complete with its invoking of Orwell) lies at the heart of the left's persistent failure to take socialist feminism to heart. Which is a polite way of saying that it allows men on the left to explain to feminists on the left that their approach (whilst interesting – political, even) is marginal, tangential to mainstream socialism, flawed, partial. We aren't speaking the male left's language, we don't share the certainties (that confident 'writing well' on the issues), of the English male socialist. Or, to quote Stedman Jones again: 'One of the things now lacking within the feminist movement is male speech. Only when men, sensitive to a feminist case, begin to speak out of their own difficulties more candidly, can there be a real chance of constructing the socialist and feminist vision of which Williams speaks.'[8] The desire for male speech, the desire to *author* the case – in other words, to write well about it – is pre-emptive. It seeks to compensate for something seen to be lacking in terms of the 'candid' and the 'visionary', when, as Williams suggests, the absence is fundamental to the socialist movement through that very commitment to masculinity. The argument tends inexorably towards the 'literary', towards a particular version of class-consciousness (the authorized account), at the very moment at which it is clearest that key assumptions there are profoundly damaging to any attempt to narrate women in relation to the labour movement (like Campbell, 'his book is all that we share').

Orwell's *The Road to Wigan Pier* (1937) belongs to 'the literary', as a key component in the formation of the narrative of English socialism.[9] As soon as we turn our attention, as feminists, to class politics and the labour movement, we find ourselves negotiating texts steeped in the traditions of the English novel, in versions of authentic working-class experience formed within the dominant culture by an intelligentsia immersed in a late nineteenth-century ideology of work and (in particular) of the domestic/the family. 'Authenticity' is problematically consolidated between the narrator and his narrative. If the romanticizing of the English working man is a failing of English socialism, it is so in part at least as a result of socialism's having claimed both a set of fictions (late nineteenth-century versions of work and experience) and an authoritative voice (the voice of the author) in which to speak about them. The question we ask in this article is: why has the labour movement allowed nineteenth-century paternalistic fiction to mediate its class history? And the reason why this question is crucial for us is because, within this account, gender is not, and cannot be, recognized as an issue. As soon as gender becomes an issue, the bond with socialism's language of class is inevitably broken (which is why Gareth Stedman Jones's review of Campbell finds her account so fraught with difficulties).

It is clear that there are many converging accounts to be given of the English labour movement's involvement with a representation of working-class life as a life of 'worth' in the fictional terms of the classic realist novel.[10] For our present purposes we choose to focus on some of the consequences of this in the discourse of the left-wing intelligentsia in England in the 1960s – and specifically the debate around Raymond Williams, concerning the relations between class and culture.

Raymond Williams's *Culture and Society* belongs to the left 'revival' of the 1950s, alongside Richard Hoggart's *The Uses of Literacy* (1957), E. P. Thompson's *William Morris, Romantic to Revolutionary* (1955),[11] and *The New Reasoner*'s metamorphosis into the politicized *New Left Review*.[12] In fact, Perry Anderson identified the 1950s as the period when the word 'culture' came to stand for a central, unifying preoccupation in English socialist thought.[13] Significantly, Anderson also goes on to argue that in the 1950s, English studies was the only discipline in which a coherent account of English society and its class and culture formations *could* be given; the only area of intellectual debate in which the boundary demarcations of the subject did not fragment the discussion beyond the point of coherent analysis:

> It is no accident that in the fifties, the one serious work of socialist theory in Britain – Raymond Williams's *The Long Revolution*[14] – should have emerged from literary criticism, of all disciplines. This paradox was not a mere quirk: in a culture which everywhere repressed the notion of totality, and the idea of critical reason, literary criticism represented a refuge. The mystified form they took in Leavis's work, which prevented him ever finding answers to his questions, may be obvious today. But it was from within this tradition that Williams was able to develop a systematic socialist thought, which was a critique of all kinds of utilitarianism and fabianism – the political avatars of empiricism in the labour movement. The detour Williams had to make through English literary criticism is the appropriate tribute to it.[15]

It wasn't a detour; the pivoting of left history and left criticism around that keyword 'culture' (in a silent agreement) has proved to be an enduring source of confusion. In the 1960s, it lay behind the confrontation between Anderson and Tom Nairn on the one hand, and Williams and Thompson on the other, over the place of theory in English left thought:

> In *The Peculiarities of the English* [writes Anderson in 1966] Thompson indignantly rejects Tom Nairn's remark that: 'Actual consciousness is mediated through the complex of superstructures, and apprehends what underlies them only partially and indirectly.' He comments virtuously: 'The mediation ... (is) not through Nairn's "complex of superstructures", but *through the people themselves*.' This 'humanist' affirmation is followed by a trumpet-call to abandon the notion of a superstructure, and to rely instead on a 'subtle, responsive social psychology'. What this amounts to is beautifully evoked by this account of historical causation working through the people themselves, unmediated by social structure, political formations, ideology – or anything more than a moralistic psychology: 'the working people of Britain could end capitalism tomorrow if they summoned up the courage and made up their minds to do it'.[16]

As we shall see, Thompson does tend not to notice the theoretical base on which his invoking of a particular version of history and culture depends. But Anderson's reaction equally fails to register that there is a context within which the calling up of individual spokesmen for an alternative cultural tradition is certainly not 'pure afflatus' ('A young left-wing journalist cannot be discussed without evoking William Morris; the comparison is no more than a slovenly gesture').[17] Williams himself later acknowledged a silent taking up of position in relation to his early writing, which he had not anticipated (but which we are suggesting was a particularly important moment in 1960s socialist thinking). Interviewed by Perry Anderson, Anthony Barnett and Francis Mulhern (and that matters; Williams is speaking to them and to a recognizable tradition of politics and letters in *New Left Review*) in 1979, Williams returned to the way in which *Culture and Society* had been 'taken up', in unexpected ways at the time of writing:

> My primary motivation in writing the book ... was oppositional – to counter the appropriation of a long line of thinking about culture to what were by now decisively reactionary positions. ... It allowed me to refute the increasing contemporary use of the concept of culture against democracy, socialism, the working class or popular education, in terms of the tradition itself. The selective version of culture could be historically controverted by the writings of the thinkers who contributed to the formation and discussion of the idea. Secondly, the possibility had occurred to me – it was very much in the back and not in the front of my mind – that this might also be a way of centring a different kind of discussion both in social-political and in literary analysis. What happened, I think, was that the second part of the project, which I had always seen as subsidiary, belonging much more to the sequel of *The Long Revolution* I was planning, assumed because of the moment of its publication a more important function than I had originally intended. The book was not primarily designed to found a new position. It was an oppositional work.[18]

What Williams is registering here is that he wrote in one sense, and was taken in another. That is to say, he wrote from within the 'tradition' an 'oppositional' work which challenged the coherently reactionary account of 'culture' as articulating the values and ideals of the dominant class (Eliot and Leavis), by offering an alternative *reading* of texts generally treated as bourgeois, to reveal, in their inner conflict (the textual version of struggle), 'democratic' values and attitudes. But at the 'moment of publication', the response to *Culture and Society* came most articulately from left historians (V. G. Kiernan and Thompson), for whom (as Perry Anderson had astutely noted) Williams's work seemed to offer (was read as offering) a domain – culture – in which politics and 'thought' were finally brought together, and in which a history of class relations could be charted with new clarity.[19]

Williams makes it clear in the *Politics and Letters* interviews that he himself, in his urge to pin down the relations between culture and class consciousness, was drawn firmly in the direction of the historians in his later writing (starting with *The Long Revolution*, and associated with his expressed admiration for Thompson's *The Making of the English Working Class*), so that he sought increasingly to anchor his 'reading' (a technical term for a methodology of analysis of texts within English Studies) in social and political history.[20] But his continued commitment to 'reading' and texts took younger left critics equally firmly in the direction of more sophisticated techniques of text analysis. Perhaps because *Culture and Society* (for the reasons Williams gives above) never explicitly makes clear the need for an historical underpinning to reading, and given the absence of any historical training within English Studies (Williams laments its absence in his formation), the result was a left criticism which in the crucially formative early years once again isolated the text from history. This is how Williams describes it:

> Distinctly, academically one had been trained to study individual writers – this was, after all, what a lot of *Scrutiny* criticism shared with the orthodox establishment.
>
> But, of course, then you can end up with Virginia Woolf, imagining that all the great writers are simultaneously present in the Reading Room of the British Museum working at their desks, and that you simply have to attend to what they are writing. In fact my work on *Culture and Society* acted as a stimulus, a self-provocation, to get completely away from that mode. The ironic thing is that by the time I was reading Kiernan's review, [21] we had already just completed the actual research for the social history of the English writer. That was the work I had immediately gone on to. Eventually, this was to lead to an explosion of the very idea of the text and of the definition of literary studies through the text, which I was not at yet. But by God when I got to it what should happen but a new and supposedly Leftist movement to revive the isolation of the text? It took another ten years to fight that back, if indeed we have yet. [22]

This problematic involvement in a specifically literary critical tradition was from the outset a crucial source of difficulty for Williams's writing in its relationship to British socialism. In an early essay review of *The Long Revolution*, published in *New Left Review* in 1961, E.P. Thompson voices his (the leftist historian's) difficulty:

> At times in *Culture and Society* I felt that I was being offered a procession of disembodied voices – Burke, Carlyle, Mill, Arnold – their meanings wrested out of their whole social context, ... the whole transmitted through a disinterested spiritual medium. I sometimes imagine this medium (and it is the churchgoing solemnity of the procession which provokes me to irreverence) as an elderly gentlewoman and near relative of Mr Eliot, [23] so distinguished as to have become an institution: The Tradition. There she sits, with that white starched affair on her head, knitting definitions without thought of recognition or reward (some of them will be parcelled up and sent to the Victims of Industry) – and in her presence *how one must watch one's LANGUAGE!* The first brash word, the least suspicion of laughter or polemic in her presence, and The Tradition might drop a stitch and have to start knitting all those definitions over again. [24]

Thompson reacts to Williams's 'oppositional' account with a critique of 'The Tradition', fails to identify the literary critical framework, and puts his finger on the fact that this is not the history of the professional historian. This early response to Williams's work sets the tone for its subsequent broader reception.

Thompson attributes this feature of Williams's writing to his institutional commitment – his (for Thompson necessarily suspect) deriving from an Old English University ('What is evident here is a concealed preference – in the name of "genuine communication" – for the language of the academy.')[25] 'Preference' suggests that this is a superficial matter, a matter of personal choice, or even taste. What we are suggesting is that this is to underestimate the difficulty. V. G. Kiernan, reviewing *Culture and Society* two years earlier in *The New Reasoner*, had already identified that disembodied voice of the medium as crucial to Williams's account:

> A procession of individuals does not add up to a class. We are not shown the *literati* in their social setting, as a congeries of clans and corporations with specific functions and specific links and points of contact with other classes. There are only scattered references to the particular kind of 'common man' who stood on one side of them in 19th century England; no reference at all to the particular kind of ruling-class man who stood on the other side; and, as the book proceeds from decade to decade, very little reference to the rapidly altering condition of England. As a result these writers have somewhat the style of disembodied intelligences, spirit-voices addressing us through the lips of a medium.[26]

In both cases 'disembodied' expresses some kind of anxiety about where materially the narrative voice is located in class terms. Williams's oppositional Tradition claims to identify a common culture which is not the unique possession of a dominant elite, but offers an authentic class consciousness. But both Thompson and Kiernan want to know what bearing the narrators have on the class consciousness which is being brought to light, and both are disturbed at the 'gentility' of the consensus which is produced. In Kiernan's case the anxiety is about Burke, Carlyle, Mill and Arnold; in Thompson's case it is again about the medium, but as the voice of Williams himself – where is he speaking from, and on behalf of whom? For Thompson this is a matter of manners and tone. Kiernan is clearer that there is a serious class issue here, and that the consensus of the disembodied voices (of Burke, Carlyle, Mill, Arnold) is a language of philanthropy deeply rooted in nineteenth-century ideology:

> It must be observed too that the men of culture, denouncing factories and Philistines, were taking their tone a good deal too easily from the landed interests which were their own old familiar employers. Their corporate existence with all its claret and amenities rested far too much on holdings of land – College estates and livings, Church glebes and tithes; in other words it rested on the depressed existence of farm labourers who could be exploited as intensively as millworkers, but more quietly and decently because they could not combine and resist. Men of culture stood in even closer contact with another depressed class, the immense army of domestic servants, which through most of the century must have been a good deal bigger than the industrial proletariat and not as a rule either better paid or better treated.[27]

If 'in the Britain of the fifties, along every road that you moved, the figure of Orwell seemed to be waiting', that was because Orwell so perfectly produces that very 'authenticity' whose class pedigree Williams, Kiernan and Thompson were debating. And nowhere is the idea of a common culture revealed to be more of a minefield than in the left's attitude towards the ubiquitous Orwell. Orwell is the subject of the final chapter of *Culture and Society*, the culmination of the alternative Tradition. In his book-length study of Orwell, Williams effectively claims Orwell's style of reportage in *The Road to Wigan Pier* as a 'documentary realism':

> But here the political point *is* the literary point. What is created in the book is an isolated independent observer and the objects of his observation. Intermediate characters and experience which do not form part of this world – this structure of feeling – are simply omitted. What is left in is 'documentary' enough, but the process of selection and organisation is a literary act: the character of the observer is as real and yet created as the real and yet created world he so powerfully describes.[28]

Yet that 'isolated independent observer' has a class profile which troubles the critic as it troubled Kiernan and Thompson.[29] It confirms ways of seeing working life from that class position (the 'squalor', the smell, the loss of human dignity), rather than ways of experiencing it. Thompson makes precisely the same moves with William Cobbett – a figure who crops up time and again on the dustjacket of *The Road to Wigan Pier*, [30] and who figures in the opening chapter of *Culture and Society* – as the spokesman for working-class consciousness at the beginning of the nineteenth century:

> It was Cobbett who *created* this Radical intellectual culture, not because he offered its most original ideas, but in the sense that he found the tone, the style, and the arguments which could bring the weaver, the schoolmaster, and the shipwright, into a common discourse. Out of the diversity of grievances and interests he brought a Radical consensus. His *Political Registers* were like a circulating medium which provided a common means of exchange between the experiences of men of widely differing attainments.[31]

At the end of *The Making of the English Working Class*, working-class consciousness acquires an enduring voice via the literate, the cultivated spokesman. At the end of *Culture and Society*, class conflict is represented in Williams's oppositional Tradition by the commissioned writing of a disenchanted English gentleman. In both cases, a common discourse is supposed to produce an equality of access to culture and experience of culture, in spite of the awkward class/political placing of the author.

Faced with the difficulty of maintaining George Orwell as any kind of hero of the left, Raymond Williams's interviewers in *Politics and Letters* interestingly displace their unease:

> Nevertheless in the last resort you seem to let Orwell off rather lightly. . . . In fact what you are saying is that Orwell got very tired and his energy ran out. But your

language – 'He had exposed himself to so much hardship and then fought so hard' – strikes a note of pathos which seems designed to exculpate him. Now it is of course true that Orwell had fought creditably in Spain, but it is not the case that there weren't other contemporaries who had fought longer and harder for socialism than Orwell, who did not switch sides so easily.[32]

We might well ask what is going on here. Are we seriously to suppose that the least sound thing about Orwell is his flagging fighting spirit?

We can, of course, sympathize with their discomfort, and with their centring that unease on some notion of 'manliness'. As Bea Campbell stresses, the most jarringly discrepant passages in *Wigan Pier* are those purporting objectively to convey the intolerable working conditions of the face-workers:

> It is impossible to watch the 'fillers' at work without feeling a pang of envy for their toughness. It is a dreadful job that they do, an almost superhuman job by the standards of an ordinary person. . . . The fillers look and work as though they were made of iron. They really do look like iron – hammered iron statues – under the smooth coat of coal dust which clings to them from head to foot. It is only when you see miners down the mine and naked that you realize what splendid men they are. Most of them are small (big men are at a disadvantage in that job) but nearly all of them have the most noble bodies; wide shoulders tapering to slender supple waists, and small pronounced buttocks and sinewy thighs, with not an ounce of waste flesh anywhere. In the hotter mines they wear only a pair of thin drawers, clogs, and knee-pads; in the hottest mines of all, only the clogs and knee-pads. You can hardly tell by the look of them whether they are young or old. They may be any age up to sixty or even sixty-five, but when they are black and naked they all look alike. No one could do their work who had not a young man's body, and a figure fit for a guardsman at that; just a few pounds of extra flesh on the waist-line, and the constant bending would be impossible. You can never forget that spectacle once you have seen it – the line of bowed, kneeling figures, sooty black all over, driving their huge shovels under the coal with stupendous force and speed.[33]

The 'spectacle', whilst ostensibly chronicling the appalling working conditions of the miners, actually elevates the working man's manly body in something close to celebration, and of course recalls D.H. Lawrence's heroic figures of masculinity.[34] But Orwell's attempt to dignify the miner by means of a rhetoric of male glamour only seems to succeed in distancing the entire class to the point at which the bourgeois commentator is absolved of all political responsibility for his labour.[35] This is most clear in the way in which Orwell repeatedly contrasts his *own* physique (that of the public-school 'boy') and manual skills with the ideal type – the deprived and underprivileged working man (supposedly typified in the miner), in terms of undisguised awe:

> Even when you watch the process of coal-extraction you probably only watch it for a short time, and it is not until you begin making a few calculations that you realize

what a stupendous task the 'fillers' are performing. ... I have just enough experience of pick and shovel work to be able to grasp what this means. When I am digging trenches in my garden, if I shift two tons of earth during the afternoon, I feel that I have earned my tea. But earth is tractable stuff compared with coal, and I don't have to work kneeling down, a thousand feet underground, in suffocating heat and swallowing coal dust with every breath I take; nor do I have to walk a mile bent double before I begin. The miner's job would be as much beyond my power as it would be to perform on the flying trapeze or to win the Grand National. ... By no conceivable amount of effort or training could I become a coal-miner; the work would kill me in a few weeks.[36]

Or again: 'All of us *really* owe the comparative decency of our lives to poor drudges underground, blackened to the eyes, with their throats full of coal dust, driving their shovels forward with arms and belly muscles of steel.'[37]

At one level, this fascination with an aesthetic of working-class manliness in Orwell is almost too obvious now for comment.[38] Campbell calls it 'the cult of masculinity in work and play and politics [which] thrives only in exclusive freemasonries of men':

Men who write about miners lavish poetic pleasure on their bodies, they seek to *explain* miners in the language of their statuesque and satanic physique. 'It is only when you see miners down the mine and naked that you realise what splendid men they are. Most of them are small (big men are at a disadvantage in that job) but nearly all of them have the most noble bodies; wide shoulders tapering to slender supple waists, and small pronounced buttocks, with not an ounce of waste flesh anywhere,' says Orwell in *Wigan Pier*. It is a familiar fascination; D.H. Lawrence had it, and more recently Vic Allen in his history of the Left's rise in the National Union of Mineworkers ... writes about his attachment to these men. They evoked for him images of hard, unrefined men, distinct and separate from other workers, hewing in the mysterious dungeons; they are dirty, strange and attractive because they are masculine and sensuous.[39]

As Campbell further points out, this cult of masculinity has devastating consequences for women:

Orwell makes miners the core of his chronicle, they are the essential man and the essential worker, but the equation between work and masculinity depends on an exclusion – women. The suppression of sexuality which is material both to his affinity for and his analysis of coal mining is also a suppression of history. The equation is represented as natural, and that gives it the force of commonsense. It is typical of Orwell – recruiting the readers' commonsense to conquer history.[40]

For the most part, indeed, the women are simply absent from his account (or bracketed with children, scrabbling for shale scraps). But at crucial points the woman appears as part of a validation of an 'authentic' ethic (in particular a family ethic) of working men, which Orwell insists is superior to that of the middle classes:

> In a working-class home ... you breathe a warm, decent, deeply human atmosphere which it is not easy to find elsewhere. I should say that a manual worker, if he is in steady work and drawing good wages ... has a better chance of being happy than an 'educated' man. His home life seems to fall more naturally into a sane and comely shape. I have often been struck by the peculiar easy completeness, the perfect symmetry as it were, of a working-class interior at its best. Especially on winter evenings after tea, when the fire glows in the open range and dances mirrored in the steel fender, when Father, in shirt-sleeves, sits in the rocking chair at one side of the fire reading the racing finals, and Mother sits on the other with her sewing, and the children are happy with a pennorth of mint humbugs, and the dog lolls roasting himself on the rag mat – it is a good place to be in, provided that you can be not only in it but sufficiently *of* it to be taken for granted.
>
> This scene is still reduplicated in a majority of English [working-class] homes.[41]

This *topos* of the 'comely' family home comes direct from nineteenth-century novel narrative, every bit as clearly as did the working man with the iron biceps; and every bit as effectively, it wipes women from the landscape of class, poverty and struggle.[42] It contrasts shockingly with Campbell's own observation:

> Women are the poorest of all. Women are responsible for family finances but they have none of the power that goes with possession. Having it in their hands never made money their own. A flinch of recognition flits across women's eyes when it comes to men and money. Sexual inequality describes their experience of the political economy of the heterosexual family, it's an open secret. Yet while we readily blame employers for their extra exploitation of women as cheap labour, and the state for regulating women's economic dependence on men, we protect men from the shame of their participation in women's poverty by keeping the secret. Family budgets are seen to be a *private* settlement of accounts between men and women, men's unequal distribution of working-class incomes within their households is a right they fought for within the working-class movement and it is not yet susceptible to *public* political pressure within the movement. ...
>
> It's old ladies who show all the signs of a long life on subsistence, though they wouldn't necessarily see themselves as having been poor, because their husbands weren't necessarily poor. I spent a wonderful afternoon with some women pensioners in Barnsley. They wear macs in midwinter: many never had winter coats. For them, getting a winter coat was a big thing, it was to many working-class women what getting a car is to many men. No winter boots – everything has to be all-purpose, for all seasons. One eats meat once a week, and only two ever ate fresh fruit. Their handbags are shopping bags, their holidays are day trips, and occasionally going to a son or daughter.[43]

But it is not just that Orwell's account is shockingly at odds with Campbell's, in ways which we recognize as having something to do with masculinity.[44] Nor that the equation of masculinity and work is secured as 'commonsense', against the grain (Campbell argues) of the evidence. *The Road to Wigan Pier* is also startlingly out of line with the diary entries which Orwell himself made during his 1936 journey north – diary entries which are much closer to Campbell's version of that northern 'reality'. Yet it is Orwell's literary *opus* (*The Road to Wigan Pier*) which the left cherishes, not the reportage in its pre-literary form.

There is little evidence in the diary of any peculiar fascination with male bodies, and plenty of vivid reporting of the physical danger and discomfort of coalmining.[45] Here, for comparison, is Orwell's description of the fillers at work, including the unique diary reference to male physique:

> The place where the fillers were working was fearful beyond description. The only thing one could say was that, as conditions underground go, it was not particularly hot. But as the seam of coal is only a yard high or a bit more, the men can only kneel or crawl to their work, never stand up. The effort of constantly shovelling coal over your left shoulder and flinging it a yard or two beyond, while in a kneeling position, must be very great even to men who are used to it. Added to this there are the clouds of coal dust which are flying down your throat all the time and which make it difficult to see any distance. The men were all naked except for trousers and knee-pads. It was difficult to get through the conveyor belt to the coal face. You had to pick your moment and wriggle through quickly when the belt stopped for a moment. Coming back we crawled on to the belt while it was moving; I had not been warned of the difficulty of doing this and immediately fell down and had to be hauled off before the belt dashed me against the props etc. which were littered about further down. Added to the other discomforts of the men working there, there is the fearful din of the belt which never stops for more than a minute or so. ....
>
> During this week G has had two narrow escapes from falls of stone, one of which actually grazed him on its way down. These men would not last long if it were not that they are used to the conditions and know when to stand from under. I am struck by the difference between the miners when you see them underground and when you see them in the street etc. Above ground, in their thick ill-fitting clothes, they are ordinary-looking men, usually small and not at all impressive and indeed not distinguishable from other people except by their distinctive walk (clumping tread, shoulders very square) and the blue scars on their nose. Below, when you see them stripped, all, old and young, have splendid bodies, with every muscle defined and wonderfully small waists. I saw some miners going into their baths. As I thought, they are quite black from head to foot. So the ordinary miner, who has no access to a bath, must be black from the waist down six days a week at least.[46]

'You can never forget that spectacle once you have seen it', but it is not the *same* spectacle. In the diary, physique takes its place on a fairly equal footing with other observed features of conditions down the mine. In *Wigan Pier* it becomes the aesthetic of romanticized manhood: those 'noble bodies; wide shoulders tapering to slender supple waists, and small pronounced buttocks, with not an ounce of waste flesh anywhere'. And where in *Wigan Pier* the contrast made is between the fillers' physique and Orwell's, the diary makes a point of the contrast between their skills: 'when I sit typing the family, especially Mrs G and the kids, all gather around to watch absorbedly, and appear to admire my prowess almost as much as I admire that of the miners.'[47]

In a movement which we (like Bea Campbell) are arguing is related to this transposition of observed working practice into a literary idyll of equatable masculinity and work, the graphic evidence of women in the diary is erased in the production of the literary text:

15 February

Went with N.U.W.M. collectors on their rounds with a view to collecting facts about housing conditions, especially in the caravans. Have made notes on these, q.v. What chiefly struck me was the expression on some of the women's faces, especially those in the more crowded caravans. One woman had a face like a death's head. She had a look of absolutely intolerable misery and degradation. I gathered that she felt as I would feel if I were coated all over with dung. All the people however seemed to take these conditions quite for granted. They have been promised houses over and over again but nothing has come of it and they have got into the way of thinking that a liveable house is something absolutely unattainable.

Passing up a horrid squalid side-alley, saw a woman, youngish but very pale and with the usual draggled exhausted look, kneeling by the gutter outside a house and poking a stick up the leaden waste-pipe, which was blocked. I thought how dreadful a destiny it was to be kneeling in the gutter in a back-alley in Wigan, in the bitter cold, prodding a stick up a blocked drain. At that moment she looked up and caught my eye, and her expression was as desolate as I have ever seen; it struck me that she was thinking just the same thing as I was. . . .

They have found lodgings for me at Darlington Rd, over a tripe shop where they take in lodgers. The husband an ex-miner (age 58), the wife ill with a weak heart, in bed on sofa in kitchen. . . . The family apart from the Fs themselves consists of a fat son who is at work somewhere and lives nearby, his wife Maggie who is in the shop nearly all day, their two kids, and Annie, fiancée of the other son who is in London. Also a daughter in Canada (Mrs F says 'at Canada'). Maggie and Annie do practically the whole work of the house and shop. Annie very thin, overworked (she also works in a dress-sewing place) and obviously unhappy. I gather that the marriage is by no means certain to take place but that Mrs F treats Annie as a relative all the same and that Annie groans under her tyranny. Number of rooms in the house exclusive of shop premises, 5 or 6 and a bathroom-w.c. Nine people sleeping here. Three in my room besides myself.[48]

In *The Road to Wigan Pier* itself, the hopelessly demoralized women of the early part of this entry have entirely disappeared, and here is Orwell's reworking of the Fs' (now become the Brookers) domestic arrangements:

The Brookers had large numbers of sons and daughters, most of whom had long since fled from home. Some were in Canada, 'at Canada', as Mrs Brooker used to put it. There was only one son living nearby, a large pig-like young man employed in a garage, who frequently came to the house for his meals. His wife was there all day with the two children, and most of the cooking and laundering was done by her and by Emmie, the fiancée of another son who was in London. Emmie was a fair-haired, sharp-nosed, unhappy-looking girl who worked at one of the mills for some starvation wage, but nevertheless spent all her evenings in bondage at the Brookers' house. I gathered that the marriage was constantly being postponed and would probably never take place, but Mrs Brooker had already appropriated Emmie as a daughter-in-law, and nagged her in that peculiarly watchful, loving way that invalids have. The rest of the housework was done, or not done, by Mr Brooker. Mrs Brooker seldom rose from her sofa in the kitchen (she spent the night there as well as the day) and was too ill to do anything except eat stupendous meals. It was Mr Brooker who attended to the shop, gave the lodgers their food, and 'did out' the bedrooms. He was always moving with incredible slowness from one hated job to another. Often the beds were still unmade at six in the evening, and at any hour of the day you were liable to meet Mr Brooker on the stairs, carrying a full chamber-pot which he gripped with his thumb well over the rim. In the mornings he sat by the fire with a tub of filthy water, peeling potatoes at the speed of a slow-motion picture. I never saw anyone who could peel potatoes with quite such an air of brooding resentment. You could see the hatred of this 'bloody woman's work', as he called it, fermenting inside him, a kind of bitter juice. He was one of those people who can chew their grievances like a cud.[49]

Here, perhaps most telling of all for our present argument, 'deprivation' is shifted from the physical circumstances chronicled at length in the diary, to 'Mr Brooker's' loss of manhood, as evidenced by the humiliatingly domestic tasks he is obliged to perform. His wife's heart condition has become 'I suspect that her only real trouble was over-eating',[50] and Maggie and Annie's drudgery has become ordinary domesticity: not 'obviously unhappy', but 'fair-haired, sharp-nosed, unhappy-looking'. Mrs F's tyranny has become 'nagged her in that loving way that invalids have'.

Campbell's response to *Wigan Pier* is to account for the difference between its manner of addressing poverty and her own in terms of the different class origins and genders of the authors:

He was an upper-class old Etonian, a southern ex-colonial. I'm from the North, from the working class. Like him, I'm white, I'm a jobbing journalist; unlike him I'm a feminist. I grew up among the kind of communists and socialists who guided him into the working-class communities and who staff some of their struggles. Politics is to me what privilege is to him.[51]

What we are suggesting is that something else mediates Orwell's experiences on his northern journey – a mediation which is part of the production of the text of *Wigan Pier* for the reader as standing in an identifiable relationship to a specifically literary tradition. And at this point we should point out that we have deliberately chosen not to speak of this mediation in terms of 'the dominant culture', in spite of the awkwardness of that notion of the 'literary'. The examples just given do show Orwell deliberately crafting his published account in terms of cultural forms and practices by means of which a position of privilege is produced as 'commonsense' (they are of course present in the diary, but are consciously honed into 'commanding' form in *Wigan Pier*). But if we label these as 'dominant culture', we tend to imagine we hold ourselves aloof from the seductive power of such discursive strategies, either as historians or as critics (and these are the categories of left intellectual to which we have been giving attention).[52] Whereas we are trying here to suggest that in its attachment to Orwell as part of a counter-tradition which provides access to 'authenticity' (even when that attachment is produced as some kind of reluctance, as in the *Politics and Letters* interview), the left continues to shape and validate its own authored/authorized version of 'experience' in those terms.[53]

The left's commitment since the 1960s to fiction as the authorized version of class-consciousness for English socialism has continually clouded the issues. It has recirculated the arguments around the literary (as the 'totalizing' context) without Williams's reservations. Some fifteen years after the left historians had first engaged with Williams, in 1976, Terry Eagleton published a version of the opening chapter of his forthcoming *Criticism and Ideology*,[54] in *New Left Review*, under the title, 'Criticism, and politics: the work of Raymond Williams', which took Williams to task in ways which are entirely symptomatic of the problem.[55] In this 'aggressive survey', as Anthony Barnett later called it,[56] Eagleton – a practising literary critic – drew explicit attention to the fact that in order to see the significance of Williams's work it was necessary to take into account its position in relation to a particular school of literary criticism (though as we suggested earlier, Perry Anderson had already pointed out the crucial role literary criticism in general, and Williams's criticism in particular, had played as the 'totalizing' context for twentieth-century English socialist thought):[57]

In [*Culture and Society*] Williams sought to extend and connect (symptomatic terms in his writing) what was still in many ways a Leavisian perspective to a 'socialist humanism' radically hostile to *Scrutiny's* political case. What the work did, in effect, was to take the only viable tradition Williams had to hand – the Romantic radical-conservative lineage of nineteenth-century England – and extract from it those 'radical' elements which could be ingrafted into a 'socialist humanism'. That is to say, the elements extracted – tradition, community, organism, growth, wholeness, continuity and so on – were interlocked with the equally corporatist, evolutionary discourse of labourism, so that the organicism of the language reproduced and elaborated the organicism of the other. The book thus paradoxically reproduced the nineteenth-century bourgeois exploitation of Romantic radical-conservative ideology for its own ends – only this time the ends in question were socialist. And it could do so, of course, because the working-class movement is as a matter of historical fact deeply infected by the Carlylean and Ruskinian ideologies in question. It was a matter of the book *rediscovering* that tradition, offering it as a richly moral and symbolic heritage to an ideologically impoverished labour movement, just as in nineteenth-century England that tradition became an ideological crutch to the industrial bourgeoisie. The manoeuvre was enabled, of course, by the fact that both Romantic and labourist ideologies are in partial conflict with bourgeois hegemony; but it is precisely that partiality which allows them to embrace. Neither tradition is purely antagonistic to bourgeois state power: the first preserves it by displacing political analysis to a moralist and idealist critique of its worst 'human' effects, the second seems to accommodate itself within it. What the book did, then, was in one sense to consecrate the reformism of the labour movement, raise it to new heights of moral and cultural legitimacy, by offering to it values and symbols drawn in the main from the tradition of most entrenched political reaction.[58]

This passage is worth quoting at length because of the way in which Eagleton polarizes Williams's critical practice and his politics. Eagleton represents Williams as appropriating a set of terms from the 'Romantic radical-conservative lineage of nineteenth-century England', to construct a 'socialist humanism' polluted by bourgeois values and ideology. In so doing Eagleton makes Williams's prior literary critical practice formative of his subsequent political outlook (which for historical reasons aligns deceptively well with that 'romantic radical-conservative' one). It is surely ironical that it should be a left critic who fractures Williams's carefully sustained connection between his criticism and his politics – the politics *in* the criticism; the critical practice as uncovering a basis for broader consensus within the hitherto protected enclosure of 'culture'. It was surely significant that Williams characterized his first encounter with 'culture' as one of inequality and exclusion:

> Culture was the way in which the process of education, the experience of literature, and – for someone moving out of a working-class family to a higher education – inequality, came through. What other people, in different situations, might experience more directly as economic or political inequality, was naturally experienced, from my own route, as primarily an inequality of culture: an inequality which was also, in an obvious sense, an uncommunity. This is, I think, still the most important way to follow the argument about culture, because everywhere, but very specifically in England, culture is one way in which class, the fact of major divisions between men, shows itself.[59]

For Williams the class politics was built into that initial encounter, the literary was simply a peculiarly rich source of political engagement and understanding:

> Literature has a vital importance because it is at once a formal record of experience, and also, in every work, a point of intersection with the common language that is, in its major bearings, differently perpetuated. The recognition of culture as the body

of all these activities, and of the ways in which they are perpetuated and enter into our common living, was valuable and timely. But there was always the danger that this recognition would become not only an abstraction but in fact an isolation. To put upon literature, or more accurately upon criticism, the responsibility of controlling the quality of the whole range of personal and social experience, is to expose a vital case to damaging misunderstanding.[60]

Here, Williams is taking issue with a particular tradition from Coleridge, through Arnold, to that pervasive dimension of Leavis which leaves his potential radicalism forgotten in favour of the celebration of an exclusive minority culture, maintained by its commitment to the literary.[61] Williams points out that, whilst Eliot comes clean about this foregrounding of the literary, Leavis operates it, possibly more dangerously, as an assumption: the centrality of English and the literary. And yet this is the very assumption which Eagleton is misreading from Williams, and which subsequently led Eagleton in search of an 'alternative terrain of scientific knowledge', within which criticism would 'break with its ideological pre-history'.[62]

We introduce this first explicitly literary critical intervention, however, largely for the response it provoked from E. P. Thompson. Thompson, publishing a 'postscript' for the revised edition of his influential political biography of Morris, took the opportunity of adding an 'afterword' in response to Eagleton. It concludes:

> The point of this note is to emphasize the *continuing* difficulty of the problems discussed in my essay [whether Morris transformed Romanticism into an influential politics, or was an isolated eccentric]. Eagleton's position is diametrically opposed to that of Morris, and arises from distinct presuppositions. Morris sought in every way to implant, encourage and enlarge new 'wants' in the present, and imbue the socialist movement with an alternative notation of value *before* the 'rupture', and he judged that socialist success or failure in this enterprise would affect not only when the revolution came but what form it would take. In the event, Morris saw (although unclearly) that 'ruptures' in values are taking place *all the time*, and not only during moments of strike and rebellion. If Eagleton is in any way representative of Marxist thinking today, we can expect the argument between traditions to go on. It may have been thought once, by the Althusserian anti-'humanists', that those of us who acknowledge our continuing relation to the transformed Romantic tradition could simply be read out of the intellectual Left: we belonged somewhere else. But that attempt has failed. We are still here: we do not mean to go. Neither the Left nor Marxism can ever belong to any set of people who put up fences and proprietary signs; it can belong only to all those who choose to stay in that 'terrain' and who mix it with their labour. I say this sharply, but not because I think that the argument should be closed. It is a serious continuing quarrel of principles, and, indeed, 'the case of William Morris' has perhaps already passed on into 'the case of Raymond Williams.'[63]

With characteristically grand theatrical sweep, Thompson takes back Eagleton's critique of Williams's literary critical undertaking, and re-identifies it as an attack on the political integrity of a socialist tradition from Morris to Williams (and, of course, as the rhetorical flourishes testify, to Thompson himself).[64] 'Culture' regains the multiple density of 'history' as opposed to the specificity of 'text'. Left criticism set off towards the 'scientific' isolation of the text in the name of a 'hard' radical alternative; the 'Old New Left' ('We are still here: we do not mean to go') remained untroubled by that important suggestion of Eagleton's, that the roots of their political discourse might bear closer scrutiny.

Ten years on again, is it surprising that Bea Campbell finds herself bemusedly ferreting through the baggage of the Orwellian tradition, for the means of conveying to her reader that 'real', that 'authenticity' of poverty and deprivation which is the experience of women and of non-white ethnic groups? Asked why 'women and the family do not make any entry at all' in *The Long Revolution*, Williams replied that he wished they had done so: 'And I also wish I understood what prevented me from doing so, because it wasn't that I was not thinking about the question.'[65] Our aim in this essay has been to begin to offer an answer to Raymond Williams's question, as to that provocative opening question of Bea Campbell's. And we close with a passage from Campbell which conveys more vividly than any more argument of ours what it is (of that 'real' with which she was struggling) that the left has lost if it refuses to acknowledge that 'literary' in its history:

> I went home to the woman I'm staying with, a single parent with three children aged between two and nine years. She doesn't get a newspaper and had to ask the social security for new shoes for the two children at school when their last pair of trainers got holes. Today she was up at the crack of dawn, 4.30, to make breakfast for her man friend. He'd come round the night before after playing pool, and they'd stayed up late, so today she is shattered. I arrived home at about tea-time, we talked a bit, the children were charging around until about 7 p.m., when they had their baths, and by 9 p.m. they were in bed. By then I was in front of the television with tea and biscuits watching the news. That felt quite odd. I've noticed how rarely women watch the news. There were two major reports on the news, one showing mass rallies in Spain on the eve of the elections there, ... and the other on the miners' ballot. ... The woman I'm staying with comes from a mining family, and as I watched the news I heard the ironing board creaking in the kitchen. She was still working, doing the ironing at ten o'clock at night. She missed the news. It had nothing to do with her anyway.[66]

We, feminists and socialists, believe that by confronting that initial question ('What have [any of us] to do with Orwell?'), we may begin to find an answer that deals with the political enormity of that final sentence: 'It had nothing to do with her anyway.'

Notes

1 This essay will also appear in Lisa Jardine and Julia Swindells, *What's Left: History, Culture and the Labour Movement* (Routledge, 1989).

2 Bea Campbell, *Wigan Pier Revisited: Poverty and Politics in the 80s* (London, 1984), p. 5.

3 Ibid., 217.

4 Gareth Stedman Jones, *Marxism Today*, July 1984, p. 39.

5 Ibid.

6 Ibid., p. 38. That 'full sense of a way of life' which Stedman Jones quotes from Williams lies at the root of the problem. As a version of 'society' it belongs firmly to the cultural sphere, where, as we shall show, it invokes both the private and domestic, but then for historical reasons excludes women as subjects.

7 Ibid., p. 39.

8 Ibid., p. 40.

9 There is an interesting lesson to be learned from the dustjackets of consecutive printings of the Penguin text (we happen to have three in front of us, identically paginated and differing only in their covers). The 1962 cover shows a crowd of working men and a pit head in a kind of photo montage, and is implicitly labelled 'literature'; the 1974 cover is a line drawing of Orwell in a cloth cap, with the pit head in the background, and is labelled 'autobiography'; the 1986 cover is a 'designer' graphic of miners in the pit cage, coloured in pastels, and is labelled 'social history'.

10 See for instance, in our own work, L. Jardine, '"Girl Talk" (for boys on the left), or marginalising feminist critical praxis', *Oxford Literary Review* 8 (1986), pp. 208–17; J. Swindells, 'Liberating the Subject? Autobiography and "Women's History": a reading of *The Diaries of Hannah Cullwick*, in *Interpreting Women's Lives: Feminist Theory and Personal Narratives*, ed. Personal Narratives Collective, Centre for Advanced Feminist Studies, University of Minnesota (University of Indiana Press, forthcoming).

11 Thompson explicitly relates *William Morris* and Williams's *Culture and Society 1780–1950* (London, 1958) in the 'postscript' to the revised 1976 edition: 'The typing of this Romantic critique as "regressive", "utopian", and "idealist" is a facile way of getting out of the problem, for an alternative way of reading that tradition had been proposed, not only in my book, in 1955, but, very cogently, by Raymond Williams in *Culture and Society* in 1958' ('Romanticism, moralism and utopianism: the case of William Morris', *New Left Review*, 99, 1976, pp. 83–111; 90).

12 Williams himself draws attention to this 'moment' in *Politics and Letters: Interviews with New Left Review* (London, 1979) – particularly to the close connection between his first two books and Thompson's *The Making of the English Working Class*, published in 1963, but under way in the late 1950s.

13 'The generalization of this use of the term [culture] characterized the Left in the fifties, and was responsible for some important insights into British society: this was the moment of Richard Hoggart's *Uses of Literacy*' (Perry Anderson, 'Components of the national culture', *New Left Review* 50, 1968, pp. 3–57; 5).

14 As per the text, but this is surely an elision; on p. 5 Anderson has specified that the 'one serious work of socialist theory' is *Culture and Society*. See also a relevant footnote in an earlier piece by Anderson: 'It is immensely significant, incidentally,

that the only major theoretical departure in English social thought in the last decade – *The Long Revolution* – has derived from a writer trained in literary criticism. This was perhaps the only source from which it could have come, since the literary tradition of *Culture and Society* was the British substitute for classical sociology or a philosophical socialism in the 19th century' ('Socialism and pseudo-empiricism', *New Left Review*, 35, 1966, pp. 2–42; 23). Both Anderson and Thompson have a tendency to run the two works together, which is, we are arguing, not at all unexpected.

15 Anderson, 'Components of the national culture', pp. 55–6.

16 Anderson, 'Socialism and pseudo-empiricism', pp. 36–7.

17 Ibid., p. 37.

18 Williams, *Politics and Letters*, pp. 97–8.

19 We tend to think that he was further read by a younger generation of Left critics as exposing the historical reality of class conflict through apparently bourgeois texts (traditionally beyond the pale for the radical critic). So, when Williams is discussing 'culture', they are discussing canonical authors; and when Williams subjects 'culture' to analysis, they are wrapped up in the nineteenth-century novel – source for them of genuine 'narrative', to be deconstructed for its social relations and cultural practices.

20 Williams himself has always been particularly upset when class has been left out in versions of his work, and his 'long revolution' has been reduced to cultural evolution. See, for example, T. Eagleton and B. Wicker (eds), *From Culture to Revolution* (London, 1968), pp. 296–7. Historically this is an interestingly symptomatic volume for the *fortuna* of Williams's work. It postdates *The Long Revolution*, and is contemporary with a period of significant student dissent, yet in its treatment of 'culture' it focuses on *Culture and Society*, and English Studies to the virtual exclusion of history.

21 See below.

22 Williams, *Politics and Letters*, p. 112.

23 It is worth noting how women habitually get invoked when there is a panic about class (see also Williams's remark about Virginia Woolf above). Mr Eliot's class might problematize the discussion, without an elderly gentlewoman to take responsibility for his Tradition.

24 E. P. Thompson, *New Left Review* 9 (1961), pp. 24–33; 24–5.

25 Ibid., p. 25.

26 V. G. Kiernan, *The New Reasoner* 9 (1959), pp. 74–83; 78.

27 Ibid., 80–1.

28 Raymond Williams, *Orwell* (London, 1971), p. 52.

29 In *Exiles and Émigrés: Studies in Modern Literature*(London, 1970), p. 73, Eagleton finds himself making this problem explicit in relation to what he calls 'the lower middle-class novel' (which Orwell supposedly writes): 'Orwell himself, of course, was not lower middle class in origin: he was born into an equally insecure stratum at the lower end of the upper class, but transplanted those tensions into what emerges, in some of his novels, as a definitively lower middle-class ethos.' A questionable assumption.

30 'Trained at Eton to be a snob but disgusted by the oppressive methods he had applied in the Burma police, George Orwell set out as deliberately as William Cobbett to make contact with the working class in England. These 'Urban Rides' of his, whether to Wigan or Sheffield, supply us with a series of factual, shocking, but

sublimely human reports on the state of the nation in a time of mass unemployment' (Penguin, 1962 dustjacket). 'Commissioned by the Left Book Club, George Orwell set out to write the urban equivalent of Cobbett's *Rural Rides* and describe the great industrial wastelands of Yorkshire and Lancashire' (Penguin, 1986 dustjacket).

31 E. P. Thompson *The Making of the English Working Class* (London, 1963) p. 820.

32 Williams, *Politics and Letters*, pp. 385–6.

33 George Orwell, *The Road to Wigan Pier* (Harmondsworth, 1962) pp. 20–1.

34 For a full account of this tendency in Orwell's text see Daphne Patai, *The Orwell Mystique: A Study in Male Ideology* (Amherst, Mass., 1984).

35 We are grateful to Dorothy Armstrong for making this point to us.

36 Orwell, *Wigan Pier*, p. 29.

37 Ibid., p. 31.

38 See in particular, Patai, *The Orwell Mystique*.

39 Campbell, *Wigan Pier Revisited*, p. 98.

40 Ibid., p. 99.

41 Orwell, *Wigan Pier*, pp. 104–5.

42 See J. Swindells, *Victorian Writing and Working Women* (Oxford, 1985), *passim*.

43 Campbell, *Wigan Pier Revisited*, pp. 57–9.

44 We would in fact argue that Campbell is misled by 'masculinity' into representing the problem as one of sexuality and involving Arthur Munby and muscular pit-girls to invalidate Orwell's account.

45 S. Orwell and I. Angus, *The Collected Essays, Journalism and Letters of George Orwell*, vol. 1, *An Age Like This 1920–1940* (Harmondsworth, 1970), pp. 210–13, 234–6, 237–40.

46 Ibid., pp. 239–40.

47 Ibid., p. 236.

48 Ibid., pp. 202–4.

49 Orwell, *Wigan Pier*, p. 11.

50 Ibid., pp. 6–7.

51 Campbell, *Wigan Pier Revisited*, p. 5.

52 Judith Williamson has drawn attention to this 'superior' stance of the critic. See particularly, 'How does girl number twenty understand ideology?', *Screen Education*, 40 (1981/2), pp. 80–7.

53 For a particularly clear account of the historically developing theories of relations between 'dominant' and 'popular' culture, see M. Shiach, *Theories of Popular Culture* (Oxford, 1989).

54 T. Eagleton, *Criticism and Ideology* (New Left Books, 1976): 'Mutations of critical ideology', pp. 11–43.

55 *New Left Review*, 95 (1976), pp. 3–23.

56 Anthony Barnett, 'Raymond Williams and Marxism: a rejoinder to Terry Eagleton', *New Left Review*, 99 (1976), pp. 47–64, 48.

57 Eagleton did so in terms which damagingly severed Williams's critical thought from his politics, to produce an unjustly harsh judgement – provoking immediate indignantly defensive replies from Anthony Barnett and E. P. Thompson: Barnett, 'Williams and Marxism'; Thompson, 'Romanticism, moralism and utopianism: the case of William Morris', *New Left Review* 99 (1976), pp. 83–111 ('Afternote', pp. 110–11).

58 Eagleton, 'Criticism and politics', p. 10.
59 Williams, 'Culture and revolution: a comment', in Eagleton and Wicker, *From Culture to Revolution*, pp. 22–34; 22.
60 Williams, *Culture and Society*, pp. 248–9.
61 See most fully, Francis Mulhern, *The Moment of Scrutiny* (London, 1979).
62 Eagleton, 'Criticism and politics', p. 23.
63 Thompson, 'Romanticism, moralism and utopianism: the case of William Morris', p. 111.
64 It did not help, of course, that Eagleton himself made overly grand claims for the 'difficulties' he had detected in Williams's work.
65 Williams, *Politics and Letters*, p. 149.
66 Campbell, *Wigan Pier Revisited*, pp. 113–4.

7

IN WHOSE VOICE?
The Drama of Raymond Williams

—— *Bernard Sharratt* ——

Throughout *Drama from Ibsen to Eliot*[1] there is an insistence upon innovative moments in the history of drama as being the result of a certain encounter with a new kind of 'experience' which results in a painful reorganization of sensibility, articulated in some new dramatic form, a new 'structure of feeling'. It is this which provides the chain upon which Williams traces the history of drama from Ibsen onwards. The book is largely organized into chapters devoted to named individual dramatists, with a prefatory chart of dates from 1850 to 1950, locating specific texts against a chronological sequence. This way of structuring the book, and the argument, rests upon an apparently obvious distinction between old and new experience, shaped as old and new structures of feeling. And, as in other parts of Williams's work, the accompanying concepts tend to cluster around age, generation, the difference between a younger and an older generation as a primary way of thinking about the nature of a period, the nature of history as succession.

By the mid-1960s, in *Modern Tragedy*,[2] that crucial notion of 'experience' seems to have come under considerable pressure. The word itself is used in a variety of ways that is peculiarly hard to pin down, as, for example, in the following two passages (emphasis added):

> However men die, the *experience* is not only the physical dissolution and ending; it is also a change in the lives and relationships of others, for we know death as much in the *experience* of others as in our own expectations and endings. And just as death enters, continually, our common life, so any statement about death is in a common language and depends on common *experience*. The paradox of 'we die alone' or 'man dies alone' is then important and remarkable: the maximum substance that can be given to the plural 'we', or to the group-name 'man' is the

singular loneliness. The common fact, in a common language, is offered as a proof of the loss of connection.

But then, as we become aware of this structure of feeling, we can look through it at the *experience* which it has offered to interpret. It is using the names of death and tragedy, but it has very little really to do with the tragedies of the past, or with death as a universal *experience*. Rather, it has correctly identified, and then blurred, the crisis around which one main kind of contemporary *tragic experience* moves. It blurs it because it offers as absolutes the very *experiences* which are are now most unresolved and most moving.

... It is characteristic of such structures that they cannot even recognise as possible any *experience* beyond their own structural limits; that such varying and possible statements as 'I die but I shall live', 'I die but we shall live', or 'I die but we do not die' become meaningless, and can even be contemptuously dismissed as evasions. (pp. 57–8).

The relationship here between experience, understanding, and language is made peculiarly difficult by the focusing upon death, but it is clear that the key term is itself stretched to cover complicatedly different areas of thought and feeling. Moreover, the whole organization of *MT* is very different from that of *DIE*: a compressed historical overview of what Williams calls Tragic Ideas in Part I; then 'Modern Tragic Literature' in Part II; and in Part III the play *Koba*. But in Part II – which covers much the same period and plays as *DIE* – there is no longer a history structured primarily round individual dramatists, but rather a series of chapters devoted to different kinds of tragedy, perhaps different structures of feeling: liberal tragedy, from Ibsen to Miller; private tragedy from Strindberg to Tennessee Williams; what is called tragic deadlock and stalemate from Chekhov to Beckett, and so on. There is now only one chapter devoted to just a single writer: a rejection of tragedy, in Brecht.

This new way of ordering authors and texts seems to indicate not any simple local revaluation or re-drawing of succession but a revision at a more basic level, in the very notion, now, of a range of options, a repertoire of responses, as constituting an overall 'period' (they are all 'modern' tragedy), so that at the same time one can find private tragedy being written alongside liberal tragedy, within the same (in some sense) cultural moment. Williams will later reformulate this in *Marxism and Literature* in terms of overlapping and contending, residual, dominant and emergent forms and feelings – though still with an implicit appeal to generational differences. But the apparently very tight relations in *DIE* between 'new' experience, new form, new structure of feeling and a 'new' period, seem to have become loosened, unhinged.

But then in *Drama from Ibsen to Brecht*, published in 1968,[3] he reverts in the title to a sense of overall succession, and in fact retains a very great deal of the actual material of *DIE*. Many of the pages are indeed identical. But the organization is again different; neither that of *DIE* nor that of *MT*. Part I of *DIB* is a 'Generation of Masters'; Part II re-orders the chapters on Yeats and Synge from *DIE*, almost wholly rewrites the comments on O'Casey, adds an essay on Joyce and groups these various pieces as a section on Irish dramatists. Part III is then, apparently rather inertly, simply 'Alternative Actions, Alternative Conventions', with Pirandello starting this section and Eliot – who had been the culmination of the whole argument in *DIE* – relegated simply to a chapter of this section, *an* alternative. Part IV, on social and political drama, includes some new material, particularly a chapter on Brecht. And then Part V, on 'Recent Drama', offers brief, almost review-like comments on ten disparate plays.

In that same year, 1968, Williams published a revised and extended edition of *Drama In Performance*, originally published in 1954.[4] The focus of that book is the charting from the Greeks to the present of the changing relations between forms of annotation, or text, and modes of performance, or realization, within different historical conditions and conventions. Yet given the scope and concision of *DIP*, it seems much less plausible than in *DIE* or *DIB* to see any such changes as arising from an individual confronting a new experience and finding a new dramatic form to encompass that experience. Indeed, *DIP* may well clarify what is intended by 'experience' in the other works. For the danger *DIE* and *DIB* both invite is to think in terms of a simple empiricist notion, of an elementary encounter with some recalcitrant particular, some inner 'I' forging a shape for its own localizable and specific 'experience' prior to the secondary act of writing this down in a formal dramatic mode, and subsequently releasing that shaped whole for inevitably partial realization in an essentially inadequate theatrical performance. This one-way model, from dramatist to final audience, with drama as the essential term in the drama-theatre coupling, would obviously be very vulnerable indeed to a charge of epistemological idealism. But in *DIP* it seems much clearer – because the individual dramatist is no longer the focus – that 'experience' might better be thought of in terms of coming to a realization of the very nature of one's own particular culture and society. The 'experience' in question is more like living through a major historical change (and not, therefore, some specifically individual experience), and only realizing the nature and scope of that change by a difficult and fundamental recasting of categories. And those categories are in part given in the dominant form of drama, whether in the relation between chorus and protagonists in the drama of the city-state or in the theological patternings of medieval mystery plays. Yet those categories are not primarily intellectual, a matter of conscious beliefs, but a shaping of emotions and feelings, of responses to particularized actions, gestures and words. Only when we do *not* 'know' in a sense what our reaction to a significant gesture is, are we perhaps on the brink of that reformulation. (It may for that reason be worth adding that even after re-reading *DIP* I don't quite know what kind of relation Williams saw between the written text of *Koba* and any possible production of it).

It might be legitimate to seek some explanation for these changing foci of attention, and in particular for those three different ways of organizing responses to what is very much the same primary material in *DIE*, *MT*, and *DIB*. It might, for example, be plausible to suggest that Williams must have encountered some profoundly new experience during these years, and that in negotiating it had emerged with a new 'structure of feeling'. After all, in the 1964 Foreward to *MT* he talks of wanting to 'get a whole structure of feeling and thinking into one book' and of how *Koba* is included, alongside other kinds of writing, because 'it seems now essentially to belong with them'. However, by 1979, in the Foreword to the Verso edition of *MT*, *Koba* seemed to 'belong to another area' of his work, and was omitted.

Alternatively, one might regard each book as an intervention, a situated response. Ibsen, after all, had aroused the attention of a number of other Cambridge critics in the late 1940s; Williams's version of Ibsen and his progeny clearly contested an emerging orthodoxy. Similarly, the argument around tragedy in the early 1960s, with Steiner's *The Death of Tragedy* occupying a commanding height for a time, was enough provocation for *MT*; and the emergence of a relatively sterilized 'designer Brecht' in the 1960s demanded, perhaps, a more sharply political reading, which then helped to foster that growth of Brecht-influenced practice and theory of the 1970s.

At this point a persistent aspect of Williams's entire output perhaps becomes relevant: that in almost every area of work there is a continuity, a carry-over, from critique to a form of practice. *Culture and Society* quite clearly, if implicitly, writes his own work into its history; *The Long Revolution* ends with a set of proposals for advancing that long revolution. *The English Novel from Dickens to Lawrence* leaves off the inquiry just at the stage, in terms of formal exploration, which his own novels might be seen as continuing. Even *Preface to Film* was a preface to Williams's own intended film-making efforts.

Whether in the study of literature or elsewhere, the problems and issues selected can always be seen as impinging upon quite definite practical tasks Williams feels it urgent to undertake. But it is then less a matter of getting the history 'right', in some impossibly positivist sense of scholarship, as of tracing the movement of which he sees himself as part. This placing of his enquiries within an overall project oriented to new forms of practice then shapes those enquiries precisely as a movement of the mind, an argument formed as history. The movement continues beyond the critique to exemplification, and it is this which gives a quite distinctive edge to Williams's 'critical' writings. It also substantially explains why he can propose, in different books, quite sharply revised judgements of particular dramatists while sometimes offering a basically unchanged analysis of their work. Clearly, the dramatic criticism might also be read in this way. The point of writing *DIE* or *DIB* is not finally to offer 'literary criticism', as a detached and spectatorial ajudication between existing texts, but is rather an attempt so to trace a selective reading of the past as to enable other work to be undertaken, other plays to be written. *MT* makes that plain precisely by including a modern tragedy.

But if this general claim holds, that Williams's 'critical' work is always at some level of analysis directed towards substantial problems of practice he is actually confronting, it may also be true that some of the dilemmas he locates in others' practice may illuminate his own critical problems. In *Politics and Letters*, Williams largely agrees with the summary offered by the *New Left Review* interviewers of his objections to Brecht's work: that 'the two terms of his drama remained the unmodified pair of the isolated individual and the overwhelming society ranged against the individual' or, in Williams's own words, that Brecht 'was hardly interested at all in intermediate relationships, in that whole complex of experience, at once personal and social, between the poles of the separated individual and the totally realised society.'[5] Yet at least in *DIE* his own argument also rests upon a certain polar relationship between the individual and a whole society, with the boundary of that whole society left undefined partly because the 'intermediate' concept he himself employs – structure of feeling – seems to act simultaneously as both a mediating term and a formulation of the totality. Ibsen, for example, is never specified as articulating the new experience of, say, a fraction of the nineteenth-century Norwegian bourgeoisie; there is an almost disdainful declining of any such sociological representativeness. Nor does the book, as in *DIP*, deploy specifically theatrical history as indicating any intermediate grouping or sector. Instead, it seems that Ibsen simply speaks for all those who share that new structure of feeling – and that can almost be everyone, or no one.

At the time of writing *DIE*, in the late 1940s and early 1950s, Williams seemed to want to refuse consideration of any kind of mediation except 'structure of feeling'; but this refusal also seemed to involve him in a certain sidestepping of the issues of determination and choice. It was in 1946–7 that he was so attracted to Ibsen, precisely because of the resonance he found in that work with his own experience, as summarized in the line he quotes so often: 'You come to a tight place and stick fast'. That very phrase indicates a kind of impasse, a sense of equilibrium between pressures and decision. The notion of a 'call' in Ibsen, which Williams also found resonant, can then be glossed within the work as effectively a kind of self-imposed vocation, a task which at some level one has set oneself and yet which seems inescapable. In particular, Williams recorded in *Politics and Letters* how he had always thought of himself since that time as primarily a writer, as having that call, that self-imposed vocation. The fact that he focused his interests upon letters rather than upon politics betokens an emphasis which runs throughout his writing, on culture not as secondary but as primary, as having a status equal to 'the economic'. Insofar as both might be offered, by contrast or opposition, as abstractions from the totality, the one has as much validity, and can be as 'determining' in any specific instance, as the other. But the very notion of being 'a writer' inevitably carries certain 'period' overtones, which could again suggest a relatively direct, unmediated relation between the individual's response and the whole social experience, while the envisaged act of writing can itself seem both chosen and imposed; Williams speaks of it taking shape as an 'impulse' and a 'disturbance'.

For someone in Williams's position shortly after the end of the war, it must indeed have seemed easier and more natural than it ever could today in England to regard himself as having in a quite palpable way 'experienced' the whole society. To have moved from a village in Wales, itself shaped by both rural capitalism and nearby mining industry, to a Cambridge college, and from there to front-line combat, indeed from student Communist Party membership to the officers' mess in the Guards Armoured Division; to have helped liberate a concentration camp and then to have returned to Cambridge; to have edited a *Daily Mirror*-style army newspaper and then a critical periodical in metropolitan literary London; to have an Oxford university appointment yet to be teaching workers in the WEA; to have married and become a father – all this in the context of a world war, and at the age when most academics today would barely be finishing a Ph.D. This must have seemed a range of experience which needed an articulated form, a conscious organization of response. To have taken the full weight of that range of social experience might well have been to risk a certain crisis or even breakdown, while any impulse to become a writer would be both deeply reinforced, and yet also deeply problematic, at the level of developing an appropriate form for that encompassing experience.

It is also clear that the specific social experiences Williams had undergone were quite unusually shaped by distinctions between older and younger generations. After the very particular experience of student life on 'borrowed time' (as Michael Orrom's filmed memories of Williams's student generation puts it) and then of war service, older not just in years but in what we call 'experience', Williams returned to a Cambridge again populated by much younger undergraduates, and went from that to teaching, in what we call 'Adult Education', men and women considerably older than himself. He later returned to Cambridge at the age of forty, to teach students this time much younger than himself. He once remarked (in *Reading and Criticism*[6]) that the problem many people face who try to write 'good' prose is that they imitate the prose norms of a generation or two previous to their own; this was perhaps acutely the case with Williams's adult students. So in those years the temptation to conceive of history in terms of individuals or generations encountering new experiences, and having to find new formulations of and forms for that experience, must have been considerable.

There is, however, another and perhaps less palatable aspect of this felt contrast between young and old; that Williams in his sixties (receiving tributes like these essays from a younger generation) can look back on an impressive, extensive and influential oeuvre, yet also glance across at figures who have wielded much more direct power in this society by the time they have reached *their* sixties. There is perhaps a strong temptation for the teacher, the academic, to think of his or her own contemporaries as either younger or older than they are. For a Wilson or a Kinnock to become leader of the Labour Party by their mid-forties can then seem mildly astonishing. For a socialist, having made the choice for 'letters', for being a 'writer', and then to realize that others who made a different choice were actually exercising the power one had spent so much time combating, might lead to some acute requestioning of the relations between 'politics' and 'letters'.

In several ways, Williams's 1966 television play *A Letter from the Country* seems to be concerned with all these intertwined problems. An obvious keyword for the structure of the play is 'correspondence'. It takes the familiar phrase, 'writing a letter to one's MP', and demonstrates an almost morality-play version of what that might involve, in the figure of a Welsh teacher, Pritchard, who writes regular letters to a particular MP, Walter Dix, reminding the MP of the distance, the lack of correspondence, between what he now says and does and what he has said in the past. Pritchard thus acts as a kind of conscience, and that structural metaphor is made explicit in the play: 'no one knows what will happen if a man meets his conscience.' Pritchard and Dix do finally meet – that is the obvious 'action' of the play. But their relationship is then crossed by the notion of the correspondent as an accredited, expert, professional – a newspaper correspondent, a lobby correspondent, someone who acts as an official channel, part of the system of communication but also of disinformation. Dix is 'guilty' of an 'indiscreet leak' to such a reporter concerning an overseas military base. Pritchard witnesses the 'leak', which is later publicly denied.

The various channels of communication, the networks of connection, are rendered visible in the play, from the process whereby a letter posted in Wales reaches a breakfast table in London, to the railway journeys following a similar route, made by Pritchard to this distant and in many ways alien centre of power. We see the intersection of systems, the ways in which, for example, the educational system is crossed by newspapers and television. There is a moment in the play when Pritchard switches on the TV in his class for a schools programme on 'Everyday Politics' and finds on the screen the MP whom he has just been to see in London. The play ends with a blockage of communication, a suppression of information, a denial of the previous, 'private' communication and then a further suppression of the newspaper report that would have made that lie public.

There are other starting points for analysis. The list of characters makes it very plain what their ages are, and the play is much concerned with the difference in response between Dix and his younger colleagues, who see the issues raised by the relationship between Pritchard and Dix in significantly different ways. There is the sisterly loyalty, to Dix, of Sally, who is prepared to see Pritchard subjected to pressure and perhaps prosecution under the Official Secrets Act, to protect the lying denial of her brother, whose 'career' is at risk. There is an inability on the part of Paul to comprehend that Pritchard's decision to try to make public his witnessing of a denied leakage is not personally directed towards Dix but is governed by a demand for democratic truth, for integrity and honesty in public life. But also, uneasily held within the play, is a worrying problem; what the effectiveness of Pritchard's intervention might or could have been. The play seems to run up against a certain impasse, since it is clear that two quite different systems of communication exist within the political formation and that one finally has power over the other. To expose that power would require access to some other system of communication, but the 'professional' or the 'public' system is not normally or easily accessible to most of us. There is in this structure a general social experience, of what we call parliamentary democracy, seen not from the perspective of the political party or parliamentary 'professional' but from the far more common viewpoint of the provincial citizen, the ordinary constituent, whose relation to 'parliament' is predominantly formal and distant, in both senses. When Pritchard gets off the train and wanders round Whitehall and Westminster, there is a distinct sense of these centres of power as decidedly not being expressions of popular will, of popular power. The formal model of parliamentary democracy is palpably at variance with the feeling one has about these buildings. They so patently belong not to oneself but to a ruling class. We can watch MPs, as Dix's TV broadcast actually recommends; we can even listen today to broadcasts directly from the House of Commons. But that is seen as a privilege, and an impotent privilege; we are basically spectators. If, then, the best we can do to modify that power is to send a letter, when in any case – through a network over which we have little control – the information upon which we might want to intervene has already been doctored, laundered, adjusted, suppressed, before it ever reaches those media which are supposed to mediate, then the relation between the individual and 'parliamentary democracy' becomes ever more one of isolated powerlessness. Television is from one angle of analysis a precise image of our powerlessness, and the fact that we can watch that very process dramatically represented *on* TV become at a certain level a reinforcement rather than a resolution of that impasse.

That this play is itself actually taking place on television indicates that it is indeed possible to appropriate some moments within the *apparently* dominant communication system. Ironically, though, we may well be watching the play in the immediate context of government denials or manipulation of information in the News which preceded its transmission. Such a juxtaposition may then become, on a particular evening, part of the 'meaning' of the play precisely as a 'television play'.

Some of these issues reappear in Williams's introduction to the *Pelican Book of English Prose* (1969), which seems to me one of the richest essays he has published.[7] It overlaps with much of his other work; it traces the same period as *Culture and Society*, from Burke to the 1950s; it evidently links up with the essay on Hume in *The English Mind*; it incorporates some of the same material as *The English Novel*. Above all, it probes very explicitly the relation between ways of speaking and writing and possible modes of political relationship, within a historical perspective. And the analysis of that deep connection begins from a comparison between *The Letters of Junius* and Burke's *Thoughts on the Causes of the Present Discontents*. One passage has immediate relevance to *A Letter from the Country*:

> What they have in common is sufficiently remarkable: the exposure of a political move made under the cover of morality. The strength of the argument in each case draws on an important assumption of public candour. Yet ... Junius relies on a distinction between public and private morality which is ultimately a matter of aristocratic convention ... the attack is then on a personal hypocrisy ... an *ad hominem* denunciation, within the moral conventions of a ruling class. [Whereas] there is a basis, in Burke, for an appeal to general principles, beyond the exposure of a personal failing within the convention. He can at least approach the moral judgement of a system of government, as something more general and important than the faults of a particular man in power.
>
> This substantial difference of political interest is embodied in the contrasted forms of writing. Junius, necessarily, extends political controversy by the device of the open letter; the personal denunciation put into general print. Burke, on the other hand, while no less immediate, is writing in a genuinely public way, not only referring the question to general principles, but describing a system of government as part of a public inquiry. The important shift from the style of eighteenth century politics, within a ruling class, to the style of a more public and open politics, can then be decisively observed. [Burke's] degree of generalization and abstraction is the necessary basis of a more general and abstract politics ... A genuinely public political argument could only begin when there was this kind of assertion of principles. (pp. 76–7)

The relevance of this passage for *A Letter from the Country* is clear. More generally, the passage anticipates a great deal of what Jürgen Habermas and others have argued in terms of the bourgeois 'public sphere'. It would be possible to go on and situate literature, criticism, critical discourse, within some such model. But there is an element in Williams's overall analysis which seems to me to be underplayed, and this is partly a matter of implicit method. At the beginning of the Introduction, he comments on the expansion of readerships, the increase in editions of books, and copies of newspapers. But this is in effect sectioned off, as a factor not then fully integrated into the analysis. The growth in readership is associated with changes in the ways of writing, and those modes of writing are then directly associated with a potentiality of democracy, as a mode of public argument and discussion. Yet to bring these two factors into further relation, to close the circle, is to raise a problem about the underlying model.

In the case of both Junius and Burke there is indeed a continuity between the mode of address and the actual power of the collective or even individual addressee; Burke, after all, is in practice addressing a very limited 'public'. That continuity still obtains for later authors, but only insofar as they are writing for a specifiable audience about particular issues in relation to which that audience has the power to act. Thus, one could recognize in Williams's emphasis on the ways in which naturalism as a dramatic form characteristically offers the room as the dramatic setting, and thereby tends to restrict its range of concerns to those which can in some sense be represented as occurring within a room, a fairly precise parallel with the kinds of control and power which the dominant audience for that form would indeed have been able to exercise. If one considers not just the readership or its size but the kinds of power exercised by that readership or audience, the kinds of domain over which they had some autonomous control, then the wider the readership, the more restricted is likely to be its actual or acknowledged power, and in particular the power of any average member of it.

One could return to the history of drama, on an 'epochal' scale, with this issue in mind. On a very broad scale, one might recognize that a fifth-century Greek *demos* watching a play does so in an arena continuous in obvious ways with the kind of assembly space in which that same audience would have taken 'political' decisions for the 'whole' society. A medieval Catholic dramaturgy might be cosmic in its reach but resolves itself into an issue of decision over one's own eternal future, a matter on which each individual is in a position to respond (at least until a theology of election and predestination prevails). Even in metropolitan Elizabethan drama, there could often have been a fairly direct continuity between the disposition of ranks of power within the auditorium and within the play; the opening of *Coriolanus* sufficiently indicates the possibilities here. English Restoration and French neo-classical drama are predominantly directed at the kinds of audience most likely to encounter precisely those entanglements of power and desire, in the marriage market or court intrigue, which are the subject of those socially claustrophobic pieces. Equally, bourgeois drama of all kinds tends to focus upon those issues a bourgeois audience has within its own control; issues are often then offered at the precisely appropriate scale of, rather than 'reduced to', apparently 'personal' dimensions, of change of heart or sentimental sympathy. Ibsen's characters, for example, often come not from a politically nondescript or insignificant middle class but from the actually ruling class. And Shaw was undoubtedly right, commercially, to postpone the opening night of his *John Bull's Other Island* till after the parliamentary recess!

The decisive extension of political audiences denoted by the term 'mass media' perhaps breaks that general congruence. For there is now a palpable strain involved in watching, say, television drama concerned with contemporary politics, where one's sense as an ordinary viewer of any direct capacity to intervene in the examined issues may be very weak indeed. The repeated experience of watching the News, those daily reports of bombings, famine, war, or high level summits, NATO conferences, ministerial meetings across a global horizon, while unable as a spectator to translate any of those problems into direct engagement, can produce a general structure of feeling in which watching the news becomes a ritualized exercise in fatalism. It can seem as if we are divided between that self which has remarkably limited individual power, and the self which can, with a historically unique privilege of access, watch not just dramatized 'representations' but real-time processes and actual events unfolding on a world-historical scale. That gap between knowledge and power becomes part of our structure of feeling. To turn from the reporting of some outrageous event (the bombing of Libya, Chernobyl, African famine) and write a passionately informed letter – a letter to Brezhnev, or one's MP – seems both perfectly possible and utterly fatuous. Yet the received 'democratic' modes of political access and engagement are also dominantly presented as continuous with that distanced world of power represented elsewhere, rather than (necessarily) as within the areas of immediate control open to the domesticated observer. A major problem of the relations between 'representation' (in both senses), forms of 'public' discourse and the actual areas of effective control available to those who constitute the audiences for that discourse, remains deeply unresolved.

Williams once told an anecdote about the only time he met Bertrand Russell. At the end of a CND meeting there had been endless discussion as to what kind of protest telegram to send, and to whom. Russell had simply slipped out of the meeting and telephoned the American President and the Russian Premier. Lord Russell had been brought up, after all, in a household in which Foreign Secretaries dropped in for lunch, and for him Whitehall and Westminster were not alien territory but familiar domestic domains. That aristocratic gesture takes us back to the letters of Junius, but also to that phrase left hanging in the comments on Burke: 'public inquiry', the title of Williams's next television play.

Public Inquiry could clearly be seen as an exercise in assigning blame for the train crash which is its focus.[8] One can imagine a family taking the play as a variant of those once-popular parlour games, and debating whose fault it was: Tom's for forgetting the starter signal, his son David's for not relieving him at the shift-change, the signalman's further up the line for arriving late, young Gareth for distracting Tom with his unnecessary hooting – or even old Andrews whose points of order and amendments so delayed the Union meeting that David was late for work. This would be the familiar linking of a moral dilemma to a chain of causality, in terms of both individual actions and characters. But the play clearly invites another reading also, in terms of a system as well as a sequence, interconnections as well as causes. Certain keywords echo across categories of context and suggest a deeper connection. 'Connection' is itself one of those keywords, linking the railway sense of 'making a connection' with the sense involved in any process of inquiry. The very word 'train' is given another dimension by its link with the kind of 'training' imposed upon yet also internalized by ordinary soldiers during the war, or by the older generation of railwaymen. That internalized training or discipline (given shape in the play in the remembered voice of Jarvis) comes through as 'Duty', but is then in some tension with the everyday sense of 'on duty', a matter of cruelly demanding shifts (three weeks of twelve-hour shift-working with no relief-man available). The Union meeting is concerned with a 'work to rule' motion, to follow the written regulations strictly, which raises the issues of how far the real 'rules', those developed by generations of railwaymen to ensure the safety of the trains, are what is actually laid down in the regulations – and whether British Rail are themselves 'following the rules', in either sense. The Union meeting has its own regulations and rules of procedure, including the 'points of order' which so lengthen it – but 'points' are also the switch-points on the track and 'orders' look two ways, to arbitrary authority and to adequate arrangements.

The crucial term is probably 'responsible'. One sense of this comes through powerfully in David's memory of his Dad's pride in his job: 'The aristocracy, he used to call it to me: all the proud skilled men, the responsible men, and the trains rushing through, the signals, the uniforms' (p. 30). But later David himself reaches for that other, narrower sense; 'A mistake under pressure. They're made all the time. But it's only a few jobs the mistakes can rear up, act in public, drivers, pilots, signalmen, seamen. All the others make their mistakes, but they can cross them out, chuck them under the bench, let them work themselves out till no one's responsible' (p. 49).

It is Jarvis, once Tom's mentor, now chairing the inquiry, who suggests a third sense, in a comment which also implicitly redefines a number of other key terms:

> The efficiency and safety of the railway system depend mainly on a system of communication, human, mechanical and electronic, which has been built up, over generations, by experience and inquiry. It might seem to those involved that the only purpose of an inquiry is to assign blame. But if we can look at an inquiry in this other way, as not only an inquiry into error or negligence by an individual, but also an inquiry into the system of communication itself, we can come face to face with our larger reponsibility. (p. 42)

Yet, as the camera cuts to a later moment, Jarvis continues with his 'next point': whether British Rail's system of recording information is detailed enough; the inquiry's recommendations will, it seems clear, include some suggestions on improving the register kept by signalmen. But this is to fall back from any adequate notion of 'our larger responsibility'.

It is the play's own system of communication, its exploitation of yet another sense of 'point', which helps to construct that larger sense of responsibility, taking us beyond Jarvis's own awareness. For the play uses the televisual possibilities of shifting points of view in order to bring home (on television, therefore in a literal sense) two different ways of seeing the entire process of which the railway is both image and part. For we see Tom both as a known, named character, with a personal, interior life to which we are given access, and also as a figure darkly glimpsed in the signal box as we rush past in the train. We glimpse other signalmen, other drivers, in the same way; but we also see ourselves, from their perspective, as another trainload safely through the signals, as brief inhabitants of lighted compartments in the night. In one extraordinary sequence we move from Tom looking at his reflection in the dark window-panes from inside the signal box, then to outside the box, looking in at Tom, and then to Tom as seen in the reflection, with Tom's voice-over: 'You get to see yourself from outside. That's the strangest part of it. You seem outside the box, looking in, and you see this man there, this man in dark clothes and you ask who he is and what exactly he's doing. What his life amounts to, up there above the line' (p. 27).

The moment is paralleled later, when Tom, looking down from the box at a passing train, tells David that when he, Tom, travels by train he stands up and waves if it's someone he knows in the signal box as they pass; but outside the 'division' (another resonant term) he just settles into it, takes the train for granted, forgets the men who man the lines. As he speaks we cut to him and Tom on the train going to the inquiry; as the train passes a signal box Tom does stand up and wave, but the signalman, a stranger, doesn't notice him.

This changing of viewpoint allows us a fuller recognition than usual of the double-facetedness of all working responsibilities: their taken-for-grantedness as an impersonal system of coordination and allocation of duties, yet also their immediate pressure as the lived experience of other people, as fully individual as ourselves. Yet in that very re-cognition is an awareness beyond the notion of 'individual' and towards a grasp of what (in two more key-terms) a 'public' 'service' might be. As the play insists, the problem is not that we 'know' this but *how* we know it. We know it, in one mode, by the value we give a life, any life. But not only when that life is over, as in the public inquiry into the fatal accident. And not only in the sharp contrasts of actual treatment when a 'working life' is over: Tom reduced to £2 10s a week pension after forty-seven years of work, while a 'failed' politician or general gets a peerage. We can sometimes grasp the deeper dependence we take for granted when 'personal' and working worlds intersect or overlap, as in the father–son relation in the play. But the crucial effort is to know the nature of public dependence and relation on an everyday basis, as ordinary an awareness as that involved in the assumption that the train will not crash. But of course that is not only a matter of some personal change of consciousness. In another memorable sequence the signal box is transformed before our eyes into a possible alternative, in its arrangements, its technology, its resources, geared this time to (as we say) both the man and the job, but now, as David says,

> a different man, controlling a different system, in a different world. . . . Not a man like us. We've sold ourselves cheap, to fit in with machines. We've felt guilty and broken when we make a mistake, the pressure too heavy on us. But not any more. We can take control, we can change the system. As we're bound to change it, to take the pressure off men. (p. 47)

Those 1960s terms, 'take control', 'change the system' again echo across, from the quite literal and specific sense of changing the system of communication and control within the signal box, to those necessary wider dimensions. If the actual ending of the play seems from this perspective like a local defeat, it is so only in the sense that a particular event seems an 'accident', merely a grotesque coincidence. Accidents, like defeats, show what has to be changed, in any fully public inquiry into their causes.

Whereas A Letter from the Country might be claimed as leading finally to a sense of political impasse, Public Inquiry seems to allow a more hopeful political possibility. At issue, indeed, seem to be two rather different models of political analysis and action. The first might be termed a 'spectatorial' model, which can take the form of thinking of oneself as a watcher, an observer, situated in a position of more or less omniscience or ignorance concerning the global society. That can lead to a dual view of one's political relation to that society: either an acute sense of impotence and impasse, or a notion of action as deliberate intervention. That model is within the Marxist tradition basically a Leninist one, and it can involve an idea of acting as representative of, and speaking on behalf of, those sections of the society thought to be strategically central, a kind of ventriloquism for (normally) the working class. This might be termed a 'spectatorial' or 'interventionist' model of politics. Its liberal version is, precisely, parliamentary politics.

The second model might be called the 'occupational' or 'conjunctural' model. Here the central emphasis would be on a different duality, on the intimate relation between power and responsibility which Public Inquiry makes clear. Insofar as one's job renders one liable to being called to account for significant consequences, it carries a degree of power, though one so routinized that it looks like powerlessness. It is an important insight of Marxism that the working class as a whole necessarily has this double-faceted power, though as in Strindberg's notion of realism it may take a crisis to reveal that underlying relation. It is often this insight which is offered as the justification, within the other model, for singling out the working class as the strategically crucial force, though any occupational role might be unexpectedly revealed as newly central or indispensable, since the extent to which a specific role or occupation becomes politically important rests not upon some general rule but upon a conjunctural combination of relations and forces. This model might be associated with Gramscian notions of 'organic' intellectuals, and perhaps even with syndicalist emphases, rather than with ideas of party intervention. One might think of combining both models in one's own political activity, by emphasizing the importance of choice of occupation as strategic in its possibilities and implications. It might then be asked, perhaps, under what circumstances becoming a Professor of Drama can be regarded as an appropriate occupation for a socialist. But a more immediately useful direction to explore might lie in connecting these two models of politics at work in the two television plays, to the underlying arguments of, respectively, DIE and MT.

The overall argument in DIE has a certain congruence with the spectatorial or interventionist model, particularly insofar as that model also describes features of the parliamentary mode of politics. The notion of history at work in *DIE* appeals to an evolutionary progression, with individuals representatively undergoing crises of articulation and integrity. The overall development has been towards verse drama as enabling a full, controlled expression of the whole range of human experience, beyond what is normally possible in speech or apparent in action. This involves the familiar ambition of 'a Writer' to be the spokesperson for the whole society, to articulate a fuller consciousness, from a position simultaneously deeply inside and above the social formation. This model then combines elements of consensus (speaking for a wholeness of society) and representation (not delegation) in a basically Enlightenment mode; at the core is a question of knowledge and, to some extent, of morality, of an integrity and adequacy of speech. John Stuart Mill's election manifesto might be the parliamentary equivalent of the dramatist's project within this structure of feeling.

The second model, the occupational-conjunctural, has an essentially different core; that of power rather than knowledge, while also emphasizing the notion of 'expertise' as the appropriate mode of 'knowledge', of competence in a specific sector. This goes with a different model of history, as constituted not by evolutionary stages but by conjunctural moments comprising several interacting layers of event, in what can sometimes seem simply accident or coincidence. Insofar as all such layers are constantly present within the social formation, and combine in unexpected ways to generate a moment of tension or creation, this model allows for a notion of 'choices' as between levels and sectors, a specification of one's position which does not seek to occupy some totalizing role. A variety of options might then constitute a particular conjuncture – until some decisive repatterning produces a wholly new conjuncture, with its own new range, as in the impact of Brecht. The model of political engagement implied here is perhaps that of delegate democracy, a range of sectoral expertise or interest groupings directly speaking from their own perspectives.

On this reading, *DIB* might be seen as dislodging both models to some extent but without firmly instituting another. The introduction of Brecht into the overall 'history' which *DIE* had constructed obviously refocuses the entire field, but only to the extent of allowing several categories of analysis to operate without clear mutual articulation: generational, national, sectorial, each perhaps with its own temporality and specificity. No overview seemed possible, and no totalizing direction for the future. There is implicitly a kind of flattening of perspectives, a loss of any shared future. A politics consonant with this model, this form and structure of feeling, would perhaps have been simply an alliance or a putatively hegemonizing politics, as in the attempt in the *May Day Manifesto* of 1967–8 to orchestrate and generalize a variety of expert analyses and single-issue interests but without any clear strategic perspective or agreed form of agency.

At this level of analysis however, the Brechtian position might also be seen quite otherwise, as offering at least a preliminary synthesis of elements from both previous models, particularly through the notion of 'complex seeing', both as denoting the attitude of the audience and as a way of registering the divided social nature of his characters. This emphasis is still held within a primarily spectatorial-interventionist model; the job of the spectator in Brecht's theatre is still to observe, from above the flow of the play as well as from within it, a critical observation registering potential alternatives, but still a spectator's role.

Yet as Williams rightly argues, the fuller contribution of Brecht lies not just in a new attitude on the part of the audience, but in a new form of action, in which within the construction of the plays themselves that contradictory constitution of the characters is embodied. In *The Good Person of Setsuan* we see a fairly simple working through of the ambivalence of occupational role, a double-facetedness made literally visible. In *Mother Courage* or *Galileo* we see a whole action in which the victims are both active and acted upon, a complex interlock of response and responsibility. (One can then see why *Koba* follows Williams's chapter on Brecht in *MT*). But this reading of Brecht, with the emphasis upon spectator or action, upon complex seeing or formal construction, still tends to underemphasize Brecht's own theatrical practice, his recognition of theatre as production, as itself one kind of working or occupation alongside others. Williams's own emphasis upon drama as distinct from theatre leads him to some extent to underplay this, but it may be where Brecht's work is now most fully resonant for socialist thought. Within the notion of theatre as an area of production, the particular occupation, the professional task, of the Brechtian actor, can be seen as having two crucial aspects. The Brechtian actor is not a 'star' but a member of an ensemble, and yet has to operate a certain distantiation from the role, a form of complex acting. The question which is always before us in a Brecht production is, precisely: who is speaking? A deliberately multi-voiced, dialogical dimension is given by our awareness of the distancing as well as the identification between authorial words, actors' performance, characters' dialogue. There is a moment in *A Letter from the Country* in which a 'crisis' is characterized as 'not being in touch with part of oneself'. The Brechtian actor, in refusing to identify with the role, maintains him or herself in a position of crisis, of critique. Hovering here, perhaps, is a quite different implicit model of political analysis and engagement, suggesting a direction for inquiry which would certainly involve those endemically Brechtian features of much television, and the deep structure of feeling which connects television and contemporary politics.

It is crucial to Brechtian practice that in a theatre, whatever the weight of any prevailing convention against the possibility, the audience can always be addressed not only by the character but by the actor. Beyond the so-called 'soliloquy' there can always be direct address, there can even be conversation. Much twentieth-century drama hovers across that possibility, as has much popular theatre of the past. In that sense drama, however naturalist or realist, is never only representational, never simply a 'show' put on for us. It is potentially an action which involves us directly. I remember, as one vivid instance, a performance of *The Resistible Rise of Arturo Ui* in Turkey, just before the 1980 *coup*, in which the final anti-Fascist speeches were wholly direct, from actor to audience. The theatre was surrounded by troops as the performance finished.

That such a possibility is always present in live theatre is one aspect of a much more fundamental dimension of drama, of work in theatre, which is brought out in Brecht's insistence upon ensemble playing. In any actual performance, there are two structures operative. There is that which is represented, acted out, made visible as an element in the diegesis, which may well be one of sharp, unrelenting conflict. And yet precisely for that to happen there must also be in control of the first structure, a second structure, of a deeply collaborative kind, a cooperative mode and endeavour, a working not against but with each other. For any actual performance to work, quite literally, the conventions must hold; one does not (completely) 'corpse' a colleague. Such basic conventions also govern the relations between performers and audience, and it is these always fundamental, though historically varying, conventions, involving audience-actor relations, actor-role relations, action-text relations, which Williams has emphasized in his work and which the term 'structure of feeling' points to.

What is then crucial is that 'socialism' for him does seem to be fundamentally conceived, at present at least, in terms of a possible structure of feeling, potential but also partly realized. Williams, more than most left thinkers, offers outlines of socialist programmes and specific proposals; but to put an emphasis on some technological level or restructured mode of production, or even upon some particular detailed arrangement of ownership or democratic control, is clearly to risk the objection that since we can't, by definition, anticipate the inventions and discoveries of the future, we can't with full confidence offer even a sketch of the material life of that future society. But that is not to say that we can have no conception of what a future socialism will be like; for we do have some conception of what that socialism *must* (rather than simply 'should') be like, in order to be 'socialism', otherwise we wouldn't be involved in trying to create it in the first place. But if we then ask what is it possible for us to imagine, if we cannot imagine specific material conditions of life, one could say that ways of relating to each other, at this basic level of shared conventions of collaborativeness which shape us more profoundly than we realize, can not only be imagined but can to some extent be realized now, against and even within the structures that tend to lock us into exploitation and determine us towards competitiveness, hostility, self-interest, at the expense of others. Without at least the possibility of that other mode of relation, notions such as class solidarity or class consciousness would have little purchase on reality. Precisely the force of those pressures warns us that for any alternative to be realized such pressures and conditions *must* not then obtain, in whatever specific form they may eventually be eradicated.

It might then be argued that though the particular achievements of dramatists may well be best explained in terms of the specific pressures upon them at a determinate historical moment, it is nevertheless palpably the case that plays are quite generally performed long after their initial moment of production, and that we can still respond to specific structures of feeling embodied in them. In a quite definite way, the embodied 'structure of feeling' of the play can be re-enacted for and by us, while the performance lasts. It has been a constant emphasis of Williams's work in several areas that conventions of response, forms of experience, structures of feeling, are operative as and recoverable in specific modes of writing, particular forms of text. But if it is possible for a past structure of feeling to be made available to a later period, it is also possible to claim in principle that a 'future' structure of feeling can also be made available to some degree in the present, in forms of writing and in forms of collaborative relationship. After all, that 'future' structure of feeling will be the result not of a mere passage of time, with predetermined forms waiting in the wings, but the result of human imagination and effort: we are not merely waiting for some hypostasized History to create it for us. No technical blueprint of the future may be possible, for the very same reason, but there can be a proleptic imaging of possible modes of social relationship and a certain partial realization of the forms of feeling appropriate to those modes. Drama, as a particularized performance of gestures, relations and feelings, reminds us of how a variety of distinct modes can be lived out and responded to in the present. Whereas the individual reader of past literature or the listener, or even the performer, of past music may well be 'reliving' an emotional mood or a moral judgement, the actual acting out of, say, a Restoration comedy upon stage is (according to one ideal of staging) far closer to the full re-present-ation of a past period's lived structure of feeling – whatever the current forms of theatre technology or production. On a more Brechtian notion of staging, of course, any such production would incorporate within itself precisely the awareness of historical difference: 'historicizing involves judging a particular social system from another social system's point of view. The standpoints in question result from the development of society.'[9]

Where this might bear more specifically upon Williams's work as a socialist is that the structure of feeling which has to be imagined, or constructed in advance, necessarily involves a relationship between the individual and the whole, even the global, society. For if socialism is to do with the supersession of various kinds of division, and most crucially of class divisions, it will necessarily involve, and be significantly constituted by, relationships between each individual and *all* others, of a qualitatively different kind, a mode of social relation which precisely does not have the present forms of mediation by class, national, ethnic and group interest (though others may obtain). To anticipate that emergent structure of feeling may well be possible only apophatically, by a kind of negation. When Oedipus (or perhaps Koba) comes to realize that the relation between himself and his whole society is one of substantial identity, that the one and the many are at a certain level interchangeable, it may be that such a recognition is available only in a negative fashion, as 'tragedy': that the crisis of society is destructive of this individual because in some sense that single person then stands for *any* individual within that society. Certain features of television coverage may already make available that difficult awareness on a genuinely global scale: a recognition of the crying child in Ethiopia as both fully real, not a 'representation', and yet as fully representative of a global system and relation. Nuclear war remains, of course, the final scenario in which this awareness might be formulated.

Let me close with a comment about Ruth's death in Williams's play *Koba*. Within the play her gesture (hardly an adequate word for her suicide) is directed at Koba or Joseph, the Stalin figure; it is a way of bringing home to him, by an undeniable particularization in terms of the single individual who matters directly to him, what is involved in the anonymous deaths of so many others. Yet insofar as the act is a dramatic gesture and therefore directed not only to the character but also towards the audience, that gesture (as, now, indeed a gesture) will have a necessarily different significance for us, the audience. We will not feel (and perhaps by Williams's very mode of dramatic writing will not have been made to feel) that the death of Ruth has any specific, particularized emotional importance or claim upon us as *Ruth's* death – because we are not in love with Ruth. In a quite literal sense her action can only work as a form of *special* pleading to Koba. For an audience to see Ruth's death as significant in the way Koba is invited to, we would have to have *already* acknowledged that *anyone's* death has indeed that significance, and we would therefore not need the message Joseph needs; in any case, since Ruth is 'only' a character, we cannot 'love' her any more than we can fully acknowledge the 'reality' of her death in the first place. However, for us truly to be convinced of that utter equality of the one and the many, in life as in death, would be to occupy already another social structure of feeling. Perhaps, however, for the present our fullest access to that possibility remains located only in the fictional, in a certain way of writing and imagining. Which is perhaps one reason why socialism needs its professors of drama.

The first letter I ever wrote to Williams was to ask him if I could join his seminar on tragedy. I had just handed it in to the porter's lodge at Jesus when the porter told me that Williams was coming across the court, into the lodge. He gave Williams a pile of mail, reminded him that a taxi was waiting, that the Arts Council had phoned, that there was an urgent message, that he had a train to catch . . . and that I had just handed in a note for him. Williams immediately put down his case and the pile of mail, stopped, relaxed, leant against the wall, smiled, and said – as if he had all the time in the world – 'Well, tell me what's in the note . . .' Across what then seemed a variety of gaps, distances and divisions, of roles, positions and powers, in that wholly alien environment of Cambridge, his welcoming response, that generous disavowal of other claims in the face of this total stranger's request and presence, seemed a gesture that needed no interpretation. I took it at the time simply as the utter generosity and patience of an exceptional teacher; I now recognize in that quietly undramatic gesture a further dimension of meaning, an anticipation of a social structure of feeling, the need for which could constantly be felt in the very rarity of the kind of relation to others which Williams so persistently embodied. Perhaps it was his capacity for that form of relation now which has made him seem throughout such an extraordinarily persuasive representative for the possibility of socialism, already a delegate from the future. It is difficult to thank him enough for that.

Notes

1 Raymond Williams, *Drama from Ibsen to Eliot* (London, 1952), hereafter cited in text as *DIE*.

2 Raymond Williams, *Modern Tragedy* (London, 1966), hereafter cited in text as *MT*.

3 Raymond Williams, *Drama from Ibsen to Brecht* (London, 1968), hereafter cited in text as *DIB*.

4 Raymond Williams, *Drama in Performance* (London, 1954; rev. ed, London, 1968), hereafter cited in text as *DIP*.

5 Raymond Williams, *Politics and Letters: Interviews with New Left Review* (London, 1979), p. 214.

6 Raymond Williams, *Reading and Criticism* (London, 1950), p. 59. This quotation is taken from the expanded version, published as 'Notes on English Prose 1780–1950', in *Writing and Society* (London, 1984).

7 Raymond Williams, *The Pelican Book of English Prose*, vol. II, *From 1780 to the Present Day* (Harmondsworth, 1969), Introduction.

8 Raymond Williams, *Public Inquiry, Stand*, 9 (1967).

9 Bertolt Brecht, *Messingkauf Dialogues*, trans. J. Willett (London 1965), p. 103.

8

JANE AUSTEN AND EMPIRE

—— *Edward W. Said* ——

We are on solid ground with V. G. Kiernan when he says that 'empires must have a mould of ideas or conditioned reflexes to flow into, and youthful nations dream of a great place in the world as young men dream of fame and fortunes.'[1] It is, I believe, too simple and reductive a proposition to argue that everything in European and American culture is therefore a preparation for, or a consolidation of, the grand idea of empire that took over those societies during 'the age of empire' after 1870 but, conversely, it will not do to ignore those tendencies found in narrative, or in political theory, or in pictorial technique that enable, encourage, and otherwise assure the readiness of the West during the earlier parts of the nineteenth century to assume and enjoy the experience of empire. Similarly, we must note that if there was cultural resistance to the notion of an imperial mission there was not much support for such resistance in the main departments of cultural thought. Liberal though he was, John Stuart Mill – as a particularly telling case in point – could still say that 'the sacred duties which civilized nations owe to the independence and nationality of each other, are not binding towards those to whom nationality and independence are certain evil, or at best a questionable good.'[2]

Why that should be so, why sacred obligation on one front should not be binding on another, are questions best understood in the terms of a culture well grounded in a set of moral, economic and even metaphysical norms designed to approve a satisfying local, that is European, order in connection with the denial of the right to a similar order abroad. Perhaps such a statement appears preposterous, or extreme. In fact, I think, it formulates the connection between a certain kind of European well-being and cultural identity on the one hand, and, on the other, the subjugation of imperial realms overseas in too fastidious and circumspect a fashion. Part of the difficulty today in accepting any sort of connection at all is that we tend to collapse the whole complicated matter into an unacceptably simple causal relationship, which in turn produces a rhetoric of blame and consequent defensiveness. But I am *not* saying that the major thing about early nineteenth century European culture was that it *caused* late nineteenth century imperialism, and I am not therefore implying that all the problems of the contemporary non-European, formerly colonial, world should be blamed on Europe. I am saying, however, that European culture often, if not always, characterized itself in such a way as simultaneously to validate its own preferences while also advocating those preferences in conjunction with distant imperial rule. Mill certainly did: he always recommended that India not be given independence. When for a variety of reasons imperial rule occupied Europe with much greater intensity after 1880, this schizophrenic practice became a useful habit.

The first thing to be done now is more or less to jettison the simple causal mode of thinking through the relationship between Europe and the non-European world. This also requires some lessening of the hold on our thought of the equally simple sequence of temporal consecutiveness. We must not admit any notion, for instance, of the sort that proposes to show that Wordsworth, Jane Austen and Hazlitt because they wrote before 1857 actually caused the establishment of formal British governmental rule over India. What we should try to discern instead is a counterpoint between overt patterns in British writing about Britain and representations of what exists in the world beyond the British Isles. The inherent mode for this counterpoint therefore is not temporal, but spatial. How do writers in the period before the great age of explicit and programmatic colonial expansion in the late nineteenth century – the scramble for Africa say – situate and see themselves and their work in the larger world? We will find some striking but careful strategies employed, most of them deriving from expected sources – the positive ideas of home, of a nation and its language, of proper order, good behaviour, moral values.

But positive ideas of this sort do more than validate 'our' world. They also tend to devalue other worlds and, perhaps more significantly from a retrospective point of view, they do not prevent or inhibit or provide a resistance to horrendously unattractive imperialist practices. No, we are right to say that cultural forms like the novel or the opera do not cause people to go out and imperialize; perhaps Carlyle did not drive Rhodes directly, and he certainly cannot be 'blamed' for the problems of today's South Africa. But the genuinely troubling issue is how little the great humanistic ideas, institutions, and monuments, which we still celebrate as having the power ahistorically to command our approving attention, how little they stand in the way of an accelerating imperial process during the nineteenth century. Are we not entitled to ask therefore how this body of humanistic ideas coexisted so comfortably with imperialism, and why until the resistance to imperialism *in the imperial domain*, among Africans, Asians, Latin Americans, developed, there was little significant opposition or deterrance to empire at home? May we suspect that what had been the customary way of distinguishing 'our' home and order from 'theirs' grew into a harsh political rule for accumulating more of 'them' to rule, study and subordinate? Do we not have in the great humane ideas and values promulgated by mainstream European culture precisely that 'mould of ideas and conditioned reflexes' of which V. G. Kiernan speaks, into which the whole business of empire would later flow?

The extent to which these ideas are actually invested in distinctions between real places has been the subject of Raymond Williams's richest book, *The Country and the City*. His argument concerning the interplay between the rural and the urban in England admits of the most extraordinary transformations, from the pastoral populism of Langland, through Ben Jonson's country-house poems, the picture of Dickens's London, right up to visions of the metropolis in twentieth-century literature. And while he does tackle the export of England into the colonies Williams does so, in my opinion, less centrally, less expansively than the practice actually warrants. Near the end of *The Country and the City*, Williams suggests that 'from at least the mid-nineteenth century, and with important instances earlier, there was this large context [the relationship between England and the colonies, and its effects on the English imagination which, Williams correctly says, 'have gone deeper than can easily be traced'] within which every idea and every image was consciously and unconsciously affected.' He goes on quickly to list 'the idea of emigration to the colonies' as one such image prevailing in various novels by Dickens, the Brontës, Gaskell, and he quite rightly shows that 'new rural societies', all of them colonial, enter the imaginative metropolitan economy of English literature via Kipling, early Orwell, Somerset Maugham. After 1880 there comes a 'dramatic extension of landscape and social relations': this corresponds more or less exactly with the great age of empire.[3]

It is dangerous to disagree with Williams. Yet I would venture to say that if one began to look for something like an imperial map of the world in English literature it would turn up with amazing centrality and frequency well before the middle of the nineteenth century. And not only turn up with an inert regularity that might suggest something taken for granted, but – much more interestingly – threaded through, forming a vital part of the texture of linguistic and cultural practice. For there were established English interests in America, the Caribbean and Asia from the seventeenth century on, and even a quick inventory will reveal poets, philosophers, historians, dramatists, novelists, travel writers, chroniclers, and fabulists for whom these interests were to be traced, cared for, prized, and regarded with a continuing concern. A similar argument could be made for France, Spain and Portugal, not only as overseas powers in their own right, but as competitors with the British. How then can we examine these interests at work in England *before* the age of empire that officially occurred during the last third of the nineteenth century?

We would do well to follow Williams's lead, and look at that period of crisis following upon wide-scale land enclosure at the end of the eighteenth century. Not only are old organic communities dissolved, and new ones forged under the impulse of parliamentary activity, industrialization, and demographic dislocation, but, I would suggest, there occurs a new process of relocating England (and in France, France) within a much larger circle of the world map. During the first half of the eighteenth century, Anglo-French competition in India was intense; in the second half there were numerous violent encounters between them in the Levant, the Caribbean and of course in Europe itself. Much of what we read today as major pre-Romantic literature in France and England contains a constant stream of references to the overseas dominions: one thinks not only of various encyclopaedists, the Abbé Reynal, de Brosses, and Volney, but also of Edmund Burke, Beckford, Gibbon, and William Jones.

In 1902 J. A. Hobson described imperialism as the expansion of nationality, implying that the process was understandable mainly by considering *expansion* to be the more important of the two terms, since 'nationality' was a fixed quantity.[4] For Hobson's purposes nationality was in fact fully formed, whereas a century before it was in the process of *being formed*, not only at home, but abroad as well. Between France and Britain in the late eighteenth century there were two contests: the battle for strategic gains in such places as India, the Nile delta and the Caribbean islands, and the battle for a triumphant nationality. Both battles place 'Englishness' in contrast with 'the French', and no matter how intimate and closeted such factors as the supposed English or French 'essence' appear to be, they were almost always thought of as being (as opposed to already) made, and being fought out with the other great competitor. Thackeray's Becky Sharp, for example, is as much an upstart as she is because of her half-French heritage. Earlier, the upright abolitionist posture of Wilberforce and his allies developed partly out of a desire to make life harder for French hegemony in the Antilles.[5]

These considerations, I think, suddenly provide a fascinatingly expanded dimension to *Mansfield Park*, by common acknowledgement the most explicit in its ideological and moral affirmations of all Austen's novels. Williams once again is in general dead right: Austen's novels all express an 'attainable quality of life', in money and property acquired, moral discriminations made, the right choices put in place, the correct 'improvements' implemented, the finely nuanced language affirmed and classified. Yet, Williams continues,

> What [Cobbett] names, riding past on the road are classes. Jane Austen, from inside the houses, can never see that, for all the intricacy of her social description. All her discrimination is, understandably, internal and exclusive. She is concerned with the conduct of people who, in the complications of improvement, are repeatedly trying to make themselves into a class. But where only one class is seen, no classes are seen.[6]

As a general description of how by the effect of her novels Austen manages to elevate certain 'moral discriminations' into 'an independent value', this is excellent. Where *Mansfield Park* is concerned, however, a good deal more needs to be said and in what follows I should like to be understood as providing greater explicitness and width to Williams's fundamentally correct survey. Perhaps then Austen, and indeed, pre-imperialist novels generally, will appear to be more implicated in the rationale for imperialist expansion than at first sight they have been.

After Lukács and Proust, we have become so accustomed to regarding the novel's plot and structure as constituted mainly by temporality that we have overlooked the fundamental role of space, geography and location. For it is not only Joyce's very young Stephen Dedalus who sees himself in a widening spiral at home, in Ireland, in the world, but every other young protagonist before him as well. Indeed we can say without exaggeration that *Mansfield Park* is very precisely about a whole series of both small and large dislocations in space that must occur before, at the end of the novel, Fanny Price, the niece, becomes the mistress of Mansfield Park. And that place itself is precisely located by Austen at the centre of an arc of interests and concerns, spanning the hemisphere, two major seas, and four continents.

As in all of Austen's novels, the central group that finally emerges with marriage and property 'ordained' is not based principally upon blood. What her novel enacts is the disaffiliation (in the literal sense) of some members of a family, and the affiliation between others and one or two chosen and tested outsiders: in other words, blood relationships are not enough for the responsibilities of continuity, heirarchy, authority. Thus Fanny Price – the poor niece, the orphaned child from the outlying port city of Portsmouth, the neglected, demure and upright wallflower – gradually acquires a status commensurate with, and even superior to, her more fortunate relatives. In this pattern of affiliation and of assumption of authority, Fanny Price is relatively passive. She resists the misdemeanours and the importunings of others, and very occasionally she ventures actions on her own: all in all, though, one has the impression that Austen has designs for her that Fanny herself can scarcely comprehend, just as throughout the novel Fanny is thought of by everyone as 'comfort' and 'acquisition' despite herself. Thus, like Kim O'Hara, Fanny is both device and instrument in a larger pattern, as well as novelistic character.

Fanny, like Kim, requires direction, requires the patronage and outside authority that her own impoverished experience cannot provide. Her conscious connections are to some people and to some places, but as the novel reveals there are *other* connections of which she has faint glimmerings that nevertheless demand her presence and service. What she comes into is a novel that has opened with an intricate set of moves all of which taken together demand sorting-out, adjustment and re-arrangement. Sir Thomas Bertram has been captivated by one Ward sister, the others have not done well, and so 'an absolute breach' opens up; their 'circles were so distinct', the distances between them were so great that they have been out of touch for eleven years (*MP*, p. 42);[7] fallen on hard times, the Prices seek out the Bertrams. Gradually, and even though she is not the eldest, Fanny becomes the new focus of attention as she is sent to Mansfield Park, there to begin her new life. Similarly, the Bertrams have given up London (the result of Lady Bertram's 'little ill health and a great deal of indolence') and come to reside entirely in the country.

What sustains this life materially is the Bertram estate in Antigua, which is not doing well. Austen takes considerable pains to show us two apparently disparate but actually convergent processes; the growth of Fanny's importance to the Bertrams' economy, including Antigua, and Fanny's own steadfastness in the face of numerous challenges, threats and surprises. In both processes, however, Austen's imagination works with a steel-like rigour through a mode that we might call geographical and spatial clarification. Fanny's ignorance, when as a frightened ten-year-old she arrives at Mansfield, is signified by her inability to 'put the map of Europe together' (*MP*, p. 54), and for much of the first half of the novel the action is concerned with a whole range of things whose common denominator, misused or misunderstood, is space. Not only is Sir Thomas in Antigua to make things better there and at home, but at Mansfield Park Fanny, Edmund, and her Aunt Norris negotiate where she is to live, read and work, where fires are to be lit, the friends and cousins concern themselves with the improvement of the estates, and the importance of chapels (of religious authority) to domesticity is debated and envisioned. When, as a device for stirring things up, the Crawfords (the tinge of France that hangs over their background is significant) suggest a play, Fanny's discomfiture is polarizingly acute. She cannot participate, although with all its confusion of roles and purposes, the play, Kotzebue's *Lovers' Vows* is prepared for anyway.

We are to surmise, I think, that while Sir Thomas is away tending his colonial garden, a number of inevitable mis-measurements (associated explicitly with feminine 'lawlessness') will occur. Not only are these apparent in innocent strolls through a park, in which people lose and catch sight of each other unexpectedly, but most clearly in the various flirtations and engagements between the young men and women left without true parental authority, Lady Bertram being too indifferent, Mrs Norris unsuitable. There is sparring, there is innuendo, there is a perilous taking on of roles: all of this of course is crystallized in preparations for the play, in which something dangerously close to libertinage is about to be (but never is) enacted. Fanny, whose earlier sense of alienation, distance and fear all derive from her first uprooting, has now assumed a sort of surrogate consciousness of what is right and how far is too much. Yet she has no power to implement her uneasy awareness, and until Sir Thomas suddenly returns from 'abroad' the rudderless drift continues.

When he does appear, preparations for the play are immediately stopped, and in a passage remarkable for its executive dispatch, Austen narrates the re-establishment of Sir Thomas's local rule:

> It was a busy morning with him. Conversation with any of them occupied but a small part of it. He had to reinstate himself in all the wonted concerns of his

Mansfield life, to see his steward and his bailiff – to examine and compute – and, in the intervals of business, to walk into his stables and his gardens, and nearest plantations; but active and methodical, he had not only done all this before he resumed his seat as master of the house at dinner, he had also set the carpenter to work in pulling down what had been so lately put up in the billiard room, and given the scene painter his dismissal, long enough to justify the pleasing belief of his being then at least as far off as Northampton. The scene painter was gone, having spoilt only the floor of one room, ruined all the coachman's sponges, and made five of the under-servants idle and dissatisfied; and Sir Thomas was in hopes that another day or two would suffice to wipe away every outward memento of what had been, even to the destruction of every unbound copy of 'Lovers' Vows' in the house, for he was burning all that met his eye. (*MP*, p. 206)

The force of this paragraph is unmistakable. This is not only a Crusoe setting things in order: it is also an early Protestant eliminating all traces of frivolous behaviour. There is nothing, however, in *Mansfield Park* that would contradict us were we to assume that Sir Thomas does exactly the same things – on a larger scale – in Antigua. Whatever was wrong there, and the internal evidence garnered by Warren Roberts suggests that economic depression, slavery, and competition with France were at issue[8] – Sir Thomas was able to fix, thereby maintaining his control over his colonial domain. Thus more clearly than anywhere else in her fiction Austen synchronizes domestic with international authority, making it plain that the values associated with such higher things as ordination, law and propriety must be grounded firmly in actual rule over and possession of territory. What she sees more clearly than most of her readers is that to hold and rule Mansfield Park is to hold and rule an imperial estate in association with it. What assures the one, in its domestic tranquillity and attractive harmony, is the prosperity and discipline of the other.

Before both can be fully secured, however, Fanny must become more actively involved. For this, I believe, Austen designed the second part of the book, which contains not only the failure of the Edmund–Mary Crawford romance as well as the disgraceful profligacy of Lydia and Henry Crawford, but Fanny Price's rediscovery and rejection of her Portsmouth home, the injury and incapacitation of Tom (the eldest) Bertram, the launching of William Price's naval career. This entire ensemble of relationships and events is finally capped with Edmund's marriage to Fanny, whose place in Lady Bertram's household is taken by Susan Price, her sister. I do not think it is an exaggeration to interpret the concluding sections of *Mansfield Park* as the coronation of an arguably *unnatural* (or at the very least, illogical) principle at the heart of a desired English order. The audacity of Austen's vision is disguised a little by her voice, which despite its occasional archness is understated and notably modest. But we should not misconstrue the limited references to the outside world, her lightly stressed allusions to work, process and class, her apparent ability to abstract (in Raymond Williams's phrase) 'an everyday uncompromising morality which is in the end separable from its social basis'. For in fact Austen is far less diffident, far more severe than that.

The clues are to be found in Fanny, or rather in how rigorously we wish to consider Fanny. True, her visit home upsets the aesthetic and emotional balance she has become accustomed to at Mansfield Park, and true, she has begun to take for granted the wonderful luxuries there as something she cannot live without. These things, in other words, are fairly routine and natural consequences of getting used to a new place. But Austen is talking about two other matters we must not mistake. One is Fanny's newly enlarged sense of what it means to be at home; this is not merely a matter of expanded space.

> Fanny was almost stunned. The smallness of the house, and thinness of the walls, brought every thing so close to her, that, added to the fatigue of her journey, and all her recent agitation, she hardly knew how to bear it. *Within* the room all was tranquil enough, for Susan having disappeared with the others, there were soon only her father and herself remaining; and he taking out a newspaper – the customary loan of a neighbour, applied himself to studying it, without seeming to recollect her existence. The solitary candle was held between himself and the paper, without any reference to her possible convenience; but she had nothing to do, and was glad to have the light screened from her aching head, as she sat in bewildered, broken, sorrowful contemplation.
>
> She was at home. But alas! it was not such a home, she had not such a welcome, as – she checked herself; she was unreasonable ... A day or two might shew the difference. *She* only was to blame. Yet she thought it would not have been so at Mansfield. No, in her uncle's house there would have been a consideration of times and seasons, a regulation of subject, a propriety, an attention towards every body which there was not here. (*MP*, pp. 375–6)

In too small a space you cannot see clearly, you cannot think clearly, you cannot have regulation or attention of the proper sort. The fineness of Austen's detail ('the solitary candle was held between himself and the paper, without any reference to her possible convenience') renders very precisely the dangers of unsociability, of lonely insularity, of diminished awareness that are rectified in larger and better administered spaces.

That such spaces are not available by direct descent, by legal title, by propinquity, contiguity or adjacence (Mansfield Park and Portsmouth are after all separated by many hours' journey) is precisely Austen's point. To earn the right to Mansfield Park you must first leave home as a kind of indentured servant, or to put the case in extreme terms, as a kind of transported commodity; this clearly is the fate of Fanny and William, but it also contains the promise for them of future wealth. I think Austen saw what Fanny does as a domestic or small-scale movement in space that corresponds to the longer, more openly colonial movements of Sir Thomas, her mentor, the man whose estate she inherits. The two movements depend on each other.

The second matter about which Austen speaks, albeit indirectly, is a little more

complex, and raises an interesting theoretical issue. To speak about Austen's
awareness of empire is obviously to speak about something very different, very
much more alluded to almost casually, than Conrad's or Kipling's awareness of
empire. Nevertheless, we must concede that Antigua and Sir Thomas's trip there
play a definitive role in *Mansfield Park*, a role which, I have been saying, is both
incidental, because referred to only in passing, and absolutely important, because
although taken for granted it is crucial to the action in many ways. How then are
we to assess the few references to Antigua, and as exactly as possible what are we
to make of them interpretively?

My contention is that Austen genuinely presages Kipling and Conrad, and that
far from being a novelist only dedicated to the portrayal and elucidation of
domestic manners, Austen by that very odd combination of casualness and stress
reveals herself to be *assuming* (just as Fanny assumes, in both senses of the word)
the importance of empire to the situation at home. Let me go further. Since
Austen refers to and uses Antigua as she does in *Mansfield Park*, there needs to be
a commensurate effort on the part of her readers to understand concretely the
historical valences in the reference. To put it differently, we should try to
understand *what* she referred to, why she gave it the role she did, and why, in a
certain sense, she did not avoid the choice, keeping in mind that she might *not*
have made use of Antigua. Let us now proceed to calibrate the signifying power
of the references to Antigua in *Mansfield Park*; how do *they* occupy the place they
do, what are they doing there?

According to Austen, no matter how isolated and insulated the English *place* is
(e.g. Mansfield Park), it requires overseas sustenance. Sir Thomas's property in
the Caribbean would have had to be a sugar plantation maintained by slave
labour (not abolished until the 1830s): these are not dead historical facts but, as
Austen certainly knew, the results of evident historical processes. Before the
Anglo-French competition to which I referred earlier, there is for Britain the
major distinguishing characteristic between its empire and all earlier ones (the
Spanish and Portuguese principally, but also the Roman). That was that earlier
empires were bent, as Conrad puts it, on loot, the transport of treasure from the
colonies to Europe, with very little attention to development, organization,
system; Britain and, to a lesser degree, France were deeply concerned with how to
make the empire a long-term profitable and, above all, an on-going concern. In
this enterprise the two countries competed, nowhere with more observable results
than in the slave colonies of the Caribbean, where the transport of slaves, the
functioning of large sugar plantations dedicated exclusively to sugar production,
the whole question of sugar markets which raised problems of protectionism,
monopolies, and price: all these were more or less constantly, competitively at
issue.

Far from being something 'out there', British colonial possessions in the
Antilles and Leeward Islands were during the last years of the eighteenth century
and the first third of the nineteenth a crucial setting for Anglo-French colonial

competition. Not only was the export of revolutionary ideas from France there to be registered, but there was a steady decline in British Caribbean profits: the French sugar plantations were producing more sugar at less cost. By the end of the century, however, the slave rebellions generated in and out of Haiti were incapacitating France and spurring British interests to more intervention, and greater power locally. Yet compared with their prominence for the home market during the eighteenth century, the British Caribbean sugar plantations of the nineteenth century were more vulnerable to such countervailing forces as the discovery of alternative sugar supplies in Brazil and Mauritius, the emergence of a European beet-sugar industry, and the gradual dominance of free trade (as opposed to monopolistic) ideology and practice.

In *Mansfield Park* – and I speak here both of its formal characteristics as well as its contents – a number of all these currents converge. The most important of course is the complete subordination of colony to metropolis. Sir Thomas is absent from Mansfield Park, and is never seen as *present* in Antigua, which requires at most a half dozen references in the novel, all of them granting the island the merest token importance to what takes place in England. There is a passage from John Stuart Mill's *Principles of Political Economy* which catches the spirit of Austen's use of Antigua:

> These are hardly to be looked upon as countries, carrying on an exchange of commodities with other countries, but more properly as outlying agricultural or manufacturing estates belonging to a larger community. Our West Indian colonies, for example, cannot be regarded as countries with a productive capital of their own ... [but are, rather,] the place where England finds it convenient to carry on the production of sugar, coffee and a few other tropical commodities. All the capital employed is English capital; almost all the industry is carried on for English uses; there is little production of anything except for staple commodities, and these are sent to England, not to be exchanged for things exported to the colony and consumed by its inhabitants, but to be sold in England for the benefit of the proprietors there. The trade with the West Indies is hardly to be considered an external trade, but more resembles the traffic between town and country.[9]

To some extent Antigua is like London or Portsmouth, a less desirable urban setting than the country estate at Mansfield Park. Unlike them, however, it is a place producing goods, sugar, to be consumed by all people (by the early nineteenth century every Britisher used sugar), although owned and maintained by a small group of aristocrats and gentry. The Bertrams and the other characters in *Mansfield Park* constitute one sub-group within the minority, and for them the island is wealth, which Austen regards as being converted to propriety, order, and at the end of the novel, comfort, an added good. But why 'added'? Because, Austen tells us pointedly in the final chapters, she wants to 'restore every body, not greatly in fault themselves, to tolerable comfort, and to have done with all the rest' (*MP*, p. 446).

This can be interpreted to mean, first, that the novel has done enough in the way of destabilizing the lives of 'everybody', and must now set them at rest: actually Austen does say this explicitly as a bit of meta-fictional impatience. Second, it can mean what Austen implicitly suggests, that everybody may now be finally permitted to realize what it means to be properly at home, and at rest, without the need to wander about or to come and go. Certainly this does not include young William, who, we are right to assume, will continue to roam the seas in the British navy on whatever missions, commercial and political, may still be required. Such matters draw from Austen only a last brief gesture (a passing remark about William's 'continuing good conduct and rising fame'). As for those finally resident in Mansfield Park itself, more in the way of domesticated advantages is given to these now fully acclimatized souls, and to none more than to Sir Thomas. He understands for the first time what has been missing in his education of his children, and he understands it in the terms paradoxically provided for him by unnamed outside forces so to speak, the wealth of Antigua and the imported example of Fanny Price. Note here how the curious alternation of outside and inside follows the pattern identified by Mill of the outside *becoming* the inside by use and, to use Austen's word, 'disposition':

> Here [in his deficiency of training, of allowing Mrs Norris too great a role, of letting his children dissemble and repress feeling] had been grievous mismanagement; but, bad as it was, he gradually grew to feel that it had not been the most direful mistake in his plan of education. Some thing must have been wanting *within*, or time would have worn away much of its ill effect. He feared that principle, active principle, had been wanting, that they had never been properly taught to govern their inclinations and tempers, by that sense of duty which can alone suffice. They had been instructed theoretically in their religion, but never required to bring it into daily practice; to be distinguished for elegance and accomplishments – the authorized object of their youth – could have had no useful influence that way, not moral effect on the mind. He had meant them to be good, but his cares had been directed to the understanding and manners, not the disposition; and of the necessity of self-denial and humility, he feared they had never heard from any lips that could profit them. (*MP*, p. 448).

What was wanting *within* was in fact supplied by the wealth derived from a West Indian plantation and a poor provincial relative, both brought in to Mansfield Park and set to work. Yet on their own, neither the one nor the other could have sufficed; they require each other and then, more important, they need executive disposition, which in turn helps to reform the rest of the Bertram circle. All of this Austen leaves to her reader to supply in the way of literal explicitation.

And that is what reading her necessarily entails. But all these things having to do with the outside brought in, seem to me unmistakably *there* in the suggestiveness of her allusive and abstract language. A 'principle wanting within' is, I believe, intended to evoke for us memories of Sir Thomas's absences in

Antigua, or the sentimental and near-whimsical vagary on the part of the three variously deficient Ward sisters by which a niece is displaced from one household to another. But that the Bertrams did become better if not altogether good, that some sense of duty was imparted to them, that they learned to govern their inclinations and tempers, and brought religion into daily practice, directed disposition: all of this did occur because outside (or rather outlying) factors were lodged properly inward, became native to Mansfield Park, Fanny, the niece, its final spiritual mistress, Edmund, the second son, its master.

An additional benefit is that Mrs Norris is dislodged from the place: this is described as 'the great supplementary comfort of Sir Thomas's life' (*MP*, p. 450). For once the principles have been interiorized, the comforts follow: Fanny is settled for the time being at Thornton Lacey 'with every attention to her comfort'; her home later becomes 'the home of affection and comfort'; Susan is brought in 'first as a comfort to Fanny, then as an auxiliary, and at last as her substitute' (*MP*, p. 456), when the new import takes Fanny's place by Lady Bertram's side. Clearly the pattern established at the outset of the novel continues, only now it has what the novel has intended to give it all along, an internalized and retrospectively guaranteed rationale. This is the rationale that Raymond Williams describes as 'an everyday, uncompromising morality which is in the end separable from its social basis and which, in other hands, can be turned against it.'

I have tried to show that the morality in fact is not separable from its social basis, because right up to the last sentence of the novel Austen is always affirming and repeating a geographical process involving trade, production, and consumption that pre-dates, underlies, and guarantees the morality. Most critics have tended to forget or overlook that process, which has seemed less important to the morality than in devising her novel Austen herself seemed to think it was. But interpreting Jane Austen depends on *who* does the interpreting, *when* it is done, and no less important, from *where* it is done. If with feminists, with great Marxist critics sensitive to history and class like Williams, with historical and stylistic critics, we have been sensitized to the issues their interests raise, we should now proceed to regard geography – which is after all of significance to *Mansfield Park* – as not a neutral fact (any more than class and gender are neutral facts) but as a politically charged one too, a fact beseeching the considerable attention and elucidation its massive proportions require. The question is thus not only how to understand and with what to connect Austen's morality and its social basis, but *what* to read of it.

Take the casual references to Antigua, the ease with which Sir Thomas's needs in England are met by a Caribbean sojourn, the uninflected, unreflective citations of Antigua (or the Mediterranean, or India, which is where Lady Bertram in a fit of distracted impatience requires that William should go 'that I may have a shawl. I think I will have two shawls' (*MP*, p. 308). They stand for something significant 'out there' that frames the genuinely important action *here*, but not for something too significant. Yet these signs of 'abroad' include, even as they repress, a complex and rich history, which has since achieved a status that the Bertrams, the Prices and Austen herself would not, could not recognize. To call this status 'the Third World' begins to deal with its realities, but it by no means exhausts its history with regard to politics or cultural activities.

There are first some prefigurations of a later English history as registered in fiction to be taken stock of. The Bertram's usable colony in *Mansfield Park* can be read proleptically as resulting in Charles Gould's San Tome mine in *Nostromo*, or as the Wilcoxes' Anglo-Imperial Rubber Company in Forster's *Howard's End*, or indeed as any of these distant but convenient treasure spots in *Great Expectations*, or in Jean Rhys's *Wide Sargasso Sea*, or *Heart of Darkness*, resources to be visited, talked about, described or appreciated – for domestic reasons, for local metropolitan benefits. Thus Sir Thomas's Antigua already acquires a slightly greater density than the discrete, almost reticent appearances it makes in the pages of *Mansfield Park*. And already our reading of the novel begins to distend and open up at those points where ironically Austen was most economical and her critics most (dare one say it?) negligent. Her 'Antigua' is therefore not just a slight but definite way of marking the outer limits of what Williams calls domestic improvements, or as a quick allusion to the mercantile venturesomeness of acquiring overseas dominions as a source for local fortunes, or one reference among many attesting to a historical sensibility suffused not just with manners and curtsies but with contests of ideas, struggles with Napoleonic France, awareness of seismic economic and social change. Not just those things, but also strikingly early anticipation of the offical age of Empire, which Kipling, Conrad and all the others, will realize a full three-quarters of a century later.

Second, we must see 'Antigua' as a reference for Austen held in its precise place in her moral geography, and in her prose, by a series of historical changes that her novel rides like a vessel sitting on a mighty sea. The Bertrams could not have been possible without the slave trade, sugar, and the colonial planter class; as a social type Sir Thomas would have been familiar to eighteenth- and early nineteenth-century readers who knew the powerful influence of the class in domestic British politics, in plays (like Cumberland's *The West Indian*), and in numerous other public ways. As the old system of protected monopoly gradually disappeared, and as a new class of settler-planter displaced the old absentee system, the West Indian interest lost its dominance: cotton manufacture, open trade, abolition reduced the power and prestige of people like the Bertrams whose frequency of sojourn in the Caribbean decreased appreciably.

Thus in *Mansfield Park* Sir Thomas's infrequent trips to Antigua as an absentee plantation-owner *precisely* reflect the diminishment of his class's power, a reduction immediately, directly conveyed in the title of Lowell Ragatz's classic *The Fall of the Planter Class in the British Caribbean, 1763–1833* (published in 1928). But we must go further and ask whether what is hidden or allusive in Austen – the reasons for Sir Thomas's rare voyages – are made sufficiently explicit in Ragatz? Does the aesthetic silence or discretion of a great novel in 1814 receive adequate explication in a major work of historical research written a full century later? If so, can we assume that the process of interpretation is thereby fulfilled, or must we go on to reason that it will continue as newer material comes to light?

Consider that for all his learning Ragatz still finds it in himself to speak of 'the Negro race' as having the following characteristics: 'he stole, he lied, he was simple, suspicious, inefficient, irresponsible, lazy, superstitious, and loose in his sexual relations.' [10] Such 'history' as this therefore gave way (as Austen gave way to Ragatz) to the revisionary work of Caribbean historians like Eric Williams and C. L. R. James, works in which slavery and empire are seen directly to have fostered the rise and consolidation of *capitalism* well beyond the old plantation monopolies, as well as a powerful ideological system whose original connection to actual economic interests may have passed, but whose effects continued for decades.

> The political and moral ideas of the age are to be examined in the very closest relation to the economic development . . .
> An outworn interest, whose bankruptcy smells to heaven in historical perspective, can exercise an obstructionist and disruptive effect which can only be explained by the powerful services it had preciously rendered and the entrenchment previously gained . . .
> The ideas built on these interests continue long after the interests have been destroyed and work their old mischief, which is all the more mischievous because the interests to which they correspond no longer exist.[11]

Thus Eric Williams in *Capitalism and Slavery* (1961). The question of interpretation, and indeed of writing itself, is tied to the question of interests, which we have seen are at work in aesthetic as well as historical work, then and now. We cannot easily say that since *Mansfield Park* is a novel, its affiliations with a particularly sordid history are irrelevant or transcended, not only because it is irresponsible to say that, but because we know too much to say so without bad faith. Having read *Mansfield Park* as part of the structure of an expanding imperialist venture, it would be difficult simply to restore it to the canon of 'great literary masterpieces' – to which it most certainly belongs – and leave it at that. Rather, I think, the novel points the way to Conrad, and to theorists of empire like Froude and Seeley, and in the process opens up a broad expanse of domestic imperialist culture without which the subsequent acquisition of territory would not have been possible.

Notes

1 V. G. Kiernan, *Marxism and Imperialism* (New York, 1974), p. 100.
2 J. S. Mill *Disquisitions and Discussions*, vol. III (London, Longmans Green, Reader & Dyer, 1875), pp. 167–8.

3   Raymond Williams, *The Country and the City* (London, 1973), p. 281.

4   J. A. Hobson, *Imperialism* (1902; repr. Ann Arbor, 1972), p. 6.

5   This is most memorably discussed in C. L. R. James, *The Black Jacobins: Toussaint L'Ouverture and the San Domingo Revolution* (1938; repr. New York, 1963), especially ch. II, 'The Owners'.

6   Williams, *The Country and the City*, p. 117.

7   Jane Austen, *Mansfield Park*, ed. Tony Tanner (1814; repr. Harmondsworth, 1966). All references to this edition of the novel are indicated parenthetically after the citation as *MP*. The best account of the novel is in Tony Tanner's *Jane Austen* (Cambridge, Mass. 1986).

8   Warren Roberts, *Jane Austen and the French Revolution* (London, 1979), pp. 97–8. See also Avrom Fleishman, *A Reading of Mansfield Park: An Essay in Critical Synthesis* (Minneapolis, 1967), pp. 36–9, and *passim*.

9   J. S. Mill, *Principles of Political Economy* vol. III, ed. J. M. Robson (Toronto, 1965), p. 693. The passage is quoted in Sidney W. Mintz *Sweetness and Power: The Place of Sugar in Modern History* (New York, 1985), p. 42.

10   Lowell Joseph Ragatz, *The Fall of the Planter Class in the British Caribbean, 1763–1833: A Study in Social and Economic History* (1928; repr. New York, 1963), p. 27.

11   Eric Williams, *Capitalism and Slavery* (New York, 1961), p. 211.

9

BASE AND SUPERSTRUCTURE IN RAYMOND WILLIAMS

—— *Terry Eagleton* ——

Few doctrines of classical Marxism have fallen into greater disrepute than the 'base/superstructure' model. However much the model may be refined and sophisticated, and however much mediation and dialectical interaction may be inserted between its twin terms, this whole binary opposition would seem to remain stubbornly reductive and mechanistic. Is it any more in the end than a mark of its authors' residual economism, still in thrall as they are to a bourgeois economic theory in which the activity of material production becomes fetishized and the rest of social life relegated to secondary status? And is it not a particularly notorious instance of what contemporary post-structuralism would brand as a 'metaphysical' mode of thought, in which a single determining essence or transcendental principle is arbitrarily isolated from the complex textuality of historical existence and elevated to some theologically privileged position?

This final point merits some further comment. There is an obvious difference between rejecting the base/superstructure model on particular historical grounds – on the basis, for example, that it is far too static and mechanistic to account for the actual complex workings of a social formation – and rejecting it, in the manner of some post-structuralist thought, for more general philosophical reasons. To criticize the model on the former grounds is not necessarily to commit oneself to the latter. If *any* such form of thought is objectionably 'metaphysical', a matter of privileged 'hierarchies' which can always be deconstructed, does this mean than one can never, in any situation, assign causal priority to a particular force or factor? Is it metaphysical to hold that the reason for my headache is the ridiculously tight bowler hat I insist on wearing? The issue is not, notice, a straightforward one of monocausality versus multicausality. The base/super-structure paradigm can certainly accommodate the later, but simply claims that, within a multitude of social determinants, some are finally more importantly determinant than others. My chronic sinus problem may well contribute to the headache, but the bowler hat is obviously the chief villain. We espouse privileged causes all the time, without necessarily denying that plurality of determinants which Louis Althusser somewhat misleadingly termed 'overdetermination'. Why should this be in principle not the case with societies too? What is so ontologically special about social formations, as opposed to headaches, that they could never conceivably be viewed as operating in accordance with such a logic? If the objection is to causal hierarchies of any kind ('hierarchy' being held to have a somewhat reactionary ring about it), does this mean that the novels of Thomas Peacock were in his day as significant a force for social change as the French Revolution? Where does a 'complex textuality' of forces end?

The assertion, following from a certain reading of Friedrich Nietzsche, that the positing of *any* privileged cause in any situation is automatically idealist, is surely dogmatic. This style of thinking is neither a very interesting nor a particularly productive line of criticism of the model in question. More challenging to classical Marxism is the belief that, although we are indeed continually confronted with privileged causes in particular circumstances, it is dangerously doctrinaire to extrapolate this truth to an object as immense as history itself. Is it not grossly implausible to believe that, in the end, one set of determinants alone has been primarily responsible for the genesis and evolution of forms of social life? My own feeling, as a defender of the classical doctrine, is that this claim has indeed a kind of implausible ring to it, which forces us to ask why anyone would want to say such a strange sort of thing in the first place. It is highly plausible to believe that in certain circumstances what we might roughly call 'material production' exerts a primary determining force on certain other social phenomena; hardly anyone would think this as silly as arguing, for example, that what makes people think the way they do is the kind of cheese they eat. The implausibility is not of *that* kind; it is its historical reach which appears most dubious. For history is not as simple a phenomenon as a headache, and to imagine that it is always ultimately determined in the same way seems to ascribe to it a spurious sort of self-identity. History, one might insist, is just not a self-identical object at all, to be determined in a consistent way; it is a kind of category mistake or false analogizing to view it as a kind of 'thing' that could ever conceivably work by a repetitive logic. The objection is not empirical but, once more, philosophical: if there *were* such a unitary ideality as 'history', then we might very well imagine it operating as the base/superstructure model supposes, but in fact there is not. There are just different kinds of historical conjuncture; and critics of the model then divide between those who hold, on what I have branded as dogmatic grounds, that none of these could for *a priori* reasons ever be considered as involving some primary causal mechanism, and those more moderate believers who think it quite likely that the model applies to some of these conditions but not to others. What would seem metaphysical about the doctrine – what would appear to rank modes of production alongside God, the *Zeitgeist*, biology, the *élan vital* and so on – is exactly its apparently overweening conceptual span.

If history has always worked according to the base/superstructure model, then there must be something very strange and peculiar about history. It must display some remarkably common features, manifest some unusually strong self-identity, if this single theoretical paradigm can account for so much of its contents. But this would seem precisely the kind of static conception of history which Marxism, along with other historicisms, is supposed to interrogate. What is it about history to date which Marxism believes to be static? The answer, for Marx at least, is surely obvious. The reason why history to date has been fairly static, and so amenable to the kind of conceptual instruments he proposes, is that it has not really been history at all. It has been, as Marx comments, 'pre-history'. History has not even started yet. All we have had so far is the realm of necessity – the ringing of changes on the drearily persistent motif of exploitation. History, or pre-history if one prefers, indeed displays a remarkable self-identity from start to finish, presents a strikingly monotonous, compulsively repetitive narrative all the way through. What all historical epochs have in common is that we can say with absolute certitude what the vast majority of men and women who populate them have spent their time doing. They have spent their time engaged in fruitless, miserable toil for the benefit of others. Arrest history at any point whatsoever, and this is what we will find. History for Marxism is indeed, as Mr Ford wisely commented, bunk, or at least the same old tedious story. Those who celebrate history as change, difference, plurality, unique conjuncture, and who hone their theoretical instruments accordingly to capture something of this precious specificity, simply blind themselves politically and intellectually to this most scandalous of all transhistorical truths. It is the mind-shaking reality of consistent, unending, unruptured oppression and exploitation which endows human history with a certain recognizable identity, not, or not just, the epistemological zeal or phallocentric metaphysical drive of its political critics. The anti-metaphysicians are right to upbraid such identities as objectionably constrictive; they are simply wrong to locate them primarily in the neatly homogenizing minds of theorists rather than in the blind, compulsive repetitions of history itself. If we are to shake them off, it will not be by evading such identities but by going right through them and coming out somewhere on the other side, in what Marx called the realm of freedom. *That* historical space is indeed, if one is to believe *The Eighteenth Brumaire*, marked by difference, plurality, heterogeneity; so that those who celebrate these things now, in opposition to what they take to be a tyrannically cohesive model, are not so much wrong as somewhat premature.

In a powerful passage in *Marxism and Literature*, Raymond Williams records his objection to the classical Marxist formulation of base and superstructure:

The social and political order which maintains a capitalist market, like the social and political struggles which created it, is necessarily a material production. From castles and palaces and churches to prisons and workhouses and schools; from weapons of war to a controlled press: any ruling class, in variable ways though always materially, produces a social and political order. These are never superstructural activities. They are the necessary material production within which an apparently self-subsistent mode of production can alone be carried on.[1]

These are wise words, emerging as they do from the steady strength of Williams's 'cultural materialism'; yet the classical Marxist response to them is not difficult to produce. 'Superstructural activities', the implication runs, are somehow immaterial and unproductive ones; and since nothing could be more material than a castle or prison, it becomes analytically true that such institutions cannot be bracketed within the superstructure. But what would an immaterial activity or institution look like in the first place? And where, in classical Marxism, has the superstructure been treated as immaterial? In *The Eighteenth Brumaire? The State and Revolution?* Engel's disquisitions on military strategy, or Trotsky's analyses of the Stalinist bureaucracy? It is true that some 'vulgar' Marxism has, so to speak, dematerialized the superstructure to a realm of pure consciousness, disembodied reflexes or mechanical effects, and the Marx of *The German Ideology* might be said on this score to be at times a vulgar Marxist. But little is to be gained by selecting a travesty of the classical concept of superstructure, and then ritually bowling it over. For all you will have done is to re-invent the wheel; and all the actual arguments will then remain just as they were before.

There is a strong implication throughout much of Williams's later work that to label a phenomenon 'superstructural' is somehow to assign it a lesser degree of effective *reality* than an element of material production. But the base/superstructure model is not in this sense an *ontological* thesis. It is perfectly possible to concede that prisons and parliamentary democracy, pedagogical techniques and sexual fantasies are just as *real* as steel mills or sterling, just as much matters of material production, without modifying the claims of the doctrine in the slightest. The specificity of the base/superstructure thesis lies not here, but in the question of determinations. It is not a thesis which is out to distinguish the more from the less material, perhaps categorizing some phenomena as 'material' and some as 'spiritual' or 'ideal'. It is a conceptual instrument for the analysis of forms of material determination in particular historical societies, for the ends of political practice. Williams's concept of 'cultural materialism', by contrast, threatens to return to an essentially philosophical emphasis. It is less an *explanatory* account of social processes, which might then be fruitfully deployed in political terms, then a *re-description* in materialist terms of certain phenomena that have been ideologically misperceived as 'ideal' or 'immaterial'. As a concept, then, cultural materialism is not a rival or alternative to historical materialism, for it occupies a quite different status. In a sense, it returns us back *before* Marx's full development of historical materialism, to the earlier philosophical contentions between materialism and idealism.

In doing so, the notion of cultural materialism is in my view of considerable value. For it is as though it extends and completes Marx's own struggle against idealism, carrying it forcefully into that realm ('culture') always most ideologically resistant to a materialist redefinition. At the same time, it has the problems and limitations of the various campaigns for 'semantic materialism' euphorically waged throughout the very period when Williams was elaborating his own concept. For what, once you have demonstrated that language, culture or even consciousness is 'material', do you then do? If *everything* is 'material', can the term logically retain any force? From what does it differentiate itself? From an actual realm of phenomena which could properly be said to be non-material, or from an ideological misperception of properly material objects as ideal ones? When one comes to speak of 'the materiality of the poem's feeling', has the term not merely reverted to its alternative meaning of 'important' or 'of some substance', dwindled to sheer emphasis or gesture? It is not that Williams's own work was ever in the least infected by those to whom the term 'material' became a modish buzz-word; but for all that, it does not entirely escape some of the difficulties of this style of thought. For there is an important sense in which, in redescribing all or most phenomena as 'material', one leaves everything just as it was. This is not true in *every* sense: Williams's cultural materialist concern for the social and material conditions of say, writing practices, once carried into the academic institutions, would make the most profound difference to what actually got done there. But cultural materialism does not make a difference in the way that *historical* materialism does, precisely because of its descriptive rather than explanatory force. The claim of historical materialism is not that 'history is material'; those philosophical battles needed to be fought out in the first place before Marxism could arrive at its own most specific contribution to social analysis. That contribution, as I have argued already, turned not on the materiality or otherwise of particular social processes, but on the question of their mutual determinations. The key point for Marxism there, crystallized in the base/superstructure doctrine, is that those determinations are not symmetrical: that in the production of human society some activities are more fundamentally determining than others.

Williams recognizes acutely the dangers of any such 'symmetrical' thinking in his critique of the concept of totality in 'Base and Superstructure in Marxist Cultural Theory'. 'It is very easy', he argues there,

> for the notion of totality to empty of its essential content the original Marxist proposition [of base and superstructure]. For if we come to say that society is composed of a large number of social practices which form a concrete social whole, and if we give to each practice a certain specific recognition, adding only that they

interact, relate and combine in very complicated ways, we are at one level much more obviously talking about reality, but we are at another level withdrawing from the claim that there is any process of determination. And this I, for one, would be very unwilling to do.[2]

The totality, in short, is loaded: and Williams's answer to what loads it, in this essay at least, is the 'intentions' of a ruling class. There is, perhaps, the suggestion of an historicist notion of the social formation in this emphasis: the unity of the society, and at the same time its specific skewedness, resides in the impositions of a dominant class, which in some formulations succeeds in removing the source of determination from base to political superstructure. The classical Marxist question, of course, is what then determines this domination, for determinacy and domination are by no means identical.

To found the unity and directedness of a social formation on the dominance of an 'intending' class-subject will throw a great deal of weight on the sheer force and effectiveness of such a class in, so to speak, holding the social formation together; and this is one reason why, within the traditions of historicist Marxism, the concept of hegemony arises. The idea of hegemony, in short, for all its undoubted theoretical and political fertility, is in part an attempt to buttress an historicist error about the nature of class power, enriching and elaborating the concept of a class subject as the key to the unity of a social formation. It is no surprise, then, that Williams's argument in 'Base and Superstructure in Marxist Cultural Theory', immediately after the points I have quoted, should turn to this notion. Williams has greeted the idea of hegemony with acclaim, and put it to powerful use in his work; but one reason why he has done so, I would suggest, is because of a certain hostility to the notion of ideology, for which hegemony has come in effect to stand in. Just as Williams sets up the idea of immaterial superstructures in what is arguably something of a straw-target way, so he has tended to entertain certain rather crude formulations of the concept of ideology only, understandably, to go on to dismiss them. In *Marxism and Literature*, ideology would seem to suggest to him certain relatively conscious and explicit systems of value and belief; and hegemony as a concept then 'goes beyond' such insufficient formulations in its depth, dynamism, plurality, comprehensiveness and subtlety. But this substitution involves two mistakes. For one thing, there is no reason to suppose that the concept of ideology can be confined to explicit systems of belief, and much of the Marxist reflection upon the notion, in the very period in which Williams was writing *Marxism and Literature*, specifically challenged any such simplification. That Williams should continue in this period to offer – only to reject – these cruder versions of the idea can perhaps largely be accounted for by his hostility – in some ways very just – to the structuralist and psychoanalytical forms of Marxism from which more intricate, deep-reaching theories of ideology were emerging. But, secondly, to replace 'ideology' with 'hegemony' entails a kind of category mistake, since the two concepts are not the same. Hegemony, in the hands of Williams and of others, becomes a kind of super-ideology, a considerably richer, more complex and persuasive account of how a ruling class disseminates its meanings and values than the mechanistic theories of ideology contained within vulgar Marxism. Hegemony, however, cannot be confined as a concept to the dissemination of ruling meanings and values, however effectively and pervasively this process is accomplished. It denotes, rather, *all* of the means by which a ruling order secures consent to its dominance, of which ideology is then, as it were, an essential sector. We can properly speak of, say, the creation of relatively affluent (and so, perhaps, relatively incorporated) layers of the working class as an aspect of hegemony; we can speak of the processes of bourgeois democracy as themselves an instrument of hegemony, since their institutional procedures foster the illusion of self-government, and so on. Hegemony, in short, can be differentiated into its various economic, political and ideological regions. It is not simply a 'deeper' version of ideology, a more profoundly internalized, experientially pervasive diffusion of meanings, as Williams would seem to have it. It is Williams, not Marxism, who would seem here constrained by an essentially idealist reading of superstructures. Hegemony, he comments in 'Base and Superstructure in Marxist Cultural Theory', is 'not merely secondary or superstructural, like the weak sense of ideology', precisely because it is so profoundly, pervasively lived. We are returned once more to the 'ontological' version of base and superstructure: hegemony cannot be superstructural because it is *real*.

At two major points in *Politics and Letters*, Williams's interviewers ask him to explain how his cultural materialism can escape a purely 'circular' notion of the social formation, in which the question of hierarchies of determination is effectively shelved. Both exchanges are essentially inconclusive on this issue; but Williams's own position emerges lucidly enough. He would seem to accept the priority of material production in social life, provided that such production is understood in the extremely broad sense posited by his theory of cultural materialism; he holds to the idea of certain central determinations, but sees these as involving the total social process rather than a narrowly abstracted economic base. What this means, in short, is that Williams does indeed hold to a 'circular' theory of the social formation, one in this respect little changed from his earlier work; what *has* changed, with the development of 'cultural materialism', is that all the elements of this totality are now, so to speak, thoroughly materialized. This position involves a particularly notably irony. For the effect of Williams's increasing *rapprochement* with Marxism during the 1970s was not, paradoxically, to lead him closer to the base/superstructure model, but to lead him further away. Essentially Marxist concepts – of practice, mode of production, material conditions of possibility – were transplanted into the cultural realm to 'materialize' cultural processes, thus rendering them equivalent with other forms of material production, and so *intensifying* Williams's pre-

Marxian 'circularity'. The circularity became theoretically elaborated in Marxian language, rather than remaining, more vulnerably, at the 'experiential' or even organicist level. In extending Marxist logic, Williams partly undoes it. The concessions made to the necessity for some 'superstructural' understanding in 1971 in effect disappear from Williams's later work.

In attempting to persuade Williams into some version of the base/super-structure argument, his interviewers at one point advance the empirical case that the vast majority of men and women in history have spent their lives in toil, which must surely lend this area of activity 'a real causal primacy over all other social activities'. Williams agrees, naturally, with the empirical claim, but he is not persuaded by it into the base/superstructure thesis, and properly so. For it is not clear why the primacy of labour in history, in the straightforward sense that this is what most people have been most of their lives compelled to do, should logically entail a *causal* primacy, in the sense that this activity then produces and conditions a superstructure. The base/superstructure question, as I have argued, is one of the privileged social determinations, not a question of empirical priorities. 'Food first, morals later', only becomes a succinct formulation of the theoretical doctrine if some determining efficacy of food for morals is being claimed. We are not discussing a mere quantitative distribution of human energy, or even a question of necessary conditions – the fact that the biological character of human beings is such that material reproduction is a *sine qua non* of other forms of human practice. All such arguments miss the specificity of the base/superstructure doctrine. There is, admittedly, a somewhat tortuous, roundabout way of getting from the justified empirical claims to the base/superstructure thesis, which is *via* the doctrine that social being determines consciousness. This latter doctrine is stated by Marx in the same breath as his promulgation of the base/superstructure notion in the Preface to *A Contribution to the Critique of Political Economy*, and Williams is one of the few Marxian thinkers to have noted, in the opening paragraph of 'Base and Superstructure in Marxist Cultural Theory', that although the two formulations are not necessarily incompatible, they make significantly different emphases. The case that social being determines consciousness is an *ontological* doctrine, consequent upon the material structure of the human body, the material nature of its environment, the necessity for a mediatory labour between the two, and the fact that consciousness is therefore always in the first place, as Marx says elsewhere, 'practical' consciousness. That this is not the same kind of claim as that made by the base/superstructure metaphor is evident in the fact that one does not need to be an historical materialist to support it. The work of Ludwig Wittgenstein, for example, lends powerful aid from a quite different philosophical quarter to this argument: when Wittgenstein states in his *Philosophical Investigations* that 'It is in language that we agree or disagree; and language is not a matter of opinions but of forms of life', it is not difficult, given a difference of idiom, to translate this deeply important insight into the Marxist claim. (It may also be noted that one could deny this case and still endorse the base/superstructure argument: some socialists have held that when we have surpassed the period of which that argument holds true, human consciousness will determine social being rather than vice-versa). Williams most certainly holds to the 'being and consciousness' thesis; and the roundabout way to get him from that to the base/superstructure position would then be to argue that, since what has historically preponderated in 'social being' has in fact been exploititative economic production, it is plausible to believe that it is this which must have been the most significant influence on human consciousness. It is something like this, presumably, which Williams's interviewers have in mind; but their point, as stated, seems unaware of the problems of demonstrating causal efficacy here.

The wider, more ambitious and ontological case about being and consciousness, then, is paradoxically the more easy to accept; but there is no *logical* entailment between it and the base/superstructure claim. By asserting the two in the same breath in his Preface, Marx runs the risk of making the latter thesis sound like an ontological claim too, or at least of making it sound as though the two go naturally together. To accept the base/superstructure argument then comes to seem like accepting, almost on faith, that this is just the way history works, just as we accept the being/consciousness case because this is just the way human animals are. But this surely obscures the historical specificity of the base/superstructure model. The question we need to pose, and which is left unanswered by Marx in his Preface, is *why* certain political, legal and other institutions, and certain definite forms of social consciousness, 'rise . . . on the real foundation' of a mode of production. To put the question another way: what is it about the mode of production which historically (rather than ontologically) *necessitates* such products? For it is not, of course, 'economic activity' which Marx claims gives rise to such superstructures; it is economic activity conducted within relations of exploitation, social relations which for Marx are the *dominant* feature of the 'base'. The answer then is that such superstructures are necessary to regulate and ratify those forms of exploitation. Superstructures are essential because exploitation exists.

But will not there be forms of law, politics, social consciousness and the rest in post-class society too? Surely Marx's thesis cannot be confined to a particular kind of historical function in class society, since he includes within the superstructure 'definite forms of social consciousness', which will presumably still exist in post-revolutionary social formations. There are two kinds of reply to this objection. The first is that if Marx believes, as he seems to in the Preface and elsewhere, that *all* forms of social consciousness can be explained by more or less direct reference to the mode of production, then he is surely mistaken to do so. There is no very significant way in which, for example, the social and ideological institutions of sexuality can be 'explained' by reference to the mode of production, interact with it though they certainly do. Marx's claim here in the Preface is considerably too universalizing, contaminated, so to speak, by its companion thesis (necessarily universal in kind) about the determinacy of social being over consciousness. A covert conflation of the two doctrines occurs, which lends the base/superstructure case an excessively global reach. The second point in answer to the objection is that a 'superstructure' is not simply a range of legal, political and ideological institutions: a settled and determinable 'realm', as it were, within the social totality. To define a superstructure as such is to reify a set of functions to an ontological region. An institution or practice is 'superstructural' when, and only when, it acts in some way as a support to the exploitative or oppressive nature of social relations. This, indeed, is exactly the point made by Williams in *Marxism and Literature*, when he writes that 'it is then ironic to remember that the force of Marx's original criticism had been mainly directed against the *separation* of "areas" of thought and activity . . . The common abstraction of "the base" and "the superstructure" is thus a radical persistence of the mode of thought which he attacked.'[3] 'Superstructural', in brief, is a *relational* term: it identifies those particular aspects of a social practice or institution which act in particular conditions as supports of exploitation and oppression, invites us to contextualize that practice or institution in a specific way. Thus, when Williams protests in 'Base and Superstructure in Marxist Cultural Theory' that he has 'great difficulty in seeing processes of art and thought as superstructural in the sense of the formula as it is commonly used',[4] he is in one sense right and in another sense wrong. He is right that cultural activity is not superstructural *tout court*: you can, for example, examine it, as he himself has so often superbly done, as part of material production in general, treat it in an 'infrastructural' way. Or you can simply count up the number of words on the page or the number of colours in the painting, which in most cases is to treat art neither infrastructurally nor superstructurally. But as soon as you come, for example, to read a literary text for symptoms of its collusion in class power, as Williams has also many times perceptively done, then you are treating it 'superstructurally'.

Williams is perfectly correct to see that the common abstraction 'the superstructure' obscures this vital point. He is incorrect, I believe, and untrue to some of his own most substantial insights, to then in effect dismiss the category out of hand. The notion that there is an isolable, relatively static realm termed the superstructure is encouraged by the strongly genetic-functional bent of Marx's own formulations in the Preface and elsewhere. For there it would seem that the superstructure is brought directly into existence by the base, and with no other purpose than to support it. The determination is a genetic one, and the consequent relation of superstructure to base is strongly functionalist. It would be incoherent, on this model, to speak of those aspects of law, culture and education which were superstructural, and those which were not. But this is a way of speaking which there is reason to believe Raymond Williams would accept.

Like many critics of the base/superstructure metaphor, Williams has occasionally protested against its static, vertical connotations. One can, perhaps, make too much of this point – models are not after all reality – but it is interesting to see what happens if the metaphor is, so to speak, horizontalized. The 'base' might then emerge as the future: that is to say, that which is *still to be done* in any process of revolutionary political change. It thus acts as both warning and reminder that the changes which one has been able so far to achieve are not enough; they are 'superstructural' in precisely this sense. The 'base' is that outer horizon or final obstacle against which a transformative politics continually presses up, that which resists its dynamic and exposes it as lacking. It is that which will not give way, whatever other achievements or concessions may occur, a final limit or threshold ceaselessly retrojected into our present struggles in the awareness that, though we have indeed (let us say) socialized much major industry, attained full equality of opportunity for all and heavily taxed the rich, 'nothing has really changed'. The 'base' on this model, is not so much an answer to the question 'What in the end causes everything else?' as an answer to the question 'What in the end do you want?'

John Milton wrote of the possibility of being a 'heretic in the truth', meaning no doubt that there are many sterile ways of being correct. There are also those who are truthtellers in heresy, deviating from a deadening orthodoxy in order to recover and revitalize what is of value in it. Raymond Williams could not have constructed the conditions for his own truthtelling without such heresy: whatever he has contributed to Marxism has been founded, necessarily, on his early break with it. It is not, then, a question of that orthodoxy looking with gracious charity upon one who, after a long detour, has re-entered the fold, for after that detour the fold will never be the same again. Long before deconstruction, Williams's work was troubling the firm demarcation between 'inside' and 'outside' in the indeterminate doubleness of its discursive sites: Wales/England, city/country, literature/culture, working class/intellectual. To include Marxist/non-Marxist within that fertile border country is to identify not an inconsistency but a source of strength.

Notes

1 Raymond Williams, *Marxism and Literature* (Oxford, 1977), p. 93.
2 Raymond Williams, *Problems in Materialism and Culture: Selected Essays* (London, 1980), p. 36.
3 *Marxism and Literature*, p. 78.
4 *Problems in Materialism and Culture*, p. 36.

10

THE POLITICS OF HOPE:
An Interview

—— *Raymond Williams and Terry Eagleton* ——

This interview with Raymond Williams was conducted for the *New Statesman* at his cottage in Saffron Walden, Essex, about six months before his death in January 1988. The immediate occasion for the interview was the General Election of 1987, in which the Conservative government was elected to a third term of office. It seemed important to establish Williams's political thoughts at that crucial moment for the left; but the conversation also ranges over a much wider area, and distils in compressed form some of Williams's characteristic political wisdom.

Terry Eagleton: You retired from the chair of drama at Cambridge University in 1983, after a long career on the political left which still continues. You fought fascism in Europe, and took a major role in the creation of the early New Left and the early years of CND. Since then you've been involved in a whole series of socialist interventions, both inside and outside the Labour party, and your intellectual work – what you've come to call 'cultural materialism' – has transformed the thinking of generations of students and workers in the cultural field.

It would have been nice to have been able to present you on your retirement, not with a gold clock, but with a socialist society. It's arguable, however, that such a goal is now as remote, if not more so, as at any time in your political career. Instead we are witnessing the most viciously anti-working-class regime of most people's political memory, the laying of the groundwork of a police state, and an apparently baffled left opposition. Militarily speaking we live in the most terrible danger. Could I ask you, then, whether after so long a struggle you now feel in any sense disillusioned? What are your political thoughts and hopes, immediately after the election of a third Thatcher government?

Raymond Williams: Disillusionment, not at all; disappointment, of course. Yet looking back it seems to me I absorbed some of these disappointments quite early on, so the recent ones didn't come as so much of a surprise. Indeed I was so thrown out of my early expectations, as a young man and a soldier in the war, by the events of 1947 that I went into a kind of retreat for a year or two, trying to work out a different kind of intellectual project, which also involved a sense of what a different political project might be. This was a time, remember, when the expectations of a Labour government, which had been the whole perspective of my childhood, had been not just disappointed but actively repulsed: the priority of the military alliance with the USA over Labour's quite real achievements in welfare, the use of troops against groups of striking workers and so on. So the crisis for me was an early one; and perhaps this partly explains why the crisis of 1956 didn't come as so much of a shock for me as it did for some of those intellectuals who had stayed in the Communist party. There was then a sense of reinvigoration in the late 1950s, which carried on throughout the 1960s in the various attempts at some new gathering of left forces. When that went down, in 1970, there was of course a sense of setback and defeat; but I think that whole history had prepared me emotionally and intellectually for the failures which the left was then to go through.

When all of this passed into the period of open reaction of the Thatcher goernments, it seemed to me that the left were repeatedly trying to reconstitute the very limited kind of hope that I'd repeatedly seen fail. The rhetoric of victory in 1945 is in a sense fair enough, but it shouldn't convince anyone unless it is immediately qualified by the realities of 1947–8. The rhetoric of the (supposedly) successful Labour governments of the 1960s is for me similarly qualified by the events of 1968 – that very confused time in which the attempt to feed new currents of ideas and feelings into the labour movement was not merely ignored but, again, actually repulsed.

Today, it's clearer to me than ever that the socialist analysis is the correct one, and its correctness has been in my view repeatedly demonstrated. But the perspectives which had sustained the main left organizations were simply not adequate to the society they were seeking to change. There was always the attempt on the left to reconstitute old models: the notion of 'uniting Britain', to take an example from recent electoral rhetoric, or of an autonomous sovereign economy – as if what's happened in international capitalism over the past forty years simply hadn't happened. When they fight in these terms, what can and should be fought for becomes much more difficult to define.

TE: What then should be fought for? Are you suggesting a wholly different strategy for the left?

RW: The strategy is all still to be found, but what blocks it, I'm saying, is this old model of creating a relatively powerful, united Britain with a 'successful' sovereign economy. That, I think, is what history has ruled out. And one consequence of this has been a retreat to certain areas, traditional strongholds of labour: Scotland, Wales, the north of England. But the shape of a genuine strategy would be to pass beyond this idea of altering such situations only in Britain. To adopt at least a west European perspective, where there are many people and regions in similar situations, penetrated and distorted by international capitalism and the military alliance. Any useful strategy would involve a great building up in autonomy in such regions of Britain, but instead of orienting that to the British state, looking out for the connections which can be made to Western Europe, at least in the first instance.

The obvious block to this is the electoral system which imposes the need for a national party – 'national' on this superannuated model of the British state. There follows the necessity for a coalition of left forces which everyone knows is impossible to sustain honestly. The range of opinion from liberal left to far left is just too broad. Socialists want to take part in defeating something uniquely vicious, and so must be friendly to the labour right, or to liberals, social democrats, even progressive Tories; but if you do so pretending that you share their perspective then you fail in one of your most basic duties: telling the truth as you see it.

Meanwhile a major obstacle to any socialist strategy is that the left makes repeated attempts to remake the whole Labour party in its own image, as distinct from maintaining, within present constraints, a socialist element. In practice, this has prevented the Labour party from achieving the kind of unity it needs for the limited jobs it has to do. But is also means a limitation on the amount of absolutely straight socialist argument and propaganda, under the pretence of consensus. When one hears a Labour candidate, as mine did, talking about loyalty to NATO, building up a fine fleet and the rest, one knows one simply isn't living in the same world with people with whom otherwise one's prepared to be comradely and cooperative, for specific objectives. Yet while the left still sees the wholesale conversion of a social democratic party to a socialist party as its objective, there's an important sense in which it silences itself.

If we had proportional representation, what we would rapidly get is a realignment of the centre. People talk of a realignment of the left, but what's already beginning to happen is actually a realignment of the centre. Now such a realignment of the centre, which I think is bound to happen, just isn't the left's business. Socialist analysis and propaganda must be made in its own terms. If there *was* a realignment of the centre which took the Labour party into some unambiguous social democratic phase, there would be in altered electoral conditions a space for some federation of socialist, Green and radical nationalist forces. It wouldn't be electorally insignificant, and above all it would be able to speak up without equivocation for its views of the world, which at present doesn't get through politically very far. It would be dreadful for the left in the Labour party to try to break it up, weaken it even further, and there's no simple question of a breakaway. But in the situation I'm describing, there will be a possibility of the left speaking in its own voice; and in a political situation as hard as this, that's not to be discounted.

TE: Indeed; though as the crisis of capitalism has tightened, we've been witnessing a steady haemorrhage of intellectuals from the far left. Individuals, groups, journals, whole parties have moved inexorably to the right, and this at a time – a bitter irony – when in a sense there's never been so obviously, so devastatingly, what one might describe as a 'total global system', which demands an appropriately radical response. To affirm such a truth in an age of post-modernist fragmentation, however, is becoming increasingly unfashionable. To mention social class in certain so-called left circles is to be unceremoniously shown the door. Defeatism and adaptation, however 'dynamically' and modernistically tricked out, seem instead the order of the day. I once heard you refer in a nicely sardonic phrase to those who 'make long-term adjustments to short-term problems'. I wonder whether it was this treason of the clerks that you had in mind.[3]

RW: Well, the strength of our enemies isn't to be doubted: yet the most intelligent operators of the system itself know just how profoundly unstable it is. The whole of a US-led, anti-Communist, anti-Third World alliance is coming under pressure, if only from its own internal divisions and the increasing inability of the USA to dominate it. The international financial system is a helterskelter economy based on frightening credit expansion and credit risk, which would have terrified an earlier generation of orthodox bankers and financiers. To say this, of course, isn't to advocate some policy of waiting for the crash; for one thing such crashes aren't automatic, and for another thing they're just as likely to produce a hard right well beyond anything we've seen so far. Those who talk of the hard right in Britain haven't really seen one. But if the system is that unstable, this clearly isn't a world to adjust to. It's not a world in which one has to settle for belonging to an eccentric minority who believe there are old socialist texts and ideas which must be kept alive, in an all too powerful and successful system. Powerful, yes; successful, no.

Meanwhile what's happened in so-called 'actually existing socialism' in Eastern Europe has done the left more damage than can be properly accounted for. It's been a key feature in many intellectual desertions, and one difficult to argue against since of course one endorses the denunciation of terror, while recalling that such terror is in fact historically outweighed by the long, systematic terror of the right. If it were a reason to desert socialism, because such terrible things have happened in its name, it would be a reason to desert every system we know. The Eastern European societies, however, aren't going to remain in their present condition; they know they can't sustain themselves without radical change. And this will be a positive factor for socialist intellectuals in the West.

TE: It would sometimes seem today that a commitment to class struggle on the one hand, and a celebration of difference and plurality on the other, have been lined up on opposite sides of the left political fence. Yet both ways of thinking would seem to have subtly co-existed in your own work almost from the beginning. You've always deeply suspected closed, monolithic theories and strategies, and from the outset your socialism has stressed difficulty, complexity, variety; yet, not least in your development over the past decade or so, in the very period of some other left intellectuals' sail-trimming or simple renegacy, you would seem to hold firmly to a class perspective. How do you see the relation between these two emphases?

RW: I've always been very aware of the complicated relationships between class and place. I've been enormously conscious of place, and still get an extraordinary amount of emotional confirmation from the sense of place and its people. Now the key argument in Marxism was always whether the proletariat would be a universal class – whether the bonds its forged from a common exploitation would be perceived as primary, and eventually supersede the more local bond of region or nation or religion. On the one hand the recognition of exploitation continually reproduces class consciousness and organization on a universal basis. On the other hand, I don't know of any prolonged struggle of that kind in which these other issues haven't been vital, and in some cases decisive. So I'm on both sides of the argument, yes: I recognize the universal forms which spring from this fundamental exploitation – the system, for all its local variety, is everywhere recognizable. But the practice of fighting against it has always been entered into, or sometimes deflected, by these other kinds of more particular bonds.

TE: Which of course vitally include gender. In your book *The Long Revolution*, right back in 1961 and long before the resurgence of the contemporary women's movement, you identified what you saw then as four interlocking systems within any society, and named one of them as the 'system of generation and nurture'. Yet your theoretical work would seem to have preserved a relative silence on those issues; instead, perhaps, they have tended to take up home in your fiction, in which the family, generation and their connections to work and politics have figured prominently.

RW: That's true. It's really all in my second novel, *Second Generation*; that's what it was really all about. But at about the same time I was writing *The English Novel from Dickens to Lawrence*, where I describe the Brontë sisters as representing interests and values marginalized by the male hegemony. Not only that, however, but representing human interests of a more general kind which showed up the limits of the extraordinarily disabling notion of masculinity. I remember how I used to embarass students in my lectures, you will doubtless remember this, by suggesting it would be interesting to locate the historical moment when men stopped crying in public. The suppression of tenderness and emotional response, the willingness to admit what isn't weakness – one's feelings in and through another: all this is a repression not only of women's experience but of something much more general. And I suppose I found it easier to explore that in more personal terms, in my novels. That's no real excuse: I ought to have been doing this in my other work too; but by the time I came to understand it in that way it was already being done by a lot of good people who were no doubt making more sense of it than I could have done.

TE: The media, or communications as you prefer to call them, have long formed a centrepiece of your work. Although the whole concept of 'media' is surely much too passive to convey the enormous power of these institutions. The editors of the *Sun*, *Mail* and *Express* were surely infinitely more important to Thatcher in the election than any members of her inner circle, and ought to be buried in Westminster Abbey. I mean as soon as possible. How are we to go about combating this formidable source of political power?

RW: Well, one can talk of course of education – of arming people's minds against that kind of journalism. But there's now been a sustained cultural attempt to show how this manipulation works, which has hardly impinged on its actual power. I don't see how the educational response can be adequate. The manipulative methods are too powerful, too far below the belt for that. These people have to be driven out. We have to create a press owned by and responsible to its readers. The increasing concentration of power in the media has been a process strangely unresisted by socialists, by the labour movement as a whole, who have actually let go of key sectors. When I was concentrating on this kind of cultural analysis in the 1950s I was sometimes told by good Marxist friends that it was a diversion from the central economic struggle. Now every trade union and political leader cries 'The media, the media'. It was correctly foreseen that this, in electoral politics, was where the battle would be fought, but the response to that was very belated. The proposals which I put forward in my book *Communications* in the early 1960s, for democratic control of the media, still seem to be a necessary programme.

TE: We both hail originally from the Celtic fringes, and both of us, relatively late in life, began turning back to those roots. You have turned increasingly to Wales both in your fictional and political work: it took us both a long time to look back to the margins because, as students of English, we'd had our heads well and truly fixed by an ideology of 'Englishness'. You still have close, active relations, personally and politically, with Wales. Is this marginality a source of strength in your work? Or is it simply convenient to have, so to speak, a different passport and identity when one sallies forth among the middle-class English natives?

RW: I think some of my Welsh friends would be kind enough to say that if I have some importance for them its precisely because I came out – because I went among the English, and got a hearing, even recognition, in their own institutions. When you're part of one of these disadvantaged nationalities you can be very bitter about people who have gone off and made it elsewhere, but it can be different if you also know they still relate to you, even if one has crossed the border rather than remained inside it. In that sense I don't altogether regret crossing the border, although there are times when I do. Coming from a border area of Wales in any case, the problem for me has always been one of what it was to be Welsh – I mean in some serious sense, rather than in one of the exportable stage Welsh versions. I suppose there was some group I thought of as the *real* Welsh, secure in their identity, who would come out in force and flail this returning migrant with all his doubts.

The response I've had, especially from young Welsh people, has been precisely the opposite: thank God someone has come out and asked who are we, what are we? All my usual famous qualifying and complicating, my insistence on depths and ambiguities, was exactly what they already knew. And this experience of ambiguity and contradiction hasn't only equipped us in Wales to understand our own situation better; it's also equipped us, emotionally and intellectually, to understand the situation of increasing numbers of people – including the once so self-assured, confident English. It's easier for us, in other words, to put questions to those simple, confident, unitary identities which really belong to an earlier historical period.

TE: Let me return finally to where we began, with the question of disappointment or despondency. What you say about the need to reject any kind of disillusion strikes me as absolutely right. Your work has always seemed to be distinguished by a kind of steady, profound humanism, which it would be too facile to describe as optimism. Beneath your political writing has always run this confident trust in human capacities – capacities so steadfast and enduring that not to see them finally triumph in some political future would seem not only unthinkable but, as it were, blasphemous. Perhaps I share that belief; but let me put to you, in the spirit of devil's advocacy, an alternative scenario. The historical record shows that such capacities have so far always been defeated. History, as Walter Benjamin might have put it, is more barbarism than progress; what you and I might consider moral and political virtue has never ruled any social order, other than briefly and untypically. The real historical record is one of wretchedness and unremitting toil; and 'culture' – your and my speciality – has its dubious roots in this. How then are we to undo such a history with the very contaminated instrument it has handed us? Is socialism, in other words, anything more than a wishful thinking which runs quite against the historical grain? To put the point more personally: how far is your own trust in human creative capacities in part the product of an unusually warm and affectionate working-class childhood, of which it's in some sense the nostalgic memory?

RW: It's true that much of my political belief is a continuation of a very early formation. I can't remember any time when I haven't felt broadly speaking as I do now, except for the period of retreat I mentioned in the 1940s, which in a sense was a kind of cancellation of the certainties I'd assumed in childhood. I ceased then to be simply a product of that culture: I don't know what I became a product of, since I couldn't accept the offered alternatives. Out of that period of radical dislocation was rebuilt what was, and I think still is, an *intellectual* conviction. Though of course it can't ever be only that. The crisis which came to me on the death of my father, who was a socialist and a railway worker – I haven't been able to explain this to people properly, perhaps I explained it partly in my novel *Border Country* – was the sense of a kind of defeat for an idea of value. Maybe this was an unreasonable response. All right, he died, he died too early, but men and women die. But it was very difficult not to see him as a victim at the end. I suppose it was this kind of experience which sent me in the end to the historical novel I'm now writing, *People of the Black Mountains*, about the movements of history over a very long period, in and through a particular place in Wales. And this history is a record of all you say: of defeat, invasion, victimization, oppression. When one sees what was done to the people who are physically my ancestors, one feels it to be almost incredible.

What do I get from this? Simply the confidence of survival? Yes, that in part. There's been a quite extraordinary process of self-generation and regeneration, from what seemed impossible conditions. Thomas Becket once asked a shrewd, worldly-wise official on the Marches about the nature of the Welsh. 'I will show you the curious disposition of the Welsh', said the official, 'that when you hold the sword they will submit, but when they hold the sword they assert themselves.' I like the deep, pokerfaced joke of that. The defeats have occurred over and over again, and what my novel is then trying to explore is simply the condition of anything surviving at all. It's not a matter of the simple patriotic answer: we're Welsh and still here. It's the infinite resilience, even deviousness, with which people have managed to persist in profoundly unfavourable conditions, and the striking diversity of the beliefs in which they've expressed their autonomy. The sense of value which has won its way through different kinds of oppression in different forms.

If I say, estimating, for example, whether we can avoid a nuclear war, 'I see it as 50–50', I instantly make it 51–49, or 60–40, the wrong way. That is why I say we must speak for hope. I don't think my socialism is simply the prolongation of an earlier existence. When I see that childhood coming at the end of milennia of much more brutal and thoroughgoing exploitation, I can see it as a fortunate time: an ingrained and indestructible yet also changing embodiment of the possibilities of common life.

A RAYMOND WILLIAMS BIBLIOGRAPHY

—— Alan O'Connor ——

References within each section of the bibliography appear in chronological order of publication, with the exception of the first and last sections (Bibliographical essays and Select bibliography), in which references appear in alphabetical order by author. The bibliography is divided into sections as follows.

Bibliographical essays

Works by Raymond Williams

Works about Raymond Williams

Selected bibliography on Williams

Bibliographical essays

Borklund, Elmer, 'Williams, Raymond (Henry)', in *Contemporary Literary Critics*, 2nd edn, Detroit, Gale Research Company, 1982.

Gilpin, George H. and Hermione de Almeida, 'Williams, Raymond (Henry)', in *Thinkers of the Twentieth Century: A Biographical, Bibliographical and Critical Dictionary*, edited by Elizabeth Devine et al., Detroit, Gale Research Company, 1983.

Page, Malcolm, Bibliography and short essay, in *Contemporary Novelists*, 3rd edn, New York, St Martin's Press, 1982.

Temple, Ruth and Martin Tucker, 'Raymond Williams (1921—)', in *A Library of Literary Criticism; Modern British Literature*, vol. III, New York, Frederick Unger, 1966.

Wakeman, John, 'Williams, Raymond (Henry)', in *World Authors 1950–1970*, New York, H. W. Wilson Company, 1975.

Works by Raymond Williams

1 Books

Reading and Criticism, Man and Society series, London, Frederick Muller, 1950. Reprinted 1962.

Drama from Ibsen to Eliot, London, Chatto and Windus, 1952. New York, Oxford University Press, 1953. Revised edn. Harmondsworth, Peregrine, 1964. London, Chatto and Windus, 1968.

Raymond Williams and Michael Orrom, *Preface to Film*, London, Film Drama, 1954.

Drama in Performance, London, Frederick Muller, 1954. Revised edn, The New Thinkers Library, London, C.A. Watts, 1968. New York, Basic Books, 1968. Harmondsworth, Pelican, 1969.

Culture and Society 1780–1950, London, Chatto and Windus, 1958. New York, Columbia University Press, 1959. New York, Doubleday, Anchor Press, 1959. Harmondsworth, Penguin, 1961; reprinted with Postscript, 1963. New York, Harper and Row (paperback edn.), 1966. New edition, New York, Columbia University Press, 1983, with a new Introduction. Translated into Italian, Japanese, Portuguese, German.

The Long Revolution, London, Chatto and Windus, 1961. New York, Columbia University Press, 1961; reissued 1983. Harmondsworth, Pelican, 1965, with additional endnotes; reissued 1984. Westport, Conn., Greenwood Press, 1975.

Britain in the Sixties: Communications, Penguin Special, Harmondsworth, Baltimore, Penguin, 1962. Danish edition. Second edition, London, Chatto and Windus, 1966. New York, Barnes and Noble, 1967. Harmondsworth, Penguin, 1968. Spanish translation. Third edition, Harmondsworth, Penguin, 1976.

Modern Tragedy, London, Chatto and Windus, 1966. Stanford, Stanford University Press,

1966. Reprinted without play 'Koba', 1977. New edition also without play 'Koba', and with new Afterword, London, Verso, 1979.

Stuart Hall, Raymond Williams, Edward Thompson (eds), *May Day Manifesto*, London, May Day Manifesto Committee, 1967. 2nd edn, Penguin Special, Harmondsworth, Penguin, 1968.

Drama from Ibsen to Brecht, London, Chatto and Windus, 1968. New York, Oxford University Press, 1969. Harmondsworth, Pelican, 1973. London, Hogarth Press, 1987.

The Pelican Book of English Prose, Volume 2: From 1780 to the present day, ed. Raymond Williams, Harmondsworth, Baltimore, Penguin, 1969.

The English Novel from Dickens to Lawrence, London, Chatto and Windus, 1970. New York, Oxford University Press, 1970. Paper edn. Marrimack, 1970. St Albans, Herts., Paladin, 1974. London, Hogarth Press, 1985.

Orwell, Fontana Modern Masters series, Fontana/Collins, 1971. New York, Viking, 1971. New York, Columbia University Press 1981. 2nd edn, Fontana, Flamingo paper editions, 1984.

The Country and the City, London, Chatto and Windus, 1973. New York, Oxford University Press, 1973. Paperback edn 1975. St Albans, Herts. Paladin, 1975. London, Hogarth Press, 1985.

Joy and Raymond Williams (eds), *D. H. Lawrence on education*, Harmondsworth, Penguin Education, 1973.

Raymond Williams (ed.), *George Orwell: A Collection of Critical Essays*, Twentieth Century Views, Englewood Cliffs, N.J., Prentice-Hall, 1974.

Television: Technology and Cultural Form, Technosphere series, Fontana/Collins, 1974 (paperback). New York, Schocken, 1975. Italian translation.

Keywords: A Vocabulary of Culture and Society, Fontana Communications series, Fontana paperbacks, 1976. London, Croom Helm, 1976. New York, Oxford University Press, 1976. 2nd edn, London, Fontana Paperbacks, 1983. New York, Oxford University Press, 1984.

Marie Axton and Raymond Williams (eds), *English Drama: Forms and Development: Essays in Honour of Muriel Clara Bradbrook*, with an Introduction by Raymond Williams, Cambridge, New York, Cambridge University Press, 1977.

Marxism and Literature, Marxist Introductions series, London, New York, Oxford University Press, 1977. Italian translation.

Politics and Letters: Interviews with New Left Review, London, New Left Books, 1979. New York, Schocken, 1979. Verso paperback edn 1981.

Problems in Materialism and Culture: Selected Essays, London, Verso, 1980. New York, Schocken, 1981.

Culture, Fontana New Sociology Series, Fontana Paperbacks, 1981. U.S. edn, *The Sociology of Culture*, New York, Schocken, 1982.

Raymond Williams (ed.), *Contact: Human Communication and its History*, London and New York, Thames and Hudson, 1981.

Cobbett, Past Masters series, Oxford, New York, Oxford University Press, 1983.

Towards 2000, London, Chatto and Windus, 1983. Harmondsworth, Penguin, 1985. US edn, *The Year 2000*, with a Preface to the American Edition, New York, Pantheon, 1984.

Writing in Society, London, Verso, 1984. US edn, 1984.

Merryn Williams and Raymond Williams (eds), *John Clare: Selected Poetry and Prose*,

Methuen English Texts, London and New York, Methuen, 1986.

Resources of Hope, London, Verso, 1988.

Raymond Williams on Television: Selected Writings, Preface by Raymond Williams, ed. Alan O'Connor, Toronto, Between the Lines; New York, London, Routledge, 1989.

2 Short stories, novels, and plays

Short stories

Short story, in *Cambridge Front*, no. 2 (1941). Perhaps 'Red Earth', listed in *Politics and Letters* chronology. Source: *Outlook: A Selection of Cambridge Writing*, Raymond Williams, Michael Orrom, Maurice James Craig (eds), Cambridge, 1941.

'Sack Labourer', in *English Story 1*, edited by Woodrow Wyatt, London, Collins, 1941.

'Sugar', in *Outlook: A Selection*, pp. 7–14.

'This Time', in *New Writing and Daylight*, no. 2, 1942–3, ed. John Lehmann, London, Collins, 1943, pp. 158–64.

'A Fine Room to Be Ill In', in *English Story 8*, ed. Woodrow Wyatt, London, Collins, 1948.

Novels

Border Country, London, Chatto and Windus, 1960. New York, Horizon Press, 1962. Book club edn, Readers Union/Chatto and Windus, London, 1962. Harmondsworth, Penguin, 1964. Reissued by Chatto and Windus, 1978.

Second Generation, London, Chatto and Windus, 1964. Reissued 1978. New York, Horizon Press, 1965.

The Fight for Manod, London, Chatto and Windus, 1979.

The Volunteers, London, Eyre Methuen, 1978. Paperback edition, London, Hogarth Press, 1985.

Loyalties, London, Chatto and Windus, 1985.

Plays

Koba, in Raymond Williams, *Modern Tragedy*, London, Chatto and Windus, 1966.

A Letter from the Country, BBC Television, April 1966, *Stand*, 12 (1971), pp. 17–34.

Public Inquiry, BBC 1 Television, 15 March 1967, *Stand*, 9 (1967), pp. 15–53.

The Country and the City (television documentary, Where We Live Now series), 1979.

Williams' unpublished plays include a television play, *The Volunteers*. See *The Listener*, 20 February 1969.

3 Chapters in books

'Culture is ordinary', in *Conviction*, ed. Norman Mackenzie, London, MacGibbon and Kee, 1958, pp. 74–92. American edn, New York, Monthly Review Press, 1959.

'The Social Thinking of D. H. Lawrence', in *A D. H. Lawrence Miscellany*, ed. Harry T.

Moore, Carbondale, Southern Illinois University Press, 1959, pp. 295–311. From *Culture and Society*.

In *Popular Culture and Personal Responsibility*, London, National Union of Teachers, 1960.

Witness for the defence, in *The Trial of Lady Chatterley: Regina v. Penguin Books Limited*, the transcript of the trial, ed. C. H. Rolph, Penguin Special, Baltimore, Harmondsworth, Penguin, 1961, pp. 133–5.

'Lawrence's Social Writings', in *D. H. Lawrence: A Collection of Critical Essays*, ed. Mark Spilka, Englewood Cliffs, N.J., Prentice-Hall, 1963, pp. 162–74. From *Culture and Society*.

'Recent English Drama', in *The Modern Age*, vol. 7 of the Pelican Guide to English Literature, ed. Boris Ford, 2nd edn, Harmondsworth, Penguin, 1963, pp. 531–45. Revised from *Twentieth Century* (1961).

'David Hume: Reasoning and Experience', in *The English Mind*, ed. Hugh Sykes and George Watson, Cambridge, Cambridge University Press, 1964, pp. 123–45. Reprinted in *Writing in Society*.

'Towards a Socialist Society', in *Towards Socialism*, ed. Perry Anderson and Robin Blackwood, London, Fontana, 1965, pp. 367–97. From *The Long Revolution*.

'Strindberg and Modern Tragedy', in *Essays on Strindberg*, published by the Strindberg Society, Sweden, Stockholm, Beckmans, 1966, pp. 7–18. From *Modern Tragedy*.

'Dylan Thomas's Play for Voices', in *Dylan Thomas: A Collection of Critical Essays*, Twentieth Century Views, ed. C. B. Cox, Englewood Cliffs, N.J., Prentice-Hall, 1966, pp. 89–98. From *Critical Quarterly*, 1959.

'General Profile'; 'Criticism', in *Your Sunday Paper*, ed. Richard Hoggart, London, University of London Press, 1967, pp. 13–29, 150–63. Book commissioned by ABC Television in relation to a series of thirteen adult-education programmes.

'Paradoxically, if the book works it to some extent annihilates itself', in *McLuhan: Hot and Cold*, ed. Gerald E. Stearn, New York, Dial Press, 1967, pp. 186–9. See response by McLuhan, pp. 283–4. Reprinted from *University of Toronto Quarterly* (1964).

'Culture and revolution: a comment', in *From Culture to Revolution: The Slant Symposium 1967*, ed. Terry Eagleton and Brian Wicker, London, Sydney, Sheed and Ward, 1968, pp. 24–34, 296–308.

'Another Pheonix', review of *Pheonix II*, by D. H. Lawrence, in *The Bedside Guardian 17: A Selection from the* Guardian *1967–68*, ed. W. L. Webb, London, Collins, 1968, pp. 246–8. From the *Guardian*.

'The Meanings of Work', concluding essay in *Work: Twenty Personal Accounts* vol. 1, ed. Ronald Fraser, Harmondsworth, Penguin in association with New Left Review, 1968, pp. 280–98.

'A social commentary', in *The Press: a case for commitment* ed. Eric Moonman, Fabian Tract 391, London, Fabian Society, 1969, pp. 1–4.

'From The May Day Manifesto', in *The New Left Reader*, ed. by Carl Oglesby, New York, Grove Press, 1969, pp. 111–43. From 1967 *May Day Manifesto*.

'Introduction', in *National Convention of the Left April 1969 Report and Proposals*, London, National Convention of the Left, 1969 (mimeo).

'Introduction', in *Three Plays*, by D. H. Lawrence, Harmondsworth, Penguin, 1969, pp. 7–14.

'The Realism of Arthur Miller', in *Arthur Miller: A Collection of Critical Essays*,

Twentieth Century Views, ed. Robert W. Corrigan, Englewood Cliffs, N.J., Prentice-Hall, 1969, pp. 69–79. From *Critical Quarterly* (1959).
'Dickens and Social Ideas', in *Dickens 1970*, ed. by Michael Slater, London, Chapman and Hall, 1970, pp. 77–98. Reprinted in *Sociology of Literature and Drama*, ed. T. and E. Burns, Harmondsworth, Penguin.
'Radical and/or Respectable', in *The Press We Deserve*, ed. Richard Boston, London, Routledge and Kegan Paul, 1970, pp. 14–26.
'The Industrial Novels: Hard Times (1958)', in *Charles Dickens*, Penguin Critical Anthologies, ed. Stephen Wall, Harmondsworth, Penguin Education, 1970, pp. 405–9. From *Culture and Society*.
'Introduction', in *Dombey and Son*, by Charles Dickens, ed. Peter Fairclough, Harmondsworth, Penguin, 1970, pp. 11–34.
'From Modern Tragedy 1966', in *Henrik Ibsen*, Penguin Critical Anthologies, ed. James McFarlane, Harmondsworth, Penguin. 1970 pp. 312–19.
'Crimes and Crimes', in *A Listener Anthology: August 1967–June 1970*, ed. Karl Miller, London, British Broadcasting Corporation, 1970, pp. 210–22. From *The Listener* (21 August 1969).
'On Reading Marcuse', in *The Cambridge Mind: Ninety Years of the Cambridge Review 1879–1969*, ed. Eric Homberger, William Janeway, Simon Schama, Boston, Little, Brown, 1970, pp. 162–6. From *The Cambridge Review* (1969).
'An Introduction to Reading in Culture and Society', in *Literature and Environment: Essays in Reading and Social Studies*, ed. Fred Inglis, London, Chatto and Windus, 1971, pp. 125–40.
'The Realism of Arthur Miller', in *Arthur Miller: The Crucible; Text and Criticism*, ed. Gerald Weales, New York, Viking, 1971, pp. 313–25. From *Critical Quarterly* (1959).
'On Solzhenitsyn', in *Literature in Revolution*, ed. George Abbott White and Charles Newman, New York, Holt, Rinehart and Winston, 1972, pp. 318–34.
'Ideas of Nature', in *Ecology: The Shaping Inquiry*, ed. J. Benthal, London, Longman, 1972. Based on a lecture at the Institute of Contemporary Arts, 1971. Reprinted in *Problems in Materialism and Culture*.
'Introduction', in *Racine*, by Lucien Goldmann, tr. Alister Hamilton, Cambridge, Rivers Press, 1972. London, Writers and Readers, 1981, pp. vii–xxii. Text of lecture, Cambridge, 26 April 1971. From *New Left Review* (1971).
'Realism and the Contemporary Novel', in *Twentieth Century Literary Criticism: A Reader*, ed. David Lodge, London, Longman, 1972. From *The Long Revolution*.
'Discussion on St. Joan of the Stockyards, 1973', in *A Production Notebook to St. Joan of the Stockyards* ed. Michael D. Bristol and Darko Suvin, Montreal, McGill University, 1973, pp. 184–98. Transcript of discussion in Montreal, March 1973.
'Social Darwinism', in *The Limits of Human Nature*, ed. J. Benthall. London, Allen Lane, 1973. From lecture at the Institute of Contemporary Arts, London, 1972.
'Thomas Hardy', in *Thomas Hardy: The Tragic Novels*, ed. R. P. Draper, pp. 341–51. From *Critical Quarterly* (1964).
'Observation and Imagination in Orwell', in *George Orwell: A Collection of Critical Essays*, ed. Raymond Williams (1974). From *Orwell*.
Untitled, in *Bookmarks*, ed. Frederic Raphael, London, Quartet Books, 1975, pp. 162–5. In connection with the Authors' Lending Rights Society.
'Welsh Culture', in *Culture and Politics: Plaid Cymru's Challenge to Wales*, Plaid Cymru,

51 Cathedral Road, Caerdydd, CF1 9HD, 1975, pp. 6–10. From talk on BBC Radio 3, 27 September 1975.

'You're a Marxist, Aren't You?' in *The Concept of Socialism*, ed. Bhikhu Parekh, London, Croom Helm, 1975, pp. 231–42.

'Sean O'Casey', in *Sean O'Casey: A Collection of Critical Essays*, Twentieth Century Views, ed. Thomas Kilroy, Englewood Cliffs, N.J., Prentice-Hall, 1975, pp. 53–60. From *Drama from Ibsen to Brecht*.

'Raymond Williams Comments (1972)', in *World Authors 1950–1970*, ed. John Wakeman, New York, H. W. Wilson Company, 1975, pp. 696–7.

'Communications as Cultural Science', in *Approaches to Popular Culture*, ed. C. W. E. Bigsby, London, Edward Arnold, 1976, pp. 27–38. From *Journal of Communication* (1974).

'Realism and Non-Naturalism', *Official Programme of the Edinburgh International Television Festival* (1977). May be Claire Johnston, ed., *Edinburgh '77 Magazine*, London, BFI, 1977.

Untitled, in *My Cambridge*, ed. Ronald Hayman, London, Robson Books, 1977, pp. 55–70. US edn *My Oxford, My Cambridge*, ed. Ann Thwaite and Ronald Hayman, New York, 1979.

'Literature in Society', in *Contemporary Approaches to English Studies*, ed. Hilda Schiff, London, Heinemann for The English Association, 1977, pp. 24–37.

'The Press We Don't Deserve', in *The British Press: A Manifesto*, Communications and Culture Series, London, Macmillan, 1978, pp. 15–28. From the Action Society Press Group presentations to the McGregor Commission on the Press.

'Foreword', in *The Critical Twilight: Explorations in the Ideology of Anglo-American Literary Theory from Eliot to McLuhan*, by John Fekete, International Library of Phenomenology and Moral Sciences, London, Routledge and Kegan Paul, 1978, pp. xi–xiv.

'The press and popular culture: an historical perspective', in *Newspaper History: From the Seventeenth Century to the Present Day*, ed. George Boyce, James Curran and Pauline Windgate, London, Constable; Beverly Hills, Sage Publications, 1978, pp. 41–50.

'Forms of English Fiction in 1848', in *1848: The Sociology of Literature*, Proceedings of the Essex Conference on the Sociology of Literature, July 1977, ed. Francis Barker et al., University of Essex, 1978, pp. 277–90. Reprinted in *Literature, Politics and Theory* ed. F. Barker et al, London, Methuen, 1986, and *Writing in Society*.

'Social environment and theatrical environment: the case of English naturalism', in *English Drama: Forms and Development*, ed. Marie Axton and Raymond Williams, 1978, pp. 203–23. Reprinted in *Problems in Materialism and Culture*.

'Wessex and the Border (1973)', in *The English Novel: Developments in Criticism since Henry James: A Casebook*, ed. Stephen Hazell, London and Basingstoke, Macmillan, 1978, pp. 190–205. From *The Country and the City*.

'The Growth and Role of the Mass Media', in *Media, Politics and Culture: A Socialist View*, ed. Carl Gardner, London, Macmillan, 1979, pp. 14–24. From *Wedge* (1977); *International* (1977).

'The Institutions of Technology', in *Communications and Class Struggle*, 2 vols, eds. Armand Mattelart and Seth Siegelaub, Vol. 1 *Capitalism, Imperialism*, New York, International General; Bagnolet, France, International Mass Media Research Centre, 1979, pp. 265–67. From *Television*.

'Utopia and Science Fiction', in *Science Fiction: A Critical Guide*, ed. Patrick Parrinder, London, Longmans, 1979. From *Science Fiction Studies* (1978).

'Effects of the technology and its uses', in *Communication Studies: An Introductory reader*, ed. John Corner and Jeremy Hawthorn, London, Edward Arnold, 1980, pp. 174–86. From *Television;* not in the 2nd edn.

'Hardy and Social Class', by Raymond Williams and Merryn Williams, in *Thomas Hardy: The Writer and His Background*, ed. Norman Page, London, Bell and Hyman, 1980, pp. 29–40.

'The Bloomsbury Fraction', in *Keynes and The Bloomsbury Group: The Fourth Keynes Seminar held at the University of Kent at Canterbury, 1978*, ed. Derek Crabtree and A. P. Thirlwall, London, Macmillan, 1980. Reprinted in *Problems in Materialism and Culture*.

'Tragedy and Contemporary Ideas (1966)', in *Tragedy: Developments in Criticism: A Casebook*, ed. R. P. Draper, London and Basingstoke, Macmillan, 1980, pp. 182–9. From *Modern Tragedy*.

'Foreword', in *A Good Night Out: Popular Theatre: Audience, Class and Form*, by John McGrath, London, Eyre Methuen, 1981, pp. vii–xi.

'Foreword', in *The Language of Television: Uses and Abuses*, New Accents Series, by Albert Hunt, London, Eyre Methuen, 1981, pp. vii–x.

'Editor's Introduction', in *Medieval Readers and Writers 1350–1400*, English Literature in History Series, London, Hutchinson; New York, Columbia University Press, 1981, pp. 9–12. General Editor's Introduction reprinted in other volumes in this series.

'Raymond Williams', in *The Forward March of Labour Halted?*, ed. Martin Jacques and Francis Mulhern, London, Verso in Association with *Marxism Today*, 1981, pp. 142–52.

'The Analysis of Culture', in *Culture, Ideology and Social Process*, ed. Tony Bennett et al., An Open University Reader, London, Batsford, 1981, pp. 43–52. From *The Long Revolution*.

'Lecture', in *The Arts Council: Politics and Policies*, London, The Arts Council of Great Britain, c.1981, pp. 9–16.

'The New Metropolis', in *Introduction to the Sociology of 'Developing Societies'*, ed. Hamza Alvai and Teodor Shanin, New York and London, Monthly Review Press, 1982. From *The Country and the City*.

'The Politics of Nuclear Disarmament', in *Exterminism and Cold War*, ed. New Left Review, London, New Left Books, 1982, pp. 65–85. Reprinted from *New Left Review* (1980).

'Region and Class in the Novel', in *The Uses of Fiction: Essays on the Modern Novel in Honour of Arnold Kettle*, ed. Douglas Jefferson and Graham Martin, Milton Keynes, The Open University Press, 1982, pp. 59–68. Reprinted in *Writing in Society*.

'Working-Class, Proletarian, Socialist: Problems in Some Welsh Novels', in *The Socialist Novel in Britain: Towards the Recovery of a Tradition*, ed. H. Gustav Klaus, Brighton, Sussex, The Harvester Press, 1982, pp. 110–21.

'Exiles', in *James Joyce: New Perspectives*, ed. Colin MacCabe, Sussex, The Harvester Press; Bloomington, Indiana University Press, 1982, pp. 105–10. Reconstruction of part of a lecture (1947).

'British Film History: New Perspectives', in *British Cinema History*, ed. James Curran and Vincent Porter, London, Weidenfeld and Nicolson, 1983, pp. 9–23.

'Cultural Revolution', in *British Socialism: Socialist Thought from the 1880's to 1960's*, ed. Anthony Wright, London and New York, Longman, 1983, pp. 170–81. From Part III of *The Long Revolution*.

'Culture', in *Marx: The First Hundred Years*, ed. David McLellan, Fontana paperbacks, 1983, pp. 15–55.

'Lecture', in *The Arts Council: Politics and Policies*, The 1981 W. E. Williams Memorial Lecture, London, Arts Council, 1983, pp. 9–16.

'Monologue in Macbeth', in *Teaching The Text*, ed. Susanne Kappeler and Norman Bryson, London, Routledge and Kegan Paul, 1983, pp. 180–202.

'Seeing a man running', in *The Leavises: Recollections and Impressions*, ed. Denys Thompson, Cambridge, Cambridge University Press, 1984, pp. 113–22.

Untitled, in *Writings on the Wall: A Radical and Socialist Anthology 1215–1984*, ed. Tony Benn, London, Faber and Faber, 1984, pp. 115, 116–17. From 'Culture is Ordinary' (1958) and *May Day Manifesto*, 1968.

'Socialists and Coalitionists', in *The Future of the Left*, ed. James Curran, Cambridge, Polity Press and New Socialist, 1984, pp. 182–94. From *New Socialist*.

'State Culture and Beyond', in *Culture and the State*, ed. Lisa Appignanesi, London, Institute of Contemporary Arts, 1984, pp. 3–5.

'Forms of English fiction in 1848', in *Literature, Politics and Theory: Papers from the Essex Conference 1976–84*, ed. Francis Barker et al., London, Methuen, 1986, pp. 1–16. Reprinted from *1848: The Sociology of Literature*, ed. F. Barker et al., University of Essex, 1978.

'Foreword', in *Languages of Nature: Critical Essays on Science and Literature*, ed. Ludmilla Jordanova, London, Free Association Books, 1986, pp. 10–14.

'Pierre Bourdieu and the sociology of culture: an introduction', by Raymond Williams and Nicholas Garnham, in *Media, Culture and Society*, ed. Richard Collins et al., London, SAGE, 1986, pp. 116–30. Reprinted from *Media, Culture and Society*, 1980.

'Towards Many Socialisms', in *Socialism on the Threshold of the Twenty-First Century*, London, Verso, 1986. First published in *Socialist Review* (1986).

'Alignment and Commitment', in *Contemporary Literary Criticism: Modernism Through Postmodernism*, ed. Robert Con Davis, New York and London, Longman, 1986, pp. 124–9. From *Marxism and Literature*.

'Base and Superstructure in Marxist Cultural Theory', and 'The Multiplicity of Writing', in *Debating Texts*, ed. Rick Rylance, Toronto: University of Toronto Press, 1987, pp. 204–16, 217–20. From *Problems in Materialism and Culture* and *Marxism and Literature*.

'Conventions', in *Twentieth-Century Literary Criticism*, ed. Vassilis Lambropoulos and David Neal Miller, Albany, State University of New York Press, 1987, pp. 185–90. From *Marxism and Literature*.

'Language and the avant-garde,' in *The Linguistics of Writing: Arguments between language and literature*, ed. Nigel Fabb, Derek Attridge, Alan Durant, Colin MacCabe, New York, Methuen, 1987, pp. 33–47. From a conference on 'The Linguistics of Writing' at Strathclyde University in 1986.

'Fact and Fiction', in *International Encyclopedia of Communications*, Oxford University Press, 1988.

'Beckett, Samuel', in *Modern Irish Literature*, ed. Denis Lane and Carol McCrory Lane, New York, Ungar, 1988, p. 10. From *Modern Tragedy*.

'Dominant, Residual, and Emersent', in *Twentieth-Century Literary Theory: A Reader*, ed. K. M. Newton, New York, St Martin's Press, 1988, pp. 121–6. From *Marxism and Literature*. 'The politics of the avant-garde', and 'Theatre as a political forum', in *Visions and Blueprints*, ed. Edward Timms and Peter Collier, Manchester, Manchester University Press, pp. 1–15, 307–20.

4 Pamphlets

Unsigned [Raymond Williams and Eric Hobsbawm]. Pamphlet on the Russo-Finnish War. Communist Party of Great Britain, 1940. This may be a pamphlet by the Russia Today Society, *Finland—the Facts*, London [Communist Party], 1939.

Communication and Community, William F. Harvey Memorial Lecture, Bedford College, University of London, 1961.

The existing alternative in communications, Fabian Tract no. 337, Socialism in the Sixties series, London, Fabian Society, 1962.

Drama in a dramatised society: An Inaugural Lecture, Cambridge, Cambridge University Press, 1975. Reprinted in *Writing in Society* and *Raymond Williams on Television*.

The Welsh Industrial Novel, Cardiff, University College Press, 1979.

Socialism and Ecology, London, Socialist Environment and Resources Association [1982].

Democracy and Parliament, with an Introduction by Peter Tatchell, London, Socialist society Pamphlet, 1982.

5 Books in translation

Catalan

Cultura i Societat, Barcelona, Laia, 1974. *Translation of Culture and Society.*

Danish

Massemedierne, Copenhagen, 1963. Translation of the first edition of *Communications* with material on the Danish press. See 1968 Penguin edition, p. 12.

German

Gesellschaftstheorie als Begriffsgeschichte: Studien z. histor. Semantik von Kultur, tr. Dt. von Heinz blumensath, Munchen, Rogner and Bernhard, 1972. Translation of *Culture and Society*.

Innovation: uber den Prozesscharakter von Literatur und Kultur, selected and tr. H. Gustav Klaus, Frankfurt am Main, Syndikat, 1979. Selections from *The Long Revolution, From Culture to Revolution, Modern Tragedy, The Country and the City*, also 'Literature and Sociology: in Memory of Lucien Goldmann,' and 'Base and Superstructure in Marxist Cultural Theory.'

Italian

Cultura e rivoluzione industriale Inghilterra, 1780–1950, Piccola bibliotech Einaudi, tr.

M. T. Grendi, Torino, G. Einaudi, 1968. Translation of *Culture and Society*.

Marxismo e letteratura, tr. by Mario Stetrema, Roma, Bari Laterza, 1979. Translation of *Marxism and Literature*.

Televisione. Technologia e forma culturale, tr. with an Introduction by Celestino E. Spada, Bari, De Donate, 1981. Translation of *Television*.

Japanese

Translation of *Culture and Society*. See 1983 Columbia University Press edition p. xi.

Portuguese

Translation of *Marxism and Literature*. *Marxismo e Literatura*, Rio, Zahar, 1979.

Spanish

Translation of *Communications*. *Los Medios de comunicacion social*, Barcelona, Peninsula, 1971.

Marxismo y Literatura, Barcelona, Peninsula, 1980. Translation of *Marxism and Literature*.

Cultura, sociologia de la communicacion y arte, Buenos Aires, Barcelona, Mexico, Paidos, 1982. Translation of *Culture*.

Hacia el Año 2000, Barcelona, Critica, 1984. Translation of *Towards 2000*.

6   Articles: general

The Cambridge University Journal (vol. 1, no. 1, 21 October 1939), Williams editor, April-June 1940.
  'Profundities for poets. The Muse in Utopia', 3 February 1940, p. 7.
  [Michael Pope] 'The Spoon in the Yellow Liver: First Act of a Great New Drama', 9 March 1940, p. 2.
  [Michael Pope.] Review of *Must the War Spread*, Penguin Special, by D. N. Pritt.
  'Commentary', 27 April 1940, p. 5.
  [Unsigned] 'Commentary', 4 May 1940, p. 5.
  'Commentary', 11 May 1940, p. 5.
  'Commentary', 18 May 1940, p. 5.
  'Commentary', 25 May 1940, p. 5.
  'Not with a Scream but with a Twitter: Trinity's "Magpie" Released', 25 May 1940.
  'Commentary', 1 June 1940, p. 5.
  'Commentary: Union Turns Left–But How', 9 November 1940, p. 2.
  [Michael Pope] 'Ralph Lynn at Arts', 9 November 1940, p. 2.

Cambridge University Socialist Club Bulletin, 1939.
  'Defence Against Air Raids'. 'Literature and the Cult of Sensibility'.

Twentyone, weekly newspaper of the 21st Anti-Tank Regiment, Royal Artillery, printed at Pinneberg, Germany. Williams editor April-October 1945. See *Politics and Letters*, p. 59. The British Library has a single copy, 1 December 1945, which includes a photograph of Williams back at Cambridge.

1947

'Dali, Corruption and His Critics', review of *Hidden Faces* by Salvador Dali, *Politics &
Letters* 1, nos 2/3 (1947), pp. 112–13.
'The Delicacy of P. H. Newby', review of *Agents and Witnesses*, by P. H. Newby, *The
Critic* 2, no. 2 (1947), pp. 79–81.
'A Dialogue on Actors', *The Critic* 1, no. 1 (1947), pp. 17–24.
Clifford Collins, Wolf Mankowitz, Raymond Williams, 'Editorial', *The Critic* 1, no. 2
(1947).
——'For Continuity in Change', editorial, *Politics & Letters* 1, no. 1 (1947), pp. 3–5.
——'Culture and Crisis', editorial, *Politics & Letters* 1, nos 2/3 (1947), pp. 5–8.
'Ibsenites and Ibsenite-Antis', review of *Ibsen: the Intellectual Background*, by Brian W.
Downs; *Ibsen the Norwegian*, by M. C. Bradbrook, *The Critic* 1, no. 2 (1947), pp.
65–8.
'Lower Fourth at St. Harry's', *Politics and Letters* 1, nos 2/3 (1947), pp. 105–6.
'Radio Drama', *Politics & Letters* 1, nos 2/3 (1947), pp. 106–9.
'Saints, Revolutionaries, Carpetbaggers', review of *The New Spirit*, by E. W. Martin;
Writers of Today, ed. Denys Val Baker, *The Critic* 1, no. 1 (1947), pp. 52–4.
'The Soviet Literary Controversy in retrospect', *Politics & Letters* 1, no. 1 (1947), pp.
21–31.

1948

'A note on Mr. Hoggart's appendices', *Adult Education* 21 (1948), pp. 96–98.
[Michael Pope] 'The American Radio', review of *The American Radio*, by Llewellyn
White, *Politics & Letters* 1, no. 4 (1948).
'And Traitors Sneer', *Politics & Letters* 1, no. 4 (1948), pp. 66–8.
'The Exiles of James Joyce', *Politics & Letters* 1, no. 4 (1948), pp. 13–21. *In Drama from
Ibsen to Brecht*, part 2, ch. 3.
[Michael Pope] Short Review of *A Skeleton Key to Finnegan's Wake*, by Campbell and
Robinson, *Politics & Letters* 1, no. 4 (1948).
'Some Experiments in Literature Teaching', *Rewley House Papers* vol. 2, no. 10 (1948–9),
pp. 9–15.
[Michael Pope] 'The State and Popular Culture', *Politics & Letters* 1, no. 4 (1948),
pp. 71–2.

1949

'Literature in relation to History: 1850–75', *Rewley House Papers* 3, no. 1 (1949–50), pp.
36–44.
'Ibsen's non-Theatrical Plays', *The Listener* 42, 22 December 1949, pp. 1098–9. From the
Third Programme.

1951

'Christopher Fry', *The Highway*, May/September 1951, pp. 42–8. A chapter in *Drama
from Ibsen to Eliot*.
'Criticism into Drama', *Essays in Criticism* 1 (1951), pp. 120–138. A chapter in *Drama
from Ibsen to Eliot*.

1953

'Film as a Tutorial Subject', *Rewley House Papers* 3, no. 2 (Summer 1953), pp. 27–37.
'The Idea of Culture', *Essays in Criticism* 1 (1953), pp. 239–66.
'Myth and Mr. O'Neill', *The Highway*, May/September 1953, pp. 42–8.
'The Teaching of Public Expression', *The Highway*, April 1953, pp. 247–50.

1954

'Editorial Commentary', *Essays in Criticism* 4 (1954), pp. 341–4. On small magazines.
'Figures and Shadows', *The Highway*, February 1954, pp. 169–72.
'Standards', *The Highway*, December 1954, pp. 43–6.

1955

'George Orwell', review of *George Orwell*, by Laurence Brander, *Essays in Criticism* 5 (1955), pp. 44–52. Early version of a *Culture and Society* chapter.

1956

'Class and Classes', *The Highway*, January 1956, pp. 84–6.
'T. S. Eliot on Culture', *Essays in Criticism* 6 (1956), pp. 302–18.
'Science Fiction', *The Highway*, December 1956, pp. 41–45.

1957

'Fiction and the Writing Public', review of *The Uses of Literacy*, by Richard Hoggart, *Essays in Criticism* 7 (1957), pp. 422–8.
'The New Party Line?', review of *The Outsider*, by Colin Wilson, *Essays in Criticism* 7 (1957), pp. 68–76.
Review of *Edward Thomas*, by H. Coombes, *The Highway*, January 1957, pp. 94–5.
'The Uses of Literacy: Working Class Culture', *Universities and Left Review* 1, no. 2 (1957): 29–32.

1958

'3B at Cement Street', review of four books for children, *New Statesman* 56, 15 November 1958, pp. 682–3.
'A Kind of Gresham's Law', *The Highway*, February 1958, pp. 107–10.
'New Verse Plays', review of *Two Plays,* by George Banker; *Helen in Egypt and Other Plays* by John Heath-Stubbs, *New Statesman*, vol. 56, 27 December 1958, p. 916.
'Poetry Today', review of six books of poetry, *New Statesman*, vol. 56, 6 December 1958, pp. 811–12.
'The Present Position in Dramatic Criticism', review of *The Art of Drama*, by Ronald Peacock, *Essays in Criticism* 8 (1958), pp. 290–98.
'The Press the People Want', *Universities and Left Review* 5 (1958), pp. 42–47. Shortened advance chapter of *The Long Revolution*.
'Realism and the Contemporary Novel', *Universities and Left Review* 4 (1958), pp. 22–5.
Review of *The Poet's Craft*, by A. F. Scott; *English Historians: Selected Passages,* by B. Newman, *The Highway,* April 1958, pp. 188–9.

'Revolution in Cambridge', review of *The Muse Unchained*, by E. M. Tillyard, *New Statesman*, vol. 56, 1 November 1958, p. 604.
'The Social Thinking of D. H. Lawrence', *Universities and Left Review* 4 (1958), pp. 66–71. Advance chapter of *Culture and Society*.

1959

'Arguing About Television', review of *Television and the Child*, Hilde T. Himmelweir, *Encounter* 12 (June 1959), pp. 56–9.
'The Bearing of Literature', review of *The Uses of the Imagination*, by William Walsh; *Poetry and Morality*, by Vincent Buckley, *New Statesman*, vol. 57, 21 March 1959, p. 410.
'The Critic as Biographer', review of *Katherine Mansfield and Other Literary Studies*, by J. Middleton Murray, *New Statesman*, vol. 57, 9 May 1959, pp. 662–3.
'Critical Forum', *Essays in Criticism* 9 (1959), pp. 171–9. Reply to Ian Gregor and Malcolm Pittock on *Culture and Society*, reviewed by Richard Hoggart.
'Definitions of Culture', review of *Culture in Private and Public Life*, by F. R. Cowell, *New Statesman*, vol. 58, 25 July 1959, p. 114.
'Dylan Thomas's Play for Voices', *Critical Quarterly* 1 (1959), pp. 18–26.
'Going on Learning', *New Statesman*, vol. 57, 30 May 1959, pp. 750–51.
'Grammar of Dissent', review of *Voices of Dissent: A selection of articles from Dissent Magazine*, *The Nation* 188 (1959), pp. 174–5.
'Literature and Morality'. Review of *Three Traditions of Moral Thought*, by Dorothea Krook; *The Ethical Idealism of Matthew Arnold*, by William Robbins, *New Statesman*, vol. 58, 31 October 1959, pp. 588–90.
'Our debt to Dr. Leavis' [Symposium], *Critical Quarterly* 1 (1959), pp. 245–7.
'The Press and Popular Education', *The Highway*, April 1959, pp. 183–8.
'Priestly Against Topside', review of *Topside, or the Future of England*, by J. B. Priestly, *New Statesman*, vol. 57, 10 January 1959, pp. 47–8.
'Realism and the Contemporary Novel', *Partisan Review* 26 (1959), pp. 200–13.
'The Realism of Arthur Miller', *Critical Quarterly* 1 (1959), pp. 140–49. Reprinted in *Universities and Left Review* 7 (1959), pp. 34–7. Reprinted in *Arthur Miller* ed. G. Weales, New York, Viking, 1971.
'Science and Culture', review of *T. H. Huxley: Scientist, Humanist and Educator*, by Cyril Bibby, *New Statesman*, vol. 57, 25 April 1959, p. 584.
'Tribune's Majority', review of *Tribune 21*, edited by Elizabeth Thomas, *New Statesman*, vol. 57, 24 January 1959, p. 124.
'Verse and Drama', review of *The Third Voice*, by Dennis Donoghue, *New Statesman*, vol. 58, 26 December 1959, p. 916.

1960

'Class and Voting in Britain', *Monthly Review* 11, no. 9 (January 1960), pp. 327–34.
'Freedom and Ownership in the Arts', *New Left Review* no. 5 (September-October 1960), pp. 53–7. Advance chapter of *The Long Revolution*.
'Ibsen restored', *New Statesman*, vol. 60, 2 July 1960, pp. 23–4.
'Labour and Culture', *New Epoch*, May 1960. Not seen. Source: *Tribune*, 13 May 1960, p. 2.

'Lawrence and Tolstoy', *Critical Quarterly* 2 (1960), pp. 33–9.

'London Letter: The New British Left', *Partisan Review* 27 (1960), pp. 341–7.

'The Magic System', *New Left Review*, no. 4 (1960), pp. 27–32. Reprinted in *Problems in Materialism and Culture*.

'Oxford Ibsen', review of *Ibsen: Volume VI*, tr. and ed. J. W. McFarlane, *New Statesman*, vol. 60, 24 September 1960, pp. 447–8.

'A Practical Critic', review of *The Truest Poetry*, by Laurence Lerner, *New Statesman*, vol. 59, 5 March 1960, pp. 338–9.

'Working Class Attitudes', Richard Hoggart and Raymond Williams, *New Left Review*, no. 1 (1960), pp. 26–30.

1961

'The Achievement of Brecht', *Critical Quarterly* 3 (1961), pp. 153–62.

'The Common Good', *Adult Education* 34 (1961), pp. 192–9.

'Definition of Culture' [Comments by Kingsley Amis, Frank Kermode, Raymond Williams, Edward Shils on *Socialism and Culture*, by Richard Wollheim], *New Statesman*, vol. 61, 2 June 1961, pp. 880–84.

'New English Drama', *Twentieth Century* 170 (1961), pp. 169–80. Reprinted in *The Pelican Guide to English Literature*, vol. 7.

'The Figure in the Rug', review of *Somerset Maugham*, by Richard Cordell, *New Statesman*, vol. 62, 7 July 1961, pp. 20–21.

'The Future of Marxism', *20th Century* 170 (1961), pp. 128–42.

'Hope Deferred', review of performance of 'Waiting for Godot', *New Statesman*, vol. 61, 19 May 1961, p. 802.

'My Performances', On the Memoirs of Thomas Bewick, *New Statesman*, vol. 62, 8 December 1961, pp. 892–3.

'Shame the World', on a performance of 'The Visions of Simone Machard', by Brecht, *New Statesman*, vol. 69, 9 June 1961, pp. 932–3.

'Thoughts on a masked stranger', review of *Between Past and Future*, by Hannah Arendt, *Kenyon Review* 23 (1961), pp. 698–702.

'Three-Quarters of a Nation', review of *English for Maturity*, by David Holbrook, *New Statesman*, vol. 61, 3 March 1961, p. 351.

'Virtuous Circle', review of *The Story of Fabian Socialism*, by Margaret Cole, *The Listener*, vol. 66, 30 November 1961, pp. 933–4.

'Work and Leisure', *The Listener*, vol. 65, 25 May 1961, pp. 926–7.

1962

'A Dialogue on Tragedy', *New Left Review*, nos 13/14 (1962), pp. 22–35.

'The deadlock', *Encounter* 18, no. 1 (1962), pp. 14–15.

'Fiction and Delusion: A note on *Auto-da-Fe*, by Elias Canetti', *New Left Review*, no. 15 (May-June 1962), pp. 103–6.

'From Scott to Tolstoy', review of *The Historical Novel*, by Georg Lukács, *The Listener*, 8 March 1962, pp. 436–7.

'Into the Wilderness', review of *The Popular Novel in England 1770–1800*, by J. M. S. Tompkins, *New Statesman*, vol. 63, 2 March 1962.

'Strong Feelings', review of *The New Radicalism*, by Bryan Magee, *The Listener*, vol. 68, 4

October 1962, pp. 529–30.

Review of *Llareggub Revisited*, by David Holbrook, *The Listener*, vol. 67, 12 April 1962, pp. 651–2.

'To the North', review of *Ibsen and Strindberg*, by F. L. Lucas, *The Listener*, vol. 67, 17 May 1962, pp. 868–70.

'Sensible People', review of *Learning and Living, 1790–1960*, by J. F. C. Harrison, *New Statesman*, vol. 63, 5 January 1962, pp. 21–2.

'Strindberg and the New Drama in Britain', *Le Theatre dans le Monde/World Theatre* 11, no. 1 (1962), pp. 61–.

'Television in Britain', *The Journal of Social Issues* 18, no. 2 (1962), pp. 6–15.

1963

'Books', *On Human Unity*, by E. E. Hirschmann, in reply to a question about what books had been neglected or undervalued in the last five years, *Twentieth Century* 172 (1963), p. 137.

'From Hero to Victim: Notes on the development of liberal tragedy', *New Left Review*, no. 20 (1963), pp. 54–68.

'Going into Europe', *Encounter* 20 (March 1963), p. 68.

'Minor Ibsen', review of *The Oxford Ibsen* Volume Two (The Vikings at Helgeland, Love's Comedy, The Pretenders), ed. J. W. McFarlane, *The Cambridge Review* 84 (19 January 1963), pp. 195, 197.

'Radical History', review of *The Making of the English Working Class*, by E. P. Thompson, *The Listener*, vol. 70, 5 December 1963, pp. 938–9.

'Liberal Breakdown', review of *The Free Spirit*, by C. B. Cox, *The Listener*, vol. 69, 30 May 1963, pp. 926–9.

Review of *The Meaning of Contemporary Realism*, by Georg Lukács, *The Listener*, vol. 69, 28 February 1963.

'Tolstoy, Lawrence, and Tragedy', *Kenyon Review* 25 (1963), pp. 633–50.

'Tragic despair and revolt', *Critical Quarterly* 5 (1963), pp. 103–15. Advance chapter of *Modern Tragedy*.

'Tragic resignation and sacrifice', *Critical Quarterly* 5 (1963), pp. 5–19. Advance chapter of *Modern Tragedy*.

'What kind of education', *The Listener*, vol. 70, 18 July 1963, p. 91.

1964

'From Hero to Victim: Ibsen, Miller and the Development of Liberal Tragedy', *Studies on the Left* 4, no. 2 (1964). pp. 83–97. Edited from *New Left Review*; to appear in *Modern Tragedy*.

'La gauche britannique', *Esprit* 32 (1964), pp. 581–92.

'Labour's cultural policy', *Views*, no. 5 (1964), pp. 40–44.

'Prelude to Alienation', *Dissent* 11 (1964), pp. 303–15. Reprinted in *Stand* vol. 7, no. 4 (1965), pp. 36–44. On Blake.

'Social Criticism in Dickens: Some problems of method and approach', *Critical Quarterly* 6 (1964), pp. 214–27. See also correspondence with J. C. Maxwell, p. 373.

'A Structure of Insights', review of *The Gutenberg Galaxy*, by Marshall McLuhan, *University of Toronto Quarterly*, April 1964. Reprinted in *McLuhan: Hot and Cold*,

edited by Gerald E. Stearn, 1967.
'Thomas Hardy', *Critical Quarterly* 6 (1964), pp. 341–51.

1965

'The British Left', *New Left Review*, no. 30 (March-April 1965), pp. 18–26. From *Esprit*.
'Other Views' [Labour in Britain], *Views*, no. 7 (1965), pp. 13–15.
'Tragic Inquiry', review of *Greek Tragedy and the Modern World*, by Leo Aylen, *The Spectator*, 8 January 1965, p. 46.
'Why I am Marching: You Can't Have It Both Ways—The Bomb *and* Democracy', *Sanity*, April 1965, p. 6.
'What is the Future of the Left', *Sanity*, April 1965, p. 9.

1966

'New Left Catholics', *New Blackfriars*, vol. 48, November 1966, pp. 74–7.

1967

'Literature and rural society', *The Listener*, vol. 78, 16 November 1967, pp. 630–32. From the Third Programme.
'Literature and the City', *The Listener*, vol. 78, 23 November 1967, pp. 653–6. From the Third Programme.

1968

'How television should be run', *The Listener*, vol. 80, 11 July 1968, pp. 33–5.
'Pastoral and counter-pastoral', *Critical Quarterly* 10 (1968), pp. 277–90. To be published in *The Country and the City*.
'Why do I demonstrate?', *The Listener*, vol. 79, 25 April 1968, pp. 521–3. From a talk broadcast on the Third Programme.

1969

'Crisis in communications: A new mood of submission', *The Listener*, vol. 82, 31 July 1969, pp. 138, 140. Reprinted in *Problems in Materialism and Culture*.
'The Knowable Community in George Eliot's Novels', *Novel* 2 (1969), pp. 255–68. To appear in a different form in *The Country and the City*.
'National Convention of the Left: Why CND must be there', *Sanity*, March 1969, p. 6.
'On Reading Marcuse', review of *Negations*, by Herbert Marcuse, *The Cambridge Review* 90 (30 May 1969), pp. 366–8. Reprinted in *The Cambridge Mind* ed. E. Homberger et al., Boston, Little, Brown, 1970.
'Dramatic changes', review of *The English Drama, 1485–1585*, Oxford History of English Literature, by F. P. Wilson; *Shakespeare's Dramatic Heritage*, by Glynne Wickham, *The Listener*, 24 April 1969, pp. 582–3.

1970

'An experimental tendency', *The Listener*, vol. 84, 3 December 1970, pp. 785–6.
'A Hundred Years of Culture and Anarchy', *The Spokesman*, no. 8, December 1970, pp. 3–5. From a talk in April 1969. Reprinted in *Problems in Materialism and Culture*.

'Ideas of nature', *Times Literary Supplement*, 4 December 1970, pp. 1419–21. Reprinted in *Problems in Materialism and Culture*.

'The Intellectual in Politics', *The Spokesman*, no. 3 (May 1970), pp. 3–5.

'The popularity of the press', *The Listener*, vol. 84, 15 October 1970, pp. 508–9. From Radio 3.

'Shadowing Orwell', *The Listener*, vol. 84, 13 August 1970, p. 218.

1971

'Dutschke and Cambridge', *Cambridge Review* 92, 29 January 1971, pp. 94–5. See also two statements, pp. 95–6.

'Going into Europe-Again?', *Encounter* 36 (June 1971), p. 13.

'In praise of films', *The Listener*, vol. 85, 20 May 1971, p. 633–5. From Radio 3.

'Literature and Sociology: In memory of Lucien Goldmann', *New Left Review*, no. 67 (1971), pp. 3–18.

'On and from any shore', review of *The Penguin Book of Socialist Verse*, ed. Alan Bold, *Stand* 12, no. 2 (1971), pp. 35–7.

'Radical Intellectuals', review of *Fellow Travellers*, by T. C. Worsley, *The Listener*, vol. 85, 24 June 1971, p. 821.

'Raymond Williams thinks well of the Open University', *The Listener*, vol. 86, 14 October 1971, pp. 507–8.

1972

'Lucien Goldmann and Marxism's alternative tradition', *The Listener*, vol. 87, 23 March 1972, pp. 375–6. From Radio 3.

'Social Darwinism', *The Listener*, vol. 88, 23 November 1972, pp. 696–700. Radio 3. One of a series of lectures at the ICA.

'What happened at Munich', *The Listener*, vol. 88, 14 September 1972, pp. 321–2. Reprinted in *Raymond Williams on Television*.

1973

'Base and Superstructure in Marxist Cultural Theory', *New Left Review*, no. 82 (1973), pp. 3–16. German translation as 'Materialistische Literaturtheorie IX', *Alternative* 101 (April 1975), pp. 77–91.

'How we lost the world we never had: the country and the city in history', introduction by Leo Marx, *Royal Institute of British Architects Journal* 80 (1973), pp. 421–31.

'Images of Solzhenitsyn', review of *Ten Years after Ivan Denisovich*, by Zhores Medvedev; *Candle in the Wind*, by Alexander Solzhenitsyn, *The Listener*, vol. 90, 29 November 1973, pp. 750–51.

'Views', *The Listener*, vol. 89, 7 June 1973, pp. 744–5. Reprinted in *Raymond Williams on Television*.

1974

'Communication as Cultural Science', *Journal of Communication* 24 (Summer 1974), pp. 17–25. Reprinted in *Approaches to Popular Culture*, ed. C. W. E. Bigsby, London, Arnold, 1976.

'The English Language and the English Tripos', *Times Literary Supplement*, 15 November

1974, pp. 1293–4.

'On High and Popular Culture', *New Republic*, vol. 171, 23 November 1974, pp. 13–16. Reprinted in *Cambridge Review* (1975).

'Pastoral Versions', review of *Rural Discontent in 19th-Century Britain*, by J. P. D. Dunbabin; *Land and Industry: The Landed Estate and the Industrial Revolution*, ed. J. T. Ward and R. C. Wilson, *New Statesman*, vol. 88, 27 September 1974, pp. 428–9.

1975

'On High and Popular Culture', *Cambridge Review*, vol. 96 (May 1975), pp. 126–9. Reprinted from *The New Republic* (1974).

'The Referendum Choice', *New Statesman*, vol. 89, 30 May 1975, p. 719.

'Variations on a Welsh Theme: On Aspects of the Welsh "Fixation on the Past"', *The Listener*, vol. 94, 2 October 1975, pp. 429–30.

1976

'The Bomb and Democracy–you can't have it both ways', *Sanity*, November 1976, pp. 10. Reprinted from *Sanity*, April 1965 as part of a special issue to celebrate CND programme on BBC-2.

'Contemporary Drama and Social Change in Britain', *Revue de Langues Vivantes* 42 (1976), pp. 624–31.

'The Cultural Contradictions of Capitalism', review of the book by Daniel Bell, *The New York Times Book Review*, 1 February 1976, p. 3.

'Developments in the sociology of Culture', *Sociology* 10 (1976), pp. 497–506. Prepared for the BSA Annual Conference, 1975.

'Legal? Decent? Honest? Truthful?–an argument about advertising', *The Listener*, vol. 96, 16 September 1976, pp. 331–2.

'Notes on Marxism in Britain since 1945', *New Left Review* 100 (1976–7), pp. 81–94.

1977

'The fiction of reform', *Times Literary Supplement*, 25 March 1977, pp. 330–31.

'The Growth and Role of the Mass Media', *International* 3, no. 3 (1977), pp. 3–6. Reprinted as 'The Role of the mass media: a discussion', *Wedge* 1 (1977). In *Media, Politics and Culture*, ed. C. Gardner (Macmillan, 1979).

'A Lecture on Realism', *Screen* 18, no. 1 (1977), pp. 61–74.

'The paths and pitfalls of ideology as an ideology', *Times Higher Education Supplement*, 10 June 1977, p. 13.

Review of *English Jacobin Novel*, by G. Kelly, *Times Literary Supplement*, 25 March 1977, pp. 330–31.

'The Role of the Mass Media', *Wedge*, no. 1 (1977), pp. 33–8.

'The Social Significance of 1926', *Llafur* 2, no. 2 (1977), pp. 5–8.

'The Sociology of Culture', *Gulliver: German-English Yearbook* 2 (1977), pp. 49–53.

'Speak for England,' review of *An Oral History of England: 1900–1975*, compiled by Melvyn Bragg, *The New York Times Book Review*, 27 February 1977, p. 3.

1978

'Commitment', *Stand* 20, no. 3 (1978), pp. 8–11.

'A man confronting a very particular kind of mystery' [On the death of F. R. Leavis], *Times Higher Education Supplement*, 5 May 1978, p. 10.

'Problems of Materialism', *New Left Review* 109 (1978), pp. 3–17.

'Utopia and Science-Fiction', *Science-Fiction Studies* 5 (1978), pp. 203–14. Reprinted in *Problems in Materialism and Culture*.

1979

'The Arts Council', *Political Quarterly* 50 (1979), pp. 157–71.

1980

'Beyond actually existing socialism', *New Left Review*, no. 120 (1980), pp. 3–19. Reprinted in *Problems in Materialism and Culture*.

'From Communism to Marxism', review of *Marxism: For and Against*, by R. L. Heilbroner, *New York Times Book Review*, 13 April 1980, p. 11.

'Gravity's Python', review of *From Fringe to Flying Circus*, by Roger Wilmut, *London Review of Books* 2, no. 23, 4–17 December 1980, p. 14.

'Isn't the news terrible?', review of *More Bad News*, Glasgow University Media Group; *The Whole World is Watching*, by Todd Gitlin, *London Review of Books* 2, no. 13, 3–16 July 1980, pp. 6–7.

'Pierre Bourdieu and the sociology of culture: an introduction', by Nicholas Garnham and Raymond Williams, *Media, Culture and Society* 2 (1980), pp. 209–23. Reprinted in *Media, Culture and Society* (1986).

'The Politics of Nuclear Disarmament', *New Left Review*, no. 124 (1980), pp. 25–42. Reprinted in *Exterminism and Cold War*, London, New Left Books, 1982.

'The Role of the Literary Magazine', *Times Literary Supplement*, 6 June 1980, p. 637.

'The Writer: Commitment and Alignment', *Marxism Today*, June 1980, pp. 22–5. Marx memorial Lecture, March 1980.

1981

'An Alternative Politics', *Socialist Register* (1981), pp. 1–10.

'Die Politik der atomaren Abrustung', *Das Argument*, no. 127 (May–June 1981), pp. 352–66. From *New Left Review*, no. 124 (1980).

'English Brecht', review of *Collected Plays*, vols. V and VI, *London Review of Books* 3, no. 13, 16 July–5 August 1981, pp. 19–20.

'Ideas and the labour movement', *New Socialist* no. 2, November/December 1981, pp. 28–33.

'Marxism, Structuralism and Literary Analysis', *New Left Review*, no. 129 (1981), pp. 51–66. Reprinted in *Writing in Society*.

Review of *George Orwell, A Life*, by Bernard Crick, *Marxism Today*, June 1981, pp. 28–9.

'Talking to Ourselves', *The Cambridge Review* 102 (27 April 1981), pp. 160–64.

'Their bark may well be lost, if it is not tempest tossed', *Guardian*, 24 January 1981, p. 11. On Cambridge English and the MacCabe dispute.

1982

'Democracy and parliament', *Marxism Today* 26, no. 6 (June 1982), pp. 14–21. Socialist Society pamphlet, 1982.

'Distance', *London Review of Books*, 17–30 June 1982, pp. 19–20.
'How to be the arrow, not the target', *Irish Broadcasting Review*, no. 15 (1982), pp. 16–21. From an address to the Festival of Film and Television in the Celtic Countries, Wexford, March 1982.

1983

'Cambridge English and Beyond', *London Review of Books* 5, no. 12, 7–20 July 1983, pp. 3–8. Reprinted in *Writing in Society*.
'Problems of the Coming Period', *New Left Review*, no. 140 (1983), pp. 7–18. Talk for the Socialist Society, May 1983.
'The Red and the Green', review of *Socialism and Survival*, by Rudloph Bahro and *Capitalist Democracy in Britain*, by Ralph Miliband; *Socialist Register 1982*, edited by Martin Eve and David Musson, *London Review of Books* 5, no. 2, 3–16 February 1983, pp. 3, 5.
'The Robert Tressel Memorial Lecture, 1982', *History Workshop*, no. 16 (Autumn 1983), pp. 74–82.

1984

'Nineteen Eighty Four in 1984', *Marxism Today*, January 1984, pp. 12–16. Reprinted in *Monthly Review* 36, no. 7 (December 1984), pp. 13–28. From 1984 edition of *Orwell*.
'Splits, pacts and coalitions', *New Socialist*, no. 16, March/April 1984, pp. 31–5. Reprinted in *The Future of the Left*, ed. J. Curran, Cambridge, Polity Press and New Socialist 1984.

1985

'Community', review of *The Taliesin Tradition: A Quest for the Welsh Identity*, by Emyr Humphries; *Jones: A Novel*, by Emyr Humphreys; *Wales! Wales?*, by Dai Smith; *The Matter of Wales: Epic Views of a Small Country*, by Jan Morris, *London Review of Books*, vol. 7, no. 1, 24 January 1985, pp. 14–15.
'Mining the meaning: Key words in the miners' strike', *New Socialist*, no. 25, March 1985, pp. 6–9.
'Ruskin among others', review of *John Ruskin: The Early Years*, by Tim Hilton, *London Review of Books* 7, 20 June 1985, p. 18.
'Torches for Superman', review of *By the Open Sea*, by August Strindberg, tr. Mary Sandbach; *August Strindberg*, by Olaf Lagercrantz, tr. Anselm Hollo; *Strindberg: a Biography*, by Michael Meyer, *London Review of Books*, vol. 7, 21 November 1985, pp. 17–18.
'Walking backwards into the future', *New Socialist*, no. 27, May 1985, pp. 21–3.

1986

'Towards Many Socialisms', *Socialist Review*, no. 85 (January-February 1986), pp. 45–65, paper delivered at Roundtable '85, 'Socialism on the Threshold of the Twenty-first Century', held at Cavtat, Yugoslavia, 21–6 October, 1985. Reprinted in *Socialism on the Threshold of the Twenty-first Century* (Verso Books, 1985).
'Desire', review of *Landscape for a Good Woman: A Story of Two Lives*, by Carolyn Steedman, *London Review of Books*, vol. 8, 17 April 1986, pp. 8–9.

'The Uses of Cultural Theory', *New Left Review* 158 (July/August 1986), pp. 19–31.

1987

'The Future of English', News From Nowhere, no. 3 (May 1987), pp. 14–25. Talk for Oxford English Limited, 28 January 1987.

'Past Masters', review of *Joachim of Fiore and the Myth of the Eternal Evangel in the 19th Century*, by Marjorie Reeves and Warwick Gould; *Beauty and Belief: Aesthetics and Religion in Victorian Literature*, by Hilary Fraser; *The Correspondance of John Ruskin and Charles Elliot Norton*, ed. John Bradley and Ian Ousby, *London Review of Books*, vol. 9, no. 12, 25 June 1987, pp. 13–14.

1988

'Art: Freedom as Duty', *planet*, 68 (April/May 1988), pp. 7–14. Lecture to a 1979 conference at UCW Aberystwyth and the Welsh Arts Council.

'The Importance of community', *Radical Wales*, No. 18 (Summer 1988), pp. 16–20. Text of lectures for 1977 Plaid Cymru Summer School at Llandudno.

7 Book reviews in the *Guardian*

[Reprint in *The Manchester Guardian Weekly* in brackets]

'The reaction to Coleridge', review of *Coleridge the Visionary*, by J. B. Beer, 17 July 1959, p. 4. [23 July 1959, p. 10]

'Messages from a spiritual storm-centre', review of *Collected Letters of Samuel Coleridge* vols 3 and 4, edited by E. L. Griggs, 11 September 1959, p. 6.

'Fiction and ideas: the case of George Eliot', review of *The Novels of George Eliot*, by Jerome Thrale, 9 October 1959, p. 6. ['Ideas and the novelist', 15 October 1959, p. 10]

'Views from the ante-rooms of power', review of *The Spare Chancellor*, by Alister Buchan, 16 October 1959, p. 9.

'The clerk without a church', review of *The Life of John Middleton Murray*, by F. A. Lea, 6 November 1959, p. 8. ['Reassembling a writer', 12 November 1959, p. 11]

'The hallmarks of American', review of *American Critical Essays, Twentieth Century*, edited by Harold Beaver, 27 November 1959. ['American critical writing', 3 December 1959, p. 10]

'A thinker in politics', review of *Coleridge: Critic of Society*, by John Colmer, 11 December 1959, p. 6. ['A thinker in politics', 24 December 1959, p. 10]

'Children and writers', review of *Young Writers, Young Readers*, edited by Boris Ford, 15 January 1960, p. 8.

'Shelley and science', review of *Shelley, his Thought and Work*, by Desmond King-Hale, 12 February 1960, p. 8.

'The Western literary heritage', review of *Literature and Western Man*, by J. B. Priestly, 19 February 1960, p. 7. ['Western literary heritage', 25 February 1959, p. 10]

'The roots of education', review of *Studies in the History of Education*, 1780–1870, by Brian Simon, 14 April 1960, p. 10.

'The necessary general view', review of *Studies in American Culture*, ed. Joseph J. Kwiat and Mary C. Turpie, 13 May 1960, p. 6. ['Taking the broad view', 19 May 1960, p. 10]

'Commentary on critics', review of *The Chartered Mirror*, by John Holloway, 27 May 1960, p. 9. [2 June 1960, p. 11]

'Common-sense romanticism', review of *Image and Experience*, by Graham Hough, 17 June 1960, p. 6.

'Mr. Winters and Professor X', review of *In Defence of Reason*, by Yvor Winters, 1 July 1960. [7 July 1960, p. 11]

'A scrapbook of reflections', review of *For Love or Money*, by Richard Rees, 12 August 1960, p. 5. [18 August 1960, p. 11]

'Literary and historical', review of *Critical History of English Literature*, by David Daiches, 23 September 1960, p. 8. [29 September 1960, p. 10]

'The uses of biology', review of *Darwin and Butler: Two versions of evolution*, by Basil Wiley, 30 September 1960, p. 8.

'Creative resources', review of *The Creative Vision: Modern European Writers on Their Art*, ed. Haskell M. Block and Herman Salinger, 25 November 1960, p. 9.

'Eliot and belief', review of *T. S. Eliot and the Idea of Tradition*, by Sean Lucy; *The Plays of T. S. Eliot*, by D. E. Jones, 9 December 1960, p. 6. ['The problem of T. S. Eliot', 15 December 1960, p. 11]

'A version of realism', review of *Realism and Imagination*, by Joseph Chiari, 23 December 1960, p. 5. [29 December 1960, p. 10]

'Orpheus and Darwin', review of *The Orphic Voice*, by Elizabeth Sewell, 10 February 1961, p. 6.

'Patterns in literature', review of *Some Mythical Elements in English Literature*, by E. M. W. Tillyard, 24 February 1961, p. 9. ['Centres of reference', 2 March 1961, p. 10]

'Creators and consumers', review of *Brecht*, by Ronald Gray; *Ionesco*, by Richard N. Coe, 24 March 1961, p. 15. [30 March 1961, p. 10]

'The recovery of Hardy', review of *Thomas Hardy*, by Douglas Brown, 28 April 1961, p. 8. ['Hardy rehabilitated', 4 May 1961, p. 11]

'The human footnote', review of *Edith Simcox and George Eliot*, by K. A. McKenzie, 26 May 1961, p. 7. [1 June 1961, p. 11]

'Writers and "the writer"', review of *The Writer's Dilemma*, ed. Times Literary Supplement, 9 June 1961, p. 8. [15 June 1961, p. 10]

'Universal brotherhood', review of *On Human Unity*, by E. E. Hirschmann, 30 June 1961, p. 7. ['A reaffirmation of brotherhood', 6 July 1961, p. 10]

'Lessons of the masters', review of S. Gorley Putt on F. R. Leavis and C. P. Snow in *Essays and Studies, 1961*, 7 July 1961. [13 July 1961, p. 12]

'Literature and society: Raymond Williams replies to Donald Davie', 11 August 1961. A response to Davie, 'Towards a New Aestheticism?', in the *Guardian*, 21 July 1961, p. 7.

'The end of a mimic', review of *The Old Man at the Zoo*, by Angus Wilson, 29 September 1961, p. 7. [5 October 1961, p. 11]

'Critical Pelican', review of *The Modern Age*, The Pelican Guide to English Literature, vol. 7, ed. Boris Ford, 6 October 1961, p. 6.

'The art of a moralist', review of *The Art of George Eliot*, by W. J. Harvey, 20 October 1961, p. 6 [26 October 1961, p. 11]

'The meaning of tragedy', review of *The Death of Tragedy*, by George Steiner, 10 November 1961, p. 7.

'Experiment in reading', review of *An Experiment in Criticism*, by C. S. Lewis, 15 December 1961, p. 7.

'Looking around Utopia', review of *Heavens Below – Utopian Expeirments in England, 1560-1960*, by W. H. G. Armytage, 5 January 1962, p. 5. [11 January 1962, p. 10]

'Critic on top', review of *The Function of Criticism*, by Yvor Winters, 9 March 1962, p. 6. ['The crack of the critical whip', 15 March 1962, p. 11]

'Letters from Lawrence', review of *The Collected Letters of D. H. Lawrence*, ed. Harry T. Moore, 2 vols, 23 March 1962, p. 8. [29 March 1962, p. 11]

'Island story', review of *Island*, by Aldous Huxley, 30 March 1962, p. 6. ['Island experiment', 5 April 1962, p. 10]

'A matter of judgement', review of *Puzzles and Epiphanies*, by Frank Kermode, 11 May 1962, p. 6. [17 May 1962, p. 10]

'A continuing dialogue', review of paperback editions of *A Modern Symposium*, by Lowes Dickinson, introduced by E. M. Forster; *Notes towards the definition of culture*, by T. S. Eliot; *Literature, Popular Culture and Society*, by Leo Lowenthal; *The House of Intellect*, by Jacques Barzun; *The Captive Mind*, by Czeslaw Milosz, 15 June 1962, p. 7.

'Meanings of romantic', review of *Classic, Romantic and Modern*, by Jacques Barzun, 24 August 1962, p. 4. ['In defence of romanticism', 30 August 1962, p. 10]

'Nightmare and normality', review of *The Dark Comedy*, by J. L. Styan, 5 October 1962, p. 13. [11 October 1962, p. 10]

'Self and place', review of *Living in Croesor* by Philip O'Connor, 26 October 1962, p. 6.

'Stratford swans or what?', review of *Contemporary Theatre*, ed. J. R. Brown and B. Harris, 30 November 1962, p. 9. [6 December 1962, p. 11]

'Books of the year', the most interesting books of 1962; reissue of *Auto-da-Fe*, by Elias Canetti; translation of *The Historical Novel*, by Georg Lukács; *The Politics of Oil*, by Robert Engler, 21 December 1962, p. 8.

'A philosophy of emotion', review of *Philosophical Sketches*, by Suzanne Langer, 28 December 1962, p. 6. [3 January 1963, p. 10]

'Contemporary', review of *Contemporaries*, by Alfred Kazin, 1 February 1963, p. 7. ['The mask of orthodoxy', 7 February 1963, p. 10]

'Monumental history', review of *English Literature 1789-1815*, by W. L. Renwick, 15 February 1963, p. 7. ['One kind of history', 21 February 1963, p. 11]

'An effect of alienation', review of *The Public Happiness*, by August Heckscher, 29 March 1963, p. 7. [4 April 1963, p. 11]

'Pulp pioneers', review of *Fiction for the Working Man 1830-1850*, by Louis James, 27 September 1963, p. 8. ['Pulp pioneers', 3 October 1963, p. 10]

'Literature and conviction', review of *The Dream and the Task*, by Graham Hough; *Logic and Criticism*, by William Righter; *Experience into Words*, by D. W. Harding, 11 October 1963, p. 9. ['Literature and morals', 17 October 1963, p. 11, first two books only]

'Scrutiny', review of *Scrutiny*, vols 1–20, 25 October 1963, p. 9.

'The Dickens argument', review of *Dickens and Education*, by Philip Collins, 22 November 1963, p. 6.

'Shaw and others', review of *Shaw and the Nineteenth Century Theatre*, by Martin Meisel; *The Drama of Chekhov, Synge, Yeats and Pirandello*, by F. L. Lucas, 3 January 1964, p. 6. ['Bernard Shaw and others', 9 January 1964, p. 11]

'Gracious mean', review of *The Age of Equipoise*, by W. L. Burn, 24 January 1964, p. 7.

'Ceremony for a radical', review of *The Radical Tradition*, by R. H. Tawney, 21 February 1964, p. 8. ['Politics and the quality of life', 27 February 1964, p. 10]

'A human abstract', review of *Science: The Glorious Entertainment,* by Jacques Barzun, 15 May 1964, p. 8.

'The rhetoric of death', review of *The Mortal No: Death and the Modern Imagination,* by Frederick J. Hoffman, 12 June 1964, p. 7. ['Rhetoric of death', 18 June 1964, p. 10]

'Strange ideology', review of *John Addington Symonds: A Biography,* by Phyllis Grosskurth, 3 July 1964, p. 7. ['A deviant ideology', 9 July 1964, p. 11]

'The believers', review of *The Unbelievers,* by A. O. J. Cockshut, 10 July 1964, p. 8. [16 July 1964, p. 10]

'Sincerity', review of *Wordsworth and the Poetry of Sincerity,* by David Perkins, 28 August 1964, p. 7.

'Edwardian illusion', review of *Edwardian England 1901–1914,* edited by Simon Nowell-Smith, 9 October 1964, p. 9. [15 October 1964, p. 11]

'Not public enough', review of *Corridors of Power,* by C. P. Snow, 6 November 1964, p. 8. ['Public and private lives', 12 November 1964, p. 10]

'Professional writer', review of *The Profession of English Letters,* by J. W. Saunders, 27 November 1964, p. 13. ['Writing to live', 3 December 1964, p. 11]

'Creative power', review of *Power in Men,* by Joyce Cary, 11 December 1964. ['Creative energy', 17 December 1964, p. 11)

'Workers College', review of *The Central Labour College,* by William W. Craik, 1 January 1965, p. 6.

'Early Dickens', review of *The Letters of Charles Dickens,* vol. 1, 1820–39 ed. Madeline House and Graham Storey; *Dickens from Pickwick to Dombey,* by Stephen Marcus, 5 February 1965. ['Dickens and his day', 11 February 1965, p. 10]

'The uses of France', review of *The View of France from Arnold to Bloomsbury,* by Christophe Campos; *A Comparative View of French and British Civilization 1850–1870,* by F. C. Green, 26 March 1965, p. 9. ['Looking across to France', 8 April 1965, p. 10]

'Exploration and commitment', review of *Further Explorations,* by L. C. Knights, 9 April 1965, p. 15.

'Conservative values', review of *Education and Values,* by G. H. Bantock, 23 April 1965, p. 9. ['A conservative view of education', 29 April 1965, p. 10]

'Old year letter', review of *New Year Letter,* by W. H. Auden, 21 May 1965, p. 9.

'Articles as books and books as articles', review of *A Sad Heart at the Supermarket,* by Randall Jarrell; *Doings and Undoings,* by Norman Podhoretz, 11 June 1965, p. 8.

'A liberal critic', review of *A Vision of Reality,* by Frederick Grubb, 2 July 1965, p. 7.

'Revolt and conformity', review of *The Theatre of Revolt,* by Robert Brustein, 9 July 1965, p. 7.

'Ideas in politics', review of *The Pursuit of Certainty,* by Shirley Robin, 24 September 1965.

'Cauldwell', review of *The Concept of Freedom,* by Christopher Cauldwell; *Poems,* by Christopher Cauldwell, 12 November 1965, p. 9. ['A young man's papers', 18 November 1965, p. 11]

'The world we have changed', review of *The World We Have Lost,* by Peter Laslett, 19 November 1965, p. 8. [25 November 1965, p. 10]

'A critic in action', review of *Writers and Politics,* by Conor Cruise O'Brien, 26 November 1965, p. 13. [2 December 1965, p. 11]

'A laurel for Hardy', review of *Thomas Hardy: The Will And The Way,* by Roy Morrell;

Hardy of Wessex, by Carl J. Weber; *The Dynasts,* by Thomas Hardy, 10 December 1965, p. 6. ['Learning about Hardy', 16 December 1965, p. 10]

'Beyond liberalism', review of *Beyond Culture,* by Lionel Trilling, 15 April 1966, p. 8. [21 April 1966, p. 10]

'Chronicles', review of *The Beginners,* by Dan Jacobsen, 27 May 1966, p. 7. [9 June 1966, p. 11]

'Tolstoy in England', review of *Tolstoy and the Novel,* by John Bayley, 21 October 1966, p. 7.

'Any old myths?', review of *The Primal Curse: the myth of Cain and Abel in the theatre,* by Honor Matthews, 13 January 1967, p. 7.

'Coleridge today', review of *Coleridge: The Work and the Relevance,* by William Walsh, 24 February 1967, p. 7.

'William Morris', review of *The Work of William Morris,* by Paul Thompson, 3 March 1967, p. 7.

'Fenland people', review of *Fenland Chronicle,* by Sybil Marshall, 31 March 1967, p. 9.

'Novels and ideas', review of *Sartre: Romantic Rationalist,* by Iris Murdoch, 12 May 1967, p. 8. ['Novels, politics and ideas', 18 May 1967, p. 11]

'Hardy in public', *Thomas Hardy's Personal Writings,* edited by Harold Orel, 19 May 1967, p. 7. [25 May 1967, p. 10]

'Father knew George Orwell', review of *The Crystal Spirit: A Study of George Orwell,* by George Woodcock, 26 May 1967, p. 7. [1 June 1967, p. 10]

'Radical landmarks', review of *The Autobiography of Samuel Bamford, Vol. 1, Early Days; Vol. 2, Passages in the Life of a Radical,* ed. W. H. Chaloner; *The Autobiography of a Working Man,* by Alexander Somerville with a preface by Brian Behan, 7 July 1967, p. 5.

'Never trust the critic', review of *'Anna Karenina' and Other Essays,* by F. R. Leavis, 1 December 1967, p. 9. ['The critic and the tale', 7 December 1967, p. 11]

'Another Pheonix', review of *Pheonix II:* Uncollected, unpublished and other prose works by D. H. Lawrence, ed. Warren Roberts and Harry T. Moore, 19 January 1968, p. 7. ['From the Lawrence ashes', 25 January 1968]

'Talking to intellectuals', review of *Intellectuals Today: Problems in a Changing Society,* by T. R. Fyvel, 1 March 1968, p. 7. [7 March 1968, p. 10]

'The left in the thirties', review of *The Left Review,* October 1934 – May 1938, reprinted in eight volumes in the series English Little Magazines, 22 March 1968, p. 9.

'A choice of worlds', review of *The Ordinary Universe: Soundings in Modern Literature,* by Denis Donoghue, 5 July 1968, p. 7. ['The man who bites the coins', 11 July 1968, p. 11]

'How we see suffering', review of *Cancer Ward,* by Alexander Solzhenitsyn, 20 September 1968, p. 9. ['Complexities of pain and pity', 26 September 1968, p. 15]

'Blair to Orwell', review of *Collected Essays, Journalism and Letters of George Orwell,* 4 vols, by George Orwell, 4 October 1968, p. 6. ['From Blair to Orwell', 10 October 1968, p. 14]

'Work on the human voice', review of *The First Circle,* by Alexander Solzhenitsyn, 15 November 1968, p. 6. ['Solzhenitsyn's courage', 21 November 1968, p. 14]

'The need for Sartre', review of *The Philosophy of Jean-Paul Sartre,* ed. and introduced by Robert Denoon Cumming, 29 November 1968, p. 11.

'Air or nothing', review of *Experiment in Autobiography,* by H. G. Wells, 24 January

1969, p. 7. ['A case of air or nothing', 30 January 1969, p. 14]

'A report on suffering', review of *Cancer Ward, Part Two*, by Alexander Solzhenitsyn, 9 March 1969, p. 9. [20 March 1969, p. 14]

'Spender on students', review of *The Year of the Young Rebels*, by Stephen Spender, 17 April 1969, p. 9. ['Mr. Spender and the students', 24 April 1969, p. 14]

'For and against Mill', review of *Mill: A Collection of Critical Essays*, ed. J. B. Schneewind, 12 June 1969, p. 9. ['Our liberal friend', 19 June 1969, p. 15]

'On structures', review of *Conversations with Claude Levi-Strauss*, by G. Charbonnier, tr. by J. Weightman and D. Weightman, 26 June 1969, p. 9.

'Getting the inside story', review of *The Right to Know: The Rise of the World Press*, by Francis Williams, 3 July 1969, p. 9. ['Getting outside the inside story', 10 July 1969, p. 14]

'Black and White', review of *Murderous Angels*, by Conor Cruise O'Brien, 10 July, p. 7. [17 July 1969, p. 18]

'Coleridge as The Friend', review of *The Friend*, by S. T. Coleridge, edited by Barbara E. Rooke, 7 August 1969, p. 5. [14 August 1969, p. 18]

'Romantic revival', review of *Romanticism*, edited by John B. Halstad, 21 August 1969, p. 7. [28 August 1969, p. 18]

'Provocations', review of *Shaw – 'The Chucker-Out'*, by Allan Chappelow, 18 September 1969, p. 9. ['No ordinary playwright', 17 September 1969, p. 19.

'In the city of apples', review of *The Keeper of Antiquities*, by Yury Dombrovsky, tr. Michael Glenny, 23 October 1969, p. 9. ['City of apples', 1 November 1969, p. 18]

'Changing the terms of reason', review of *American power and the new mandarins*, by Noam Chomsky, 30 October 1969, p. 8. ['The moments of decision', 8 November 1969, p. 16]

'Dickens at 157', review of *The Uncollected Writings of Charles Dickens: Household Words, 1850–1859*, ed. Harry Stone; *The Letters of Charles Dickens, Volume Two, 1840–1841* ed. Madelaine House and Graham Storey; *Charles Dickens, 1812–1870, A Centenary Volume*, ed. E. W. F. Tomlin, 20 November 1969, p. 8.

'The ruling class', review of *The English Ruling Class*, ed. W. L. Guttsman, 27 November 1969, p. 10. ['The class apart', 6 December 1969, p. 18]

'A refusal to be resigned', review of *English Literature in Our Time and the University*, by F. R. Leavis, 18 December 1969, p. 7.

'Beyond protest', review of *The Limits of Protest*, by Peter Buchman, 8 January 1970.

'Masters and others', review of Fontana Modern Masters series, ed. Frank Kermode: *Camus*, by Conor Cruise O'Brien; *Fanon*, by David Caute; *Levi-Strauss*, by Edmund Leach; *Marcuse*, by Alasdair MacIntyre; *Guevara*, by Andrew Sinclair, 15 January 1970, p. 9. ['Mixed bag', 24 January 1970, p. 19]

'Practical critic', review of *Speaking to Each Other*, vol. 1, *About Society*; vol. 2, *About Literature*, by Richard Hoggart, 26 February 1970. ['Keeping up with Hoggart', 7 March 1970, p. 18]

'Young Brecht', review of *Bertolt Brecht: Collected Plays*, vol. 1, 1918–23, ed. John Willet and Ralph Manheim, 22 April 1970, p. 9. [9 May 1970, p. 19]

'Dickens celebrations', review of *The World of Charles Dickens*, by Angus Wilson; *Inimitable Dickens*, by A. E. Dyson; *Dickens's England*, by Michael and Mollie Hardwick, 28 May 1970, p. 15. ['The Dickens Celebrations', 6 June 1970, p. 18]

'Violence and confusion', review of *On Violence*, by Hannah Arendt, 25 June 1970, p. 14

['Violence defined', 4 July 1970, p. 18]

'Report in repertory', review of *Brief Chronicles: Essays on Modern Theatre*, by Martin Esslin, 2 July 1970, p. 9. [11 July 1970, p. 18]

'Notes on a campaign'. Review of *Fears of Fragmentation*, by Arnold Wesker, 16 July 1970.

'Theory and practice', review of *A Theory of Communication*, by Philip Hobsbaum, 3 September 1970, p. 7.

'Myth and intimations', review of *The Rape of Tamar*, by Dan Jacobson, 1 October 1970, p. 9.

'Teletalk', review of *The New Priesthood: British Television Today*, by Joan Bakewell and Nicholas Garnham, 5 November 1970, p. 9.

'A power to fight', review of *The Stubborn Structure: Essays on Criticism and Society*, by Northrop Frye, 12 November 1970, p. 9.

'Varieties of protest', review of *Protest and Discontent*, edited by Bernard Crick and William A. Robson, 26 November 1970, p. 12.

'Open change', review of *Industrialization and Culture, 1830–1914*, ed. Christopher Harvie, Graham Martin and Aaron Scharf, 31 December 1970, p. 7.

'Working class politics', review of *Respectable Radical: George Howell and Victorian Working Class Politics*, by F. M. Leventhal; *The Decline of Working Class Politics*, by Barry Hindess, 28 January 1971, p. 7. [6 February 1971, p. 16]

'Socialism active and passive', review of *History and Class Consciousness*, by Georg Lukács; *Solzhenitsyn*, by Georg Lukács, 25 February 1971, p. 8.

'Good societies', review of *The Good Society. A book of readings*, ed. Anthony Arblaster and Stephen Lukes, 13 May 1971, p. 9. [22 May 1971, p. 18]

'Who speaks for Wales', review of *The Welsh Extremist: A Culture in Crisis*, by Ned Thomas, 3 June 1971.

'Labour and/or socialism', review of *The Crisis of British Socialism*, by Ken Coates, 1 July 1971, p. 9. ['The shame of the sixties', 10 July 1971, p. 18]

'Reading Carlyle', *Thomas Carlyle: Selected Writings*, ed. Alan Shelston; *Thomas Carlyle: Critical heritage*, ed. Jules Paul Seigel; *The Carlyles*, by John Stewart Collis, 18 November 1971, p. 11. [27 November 1971, p. 25]

'Radical categories', review of *Radical Man*, by Charles Hampden-Turner, 9 December 1971, p. 8. [27 January 1972]

'The novel and the people', *Working-Class Stories of the 1890s*, ed. P. J. Keating; *The Working-Classes in Victorian Fiction*, by P. J. Keating, 30 December 1971, p. 13. [8 January 1972]

'General studies?', review of *The Twentieth Century Mind: Vol. 1: 1900–1918*, ed. C. B. Cox and A. E. Dyson, 20 January 1972, p. 11.

'Beyond social abstractions', review of *Beyond Freedom and Dignity*, by B. F. Skinner, 9 March 1972, p. 14.

'Open-circuit television', review of *Television and the People: a program for democratic participation*, by Brian Groombridge, 27 April 1972, p. 14. [6 May 1972, p. 22]

'Suspecting the left', review of *The Suspecting Glance*, by Conor Cruise O'Brien, 8 June 1972, p. 16. ['Illiberal reactions', 17 June 1972, p. 23]

'Creative quarrelling?', review of *Nor Shall My Sword: Discourses on pluralism, compassion, and social hope*, by F. R. Leavis, 13 July 1972, p. 14. [29 July 1972, p. 22]

'Russia betrayed', review of *August 1914*, by Alexander Solzhenitsyn, tr. Michael Glenny,

21 September 1972, p. 14. [30 September 1972, p. 22]

'Stand up for what?', review of *The Obscenity Report*, introduced by John Trevelyn, preface by Maurice Girodias; *Pornography: The Longford Report; The Case against Pornography*, ed. David Holbrook, 28 September 1972, p. 16. [7 October 1972, p. 29]

'A radical miscellany', review of *Radical Perspectives in the Arts*, ed. Lee Baxindall, 26 April 1973, p. 26. ['The Marx Arts', 5 May 1973, p. 26]

'No wealth but life', review of *Interpretations and Forecasts, 1922–1972*, by Lewis Mumford, 23 August 1973, p. 9. ['The other Mumford', 1 September 1973, p. 23]

'A city and its writers', review of *Charles Baudelaire: A Lyric Poet in the Era of High Capitalism*, by Walter Benjamin, tr. Harry Zohn, 30 August 1973, p. 12. ['Baudelaire's Paris', 8 September 1973, p. 22]

'Against monopoly', review of *Tools for Conviviality*, by Ivan D. Illich, 27 September 1973, p. 11.

'Systems of error', review of *For Reasons of State*, by Noam Chomsky; *The Backroom Boys*, by Noam Chomsky; *Problems of Knowledge and Freedom*, by Noam Chomsky, 1 November 1973, p. 11.

'Radical Blake', review of *The Notebook of William Blake: A photographic and typographic facsimile*, ed. David V. Erdman; *The 'Heaven' and 'Hell' of William Blake*, by G. R. Sabri-Tabrizi, 29 November 1973, p. 15.

'Developing what?', review of *Education For Liberation*, by Adam Curle, 27 December 1973, p. 7. [12 January 1974, p. 24]

'The Frankfurt School', review of *The Dialectical Imagination*, by Martin Jay; *Aspects of Sociology*, by Frankfurt Institute for Social Research, with a preface by Max Horkheimer and Theodor Adorno; *Negative Dialectics*, by Theodor Adorno, tr. E. B. Ashton; *The Jargon of Authenticity*, by Theodor Adorno, tr. Knut Tarnowski and Frederick Will, 14 February 1974, p. 14. [26 January 1974, p. 23]

'Knots of socialism', review of *The Socialist Register 1973*, ed. Ralph Miliband and John Saville, 14 February 1974, p. 14. [23 February 1974, p. 24]

'Who are the intellectuals?', review of *Between Existentialism and Marxism*, by Jean-Paul Sartre; *Sartre*, by Hazel E. Barnes; *Camus and Sartre*, by Germaine Bree, 25 April 1974, p. 17.

'Working lives', review of *Useful Toil: Autobiographies of Working People from the 1820s to the 1920s*, ed. John Burnett, 13 June 1974, p. 9.

'Shelley plain', review of *Shelley: The Pursuit*, by Richard Holmes; *Shelley*, selected by Kathleen Raine, 25 July 1974, p. 9. [3 August 1974, p. 21]

'In the great tradition', review of *The Great Web: the form of Hardy's major fiction*, by Ian Gregor; *Thomas Hardy and History*, by R. J. White, 8 August 1974, p. 9. [17 August 1974, p. 22]

'Vindication of a radical', review of *The Life and Death of Mary Wollstonecraft*, by Claire Tomalin, 5 September 1974, p. 14. [14 September 1974, p. 22]

'When myth meets myth', review of *The Eating of the Gods: An Interpretation of Greek tragedy*, by Jan Kott, 10 October 1974, p. 16. [19 October 1974, p. 20]

'Is there anything wrong?', review of *The Socialist Idea: A Reappraisal*, ed. Leszek Kolakowski and Stuart Hampshire, 28 November 1974, p. 11. ['Defining socialism', 7 December 1974, p. 18]

'What the papers don't say', review of *Newspaper Money: Fleet Street and the search for the Affluent Reader*, by Fred Hirsch and David Gordon; *Paper Voices: The Popular Press and Social Change*, by A. C. H. Smith, with Elizabeth Immirzi and Trevor Blackwell, 22 May 1975, p. 14. [31 May 1975, p. 17]

'A little more on Hardy', review of *Desperate Remedies; A Pair of Blue Eyes; The Hand of Ethelberts; A Laodicean; Two on a tower; The Well-Beloved* (New Wessex Edition), by Thomas Hardy; *Thomas Hardy: The Forms of Tragedy*, by Dale Kramer; *Thomas Hardy: An Illustrated Biography*, by Timothy O'Sullivan; *The Genius of Thomas Hardy*, ed. Margaret Drabble, 5 February 1976, p. 7. [15 February 1976, p. 21]

'Only yesterday', review of *The Left in Britain, 1956–1968*, by David Widgery, 12 February 1976, p. 12. ['Left with nothing to celebrate', 22 February 1976, p. 21]

'The anger of exile', review of *Lenin in Zurich*, by Alexander Solzhenitsyn, tr. H. T. Williams, 22 April 1976, p. 9. [9 May 1976, p. 22]

'Meanings of dialectic', review of *Critique of Dialectical Reason*, by Jean-Paul Sartre, tr. Alan Sheridan, 20 January 1977, p. 14.

'All power to the poem', review of *The Spirit Ascent, a trilogy*, by Edward Upward, 28 July 1977, p. 9. ['Power to the poem', 7 August 1977, p. 22]

'A radical perspective', review of *Milton and the English Revolution*, by Christopher Hill, 6 October 1977, p. 9. [16 October 1977, p. 21]

'Politics and letters', review of *Edmund Wilson: Letters on Literature and Politics, 1912–1972*, ed. Elena Wilson, 17 November 1977, p. 10. [1 January 1978, p. 22]

'Enduring ghost', review of *Ibsen: A Dissenting View*, by Ronald Gray, 8 December 1977, p. 10.

'The Englishness of Chaucer', review of *The Life and Times of Chaucer*, by John Gardner, 5 January 1978, p. 7. [15 January 1978, p. 22]

'Rural yet shrewd', review of *The Older Hardy*, by Robert Gittings; *An Essay on Hardy*, by John Bayley, 9 March 1978, p. 11. [19 March 1978, p. 22]

'Explaining the word', review of *Aesthetics and Politics*, ed. New Left Books, 23 March 1978, p. 11.

'The link in Tolstoy', review of *Tolstoy's Letters*, ed. in two volumes by R. F. Christian, 20 April 1978, p. 9. [30 April 1978, p. 22]

'Most generally known', review of *Samuel Johnson*, by W. Jackson Bate, 18 May 1978, p. 10. ['A life of Johnson', 28 May 1978, p. 22]

'The black domain', review of *The Merthyr Rising*, by Gwyn A. Williams, 8 June 1978. ['Black domain', 18 June 1978, p. 22]

'The yapping pack', review of *The Policies of Information*, by Anthony Smith, 3 August 1978, p. 7.

'A call to struggle', review of *The Moment of Scrutiny*, by Francis Mulhern, 17 May 1979, p. 9.

'Dreams and sea', review of *Conrad in the Nineteenth Century*, by Ian Watt, 29 May 1979, p. 16.

'The book of Governors', review of *Governing the BBC*, by Asa Briggs, 29 November 1979, p. 10. [23 December 1979, p. 14]

'Lawrence in the '80s', review of *D. H. Lawrence Country*, by Roy Spencer; *The Life of D. H. Lawrence*, by Keith Sagar, 28 February 1980, p. 7. [9 March 1980, p. 21]

'The Greeks in England', review of *The Victorians and Ancient Greece*, by Richard Jenkyns, 7 August 1980, p. 9. [24 August 1980, p. 22]

'Life on the other side of the tracks', review of *The Railway Workers, 1840–1970*, by Frank McKenna, 16 October 1980, p. 9. [26 October 1980, p. 21]

'The little green book', review of *Edward Carpenter 1844–1929*, by Chushichi Tsuzuki, 20 November 1980, p. 18.

'Straddling the chasm', review of *Mediations: Essays on Brecht, Beckett, and the Media*, by Martin Esslin, 29 January 1981, p. 7.

'1956 and all that', review of *In Anger: Culture in the Cold War, 1945–60*, by Robert Hewison, 2 April 1981, p. 11.

'A future for Europe?', review of *The Dynamics of European Nuclear Disarmament*, by Alva Mydral et al., 13 August 1981, p. 12.

'Writers' reading in 1981', 10 December 1981, p. 14. Eleven *Guardian* writers and readers recall the books that have meant the most to them during the year. [27 December 1981, p. 22]

'Close friends', review of *A Memoir of D. H. Lawrence (The Betrayal)*, by G. H. Neville, 14 January 1982, p. 16. [24 January 1982]

'The reasonable Englishman', review of *An English Temper*, by Richard Hoggart, 8 April 1982, p. 16.

'Danger: intellectuals!', review of *The Transformation of Intellectual Life in Victorian England*, by T. W. Heyck; *Fabianism and Culture*, by Ian Britain, 1 July 1982, p. 8. [11 July 1982, p. 21]

'Putting the Welsh in their place', review of *The Welsh in Their History*, by Gwyn A. Williams, 9 September 1982, p. 8. [19 September 1982, p. 21]

'Movement of faith', review of *The Critic as Anti-Philosopher*, by F. R. Leavis, 11 November 1982, p. 10. [21 November 1982, p. 22]

'Generations out of joint', review of *A Margin of Hope*, by Irving Howe, 10 March 1983, p. 10. [20 March 1983, p. 22]

'The new morality', review of *Eve and the New Jerusalem*, by Barbara Taylor, 17 March 1983, p. 16.

'Ours and not ours', review of *The World, the Text and the Critic*, by Edward Said, 8 March 1984, p. 10.

'The politics of poverty', review of *The Ideas of Mass Poverty: England in the Early Industrial Age*, by Gertrude Himmelfarb, 5 April 1984, p. 18.

'The resonance of Antigone', review of *Antigone*, by George Steiner, 20 July 1984, p. 14.

'Feeling the draft', review of *Mr. Noon*, by D. H. Lawrence, ed. Lindeth Vasey, 13 September 1984, p. 20. [23 September 1984, p. 21]

'Two faces of liberalism', review of *The Rise and Decline of Western Liberalism*, by Anthony Arblaster; *An End to Allegiance*, by Geoffrey Sampson, 11 October 1984, p. 20. [21 October 1984, p. 21]

'Had your letter, yesterday', review of *The Letters of D. H. Lawrence*, Vol. 3, 1916–21, ed. James T. Boulton and Andrew Robertson, 29 November 1984, p. 13.

'The shadow of the dragon', review of *When was Wales?*, by Gwyn A. Williams; *Wales: A History*, by Winford Vaughan-Thomas, 24 January 1985, p. 20.

'The literary civil war', review of *Writing and Revolution in 17th Century England*, vol. 1 of the collected essays of Christopher Hill, 11 April 1985, p. 21.

'Lawrence's century', review of *D. H. Lawrence and Tradition*, ed. Jeffrey Meyers; *D. H. Lawrence: Life into Art*, by Keith Sagar; *Flame into Being: the Life and Work of D. H. Lawrence*, by Anthony Burgess, 19 September 1985, p. 10.

'The better half of Lev Tolstoy', Review of *The Diaries of Sofia Tolstaya*, tra. Cathy Porter; *Tolstoy's Diaries*, tr. R. F. Christian, 28 November 1985, p. 11.

'Clare's voices', review of *The Letters of John Clare*, ed. Mark Storey, 13 February 1986, p. 21.

'A Welsh companion', review of *The Oxford Companion to the Literature of Wales*, ed. Meic Stephens, 27 February 1986, p. 23.

'Elites and loyalties', review of *The Red and the Blue: Intelligence Treason, and the Universities*, by Andrew Sinclair, 19 June 1986, p. 21. [29 July 1986, p. 21]

'How Bloomsbury contrived to borrow time', review of *Victorian Bloomsbury: the early literary history of the Bloomsbury Group*, vol. 1, by S. P. Rosenbaum, 20 February 1987, p. 13.

'The word and the dictator', review of *I The Supreme*, by Augusto Roa Bastos, 13 March 1987, p. 13.

'A novel out of this world', review of *Women in Love*, by D. H. Lawrence, ed. David Farmer; *The Letters of D. H. Lawrence*, vol. IV, 1921–24, ed. Warren Roberts, James T. Boulton and Elizabeth Mansfield, 22 May 1987, p. 13.

'Doing despair', review of *Vladimir's Carrot: Modern Dance and the modern imagination*, by John Peter; *The Field of Drama*, by Martin Esslin, 17 July 1987, p. 13.

8   Articles in *Tribune*

'Man on the run from himself', 27 March 1959, p. 13. See letter from Frederick Harper, 27 April 1959, p. 4.

'Investigator, first investigate yourself!', review of *Britain Revisited*, by Tom Harrison, 21 April 1961, pp. 6–7.

'Sociology's range', review of *Ideology and Society*, by Donald Macrea, 4 August 1961, p. 9.

'Culture and Labour', letter, 14 August 1964, p. 2.

'R. H. Tawney', Voices of Socialism series, 1 January 1965, p. 13. See letter from David Elstein, 15 January 1965, p. 2.

'Tawney's Christianity', letter, 22 January 1965, p. 2.

'We are starting to use our own voices!', 5 March 1965, pp. 1, 6.

'Communications: Just what is Labour's policy for radio?', 18 February 1966, p. 8. See letter from J. R. Grierson, 4 March 1966, p. 11.

'Policy for radio', letter, 11 March 1966, p. 11.

'Oxbridge *Their* Oxbridge', 3 June 1966, p. 6. Invited comment with Stephen Lukes and John Saville on the Franks Report on British Universities.

'Expulsion of Ken Coates', letter with others, 23 September 1966, p. 8.

'The future of broadcasting: what happens after the "pirates" walk the plank?', 7 October 1966, p. 9.

'"Bemused liberalism" from Hugh Jenkins', 21 October 1966, p. 6. See letters from Ronan O'Rahilly and Brian Blain, 14 October 1966.

'Communications put in order', letter, 2 December 1966, p. 8.

'May Day Manifesto 1967', 28 April 1967, p. 5. See letter from John Sheridan, 26 May 1967, p. 9.

'May Day Manifesto', letter, 2 June 1967, p. 8.

'Commercial radio: the thin edge of the wedge?', 2 August 1968, pp. 6–7.

'A National Convention of the Left', 28 March 1969, p. 5.

9 Articles on politics in Britain in *The Nation*

'The culture of politics', vol. 188, 3 January 1959, pp. 10–12.

'The British elections', vol. 199, 28 September 1964, pp. 154–7.

'Letter from Britain' vol. 203, 4 July 1966, pp. 18–19. See correction, p. 90.

'Significance of economic-political crisis; illusions lost', vol. 203, 5 September 1966, pp. 185–7.

'Affluence after anger: on the development of the British "cultural generation" of the 1950's', vol. 203, 19 December 1966, pp. 676–7.

'Britain's press crisis; trend to monopoly', vol. 204, 10 April 1967, pp. 466–7.

'The Catholic crisis: tension between hierarchy and reformers', vol. 205, 17 July 1967, pp. 51–2.

'Socialism's crisis of theory', vol. 206, 26 February 1968, pp. 274–6.

'Great Britain: saying "no" to the Labour Party', vol. 210, 15 June 1970, pp. 710–12.

'Downhill to Dutschke', vol. 212, 15 February 1971, pp. 210–12.

'The Liberals move up fast; Britain's third party', vol. 217, 29 October 1973, pp. 432–4.

'Crisis in Britain: reality behind the appearance', vol. 218, 19 January 1974, pp. 73–4.

'British elections: muddling through to hope', vol. 218, 23 March 1974, pp. 359–61.

'The size of the crisis: Britain after the election', vol. 219, 2 November 1974, pp. 428–30.

'The impossible society: Britain needs a New Left', vol. 220, 28 June 1975, pp. 780–82.

'Structural unemployment: Britain's small deal', vol. 222, 20 March 1976, pp. 330–32.

See section 6 for book review in The Nation, 1959.

10 Television column in *The Listener*

All of these columns are reprinted in *Raymond Williams on Television*, ed. A. O'Connor, Toronto, Between The Lines; London and New York, Routledge, 1989.

'As we see others', 1 August 1968, pp. 154–5.

'Private worlds', 12 September 1968, pp. 346–8.

'Shoot the Prime Minister', 10 October 1968, p. 483.

'The miner and the city', 7 November 1968, p. 623.

'A moral rejection', 5 December 1968, pp. 771–2.

'A new way of seeing', 2 January 1969, pp. 27–8.

'Persuasion', 30 January 1969, pp. 155.

'To the last word: on *The Possessed*', 20 February 1969, pp. 248–9.

'Personal relief time', 20 March 1969, p. 399.

'A noble past', 17 April 1969, p. 543.

'Combined operations', 15 May 1969, p. 697. Reprinted in *Communications*, 3rd edn.

'Based on reality', 12 June 1969, pp. 838–9.

'Watching from elsewhere', 10 July 1969, pp. 59–60.

'Crimes and crimes', 21 August 1969, p. 235. Reprinted in *A Listener Anthology*, ed. K. Miller, London, BBC, 1970.

'Death wish in Venice', 4 September 1969, pp. 322–3.

'Science, art and human interest', 2 October 1969, pp. 462–3.

'Pitmen and pilgrims', 30 October 1969, p. 611.

'Most doctors recommend', 27 November 1969, pp. 770–71.
'A bit of a laugh, a bit of glamour', 25 December 1969, p. 903.
'Brave Old World', 22 January 1970, pp. 126–7.
'The green language', 19 February 1970, pp. 259–60.
'The best things in life aren't free', 19 March 1970, pp. 386–7.
'There's always the sport', 16 April 1970, pp. 522–3.
'Going places', 7 May 1970, pp. 626–7.
'Against adjustment', 4 June 1970, pp. 770–71.
'Back to the world', 2 July 1970, p. 27.
'ITV's domestic romance', 30 July 1970, pp. 159–60. Reprinted in *Communications*, 3rd edn.
'Breaking out', 27 August 1970, pp. 286–7.
'Between us and chaos', 24 September 1970, pp. 432–3.
'The decadence game', 22 October 1970, pp. 557–8.
'A very late stage in bourgeois art', 12 November 1970, pp. 678–9.
'Galton and Simpson's *Steptoe and Son*', 17 December 1970, pp. 854–5.
'Being serious', 14 January 1971, pp. 60–61.
'Billy and Darkly', 11 February 1971, p. 188.
'Programmes and sequences', 11 March 1971, pp. 314–15. Reprinted in *Communications*, 3rd edn.
'Remembering the thirties', 8 April 1971, pp. 463–4.
'Open teaching', 6 May 1971, pp. 594–5.
'Terror', 3 June 1971, pp. 731–2.
'Cowboys and missionaries', 1 July 1971, p. 27.
'Careers and jobs', 29 July 1971, pp. 155–6.
'China-watching', 26 August 1971, p. 281.
'An English autumn', 23 September 1971, pp. 423–4.
'Judges and traitors', 21 October 1971, p. 552.
'Seasame Street', 18 November 1971, p. 700.
'Three documentaries', 16 December 1971, p. 850.
'Raymond Williams writes that free speech is being curtailed, and in ways that are not generally understood', 13 January 1972, pp. 60–61. See reply from Noel Annan, 3 February 1972, pp. 131–3.
'Culture', 10 February 1972, pp. 191.
'Old times and new', 16 March 1972, pp. 351–2.
'Hardy annuals', 6 April 1972, p. 463.
'Where does Rozanov come in?', 4 May 1972, pp. 599–600.
'The golden lotus', 1 June 1972, pp. 739–40.
'Hassle', 27 July 1972, p. 124.
'Natural breaks', 24 August 1972, pp. 251–2. Reprinted in *Communications*, 3rd edn.
'Ad hominem', 14 September 1972, pp. 347–8.
'Versions of Webster', 19 October 1972, pp. 515.
'Intellectual superiority', 16 November 1972, pp. 684–5.
'Why the BBC is like Monty Python's Flying Circus?', 14 December 1972, pp. 839–40.
'The top of the laugh', 10 January 1974, pp. 58–9.
'Isaac's urges', 31 January 1974, p. 155.

Williams's other contributions to *The Listener* are listed in section 6.
For a column on American television see 'Views', *The Listener* (1973).

11 Book reviews in *New Society*

'Mill, Arnold and the Zeitgeist', review of *Matthew Arnold and John Stuart Mill*, by
Edward Alexander, 10 June 1965, pp. 31–2.

'The achievement of Balzac', review of *Prometheus*, by Andre Maurois, 4 November 1965,
pp. 28–9.

'The pain of industrial relations', review of *It Was Not in the News*, by Max Cohen, 2
December 1965, pp. 33–4.

'A critic in business', review of *The Collected Works of Walter Bagehot*, vols 1 and 2, ed.
Norman St John-Stevas, 6 January 1966, pp. 23–4.

'Ordinary letters', review of *The letters of Mrs. Gaskell*, ed. J. A. V. Chapple and Arthur
Pollard, 1 December 1966, pp. 843–4.

'Shifting barriers', review of *Class*, ed. Richard Mabey, 2 March 1967, pp. 324–5.

'A Northampton family', review of *The Underprivileged*, by Jeremy Seabrook, 27 April
1967, p. 621.

'Cambridge reforms', review of *The Revolution of the Dons: Cambridge and Society in
Victorian England*, by Sheldon Rothblatt, 8 February 1968, p. 204.

'Against academic orthodoxy', review of *The Dissenting Academy*, ed. Theodore Roszak, 4
April 1968, p. 507.

'Up north', review of *Working Class Community*, by Brian Jackson, 25 April 1968, pp.
611–12.

'Secondary stuff', review of *The Victorian Debate*, by Raymond Chapmen, 25 July 1968,
pp. 134–5.

'Man of letters', review of *The Rise and Fall of the Man of Letters*, by John Gross, 22 May
1969, p. 809.

'Beyond words', review of *The Sociology of Literature*, by Diana T. Laurenson and Alan
Swingswood, 24 August 1972, p. 404.

'Television and the mandarins', on the Annan Report, *The Future of Broadcasting*, 31
March 1977, pp. 651–2. See letters 14 April 1977, p. 79; 21 April 1977, p. 131.

'French connection', review of *Reproduction in Education, Society and Culture*, by Pierre
Bourdieu and Jean-Claude Passeron; *Society, State and Schooling*, ed. Michael F. D.
Young and Geoff Whitty, 5 May 1977, pp. 239–40.

'Class of the conscious', review of *Cultural Creation in Modern Society*, by Lucien
Goldmann; *Lukács and Heidegger: towards a new philosophy*, by Lucien Goldmann, 5
January 1978, pp. 26–7.

'A book at bedtime', review of *Fiction and the Fiction Industry*, by J. A. Sutherland, 4
May 1978, pp. 264–5.

'"The god that failed" all over again', review of *Main Currents of Marxism*, 3 vols., by
Leszek Kolakowski, 23 November 1978, pp. 469–70. See correction 30 November
1978, pp. 533.

'What is anti-capitalism?', review of *Georg Lukács – From Romanticism to Bolshevism*,
by Michael Lowy, 24 January 1980, pp. 189–90.

'The popularity of melodrama', review of *Performance and Politics in Popular Drama*, ed.

David Bradby, Louis James and Bernard Sharratt, 24 April 1980, pp. 170–71.

'Realism again', review of *Essays on Realism*, by Georg Lukács, 20 November 1980, pp. 381–2.

'Radical drama', review of *Stages in the Revolution: political theatre in Britain since 1968*, by Catherine Itzin, 27 November 1980, pp. 432–3.

'The rise of the careerist intelligentsia', review of *Teachers, Writers, Celebrities: the Intellectuals of Modern France*, by Regis Debray, tr. David Macey, 21 May 1981, pp. 322–3.

'The man who shifted against the tide', review of *William Cobbett: the poor man's friend*, by George Spater, 29 April 1982.

'The need to get beyond the past', review of *Destiny Obscure: autobiographies of childhood, education and family from the 1820s to the 1920s*, by John Burnett; *Working Class Childhood: an oral history*, by Jeremy Seabrook, 7 October 1982, pp. 37–8.

'The estranging language of post-modernism', review of *The Naked Artist*, by Peter Fuller; *Aesthetics after Modernism*, by Peter Fuller, 16 June 1983, pp. 439–40.

'Double Default', review of *Dockers and Detectives*, by Ken Worpole, 5 January 1984, pp. 17–18.

'Goodbye to Sartre', review of *Adieux: a farewell to Sartre*, by Simone de Beauvoir, tr. Patrick O'Brien, 21 June 1984, pp. 470–71.

'The Collier's Letter', review of *The Literature of Labour: 200 years of working class writing*, by H. Gustav Klaus, 28 February 1985, pp. 335–6.

'Signs of the time', review of *The Grain of the Voice*, by Roland Barthes, tr. Linda Coverdale, 11 October 1985, p. 65.

'West of Offa's Dyke', review of *Wales: The Imagined Nation*, ed. Tony Curtis, 4 July 1986.

12   Published interviews

'Two interviews with Raymond Williams', *Red Shift* [Cambridge] (1977), no. 2, pp. 12–17; no. 3, pp. 13–15.

'Making It Active', an interview with Ken Worpole, *The English Magazine*, no. 1 (Spring 1979), pp. 4–7.

'Raymond Williams: building a socialist culture', interview with Dave Taylor, *The Leveller*, 24 (March 1979), pp. 25–7.

'Television and Teaching: An Interview with Raymond Williams', *Screen Education*, no. 31 (Summer 1979), pp. 5–14. Reprinted in *Raymond Williams on Television*.

'The Labour Party and Beyond', an interview with Raymond Williams, by Peter Anderson and Martin Steckelmacher, *Revolutionary Socialism*, no. 5 (Summer 1980), pp. 3–7.

'This Sadder Recognition', Sue Aspinal talks to Raymond Williams about *So That You Can Live*, *Screen*, vol. 23, nos 3–4 (September/October 1982), pp. 144–52.

'Nationalisms and Popular Socialism: Phil Cooke talks to Raymond Williams', *Radical Wales*, no. 2 (Spring 1984), pp. 7–8.

'An Interview with Raymond Williams', Stephen Heath and Gillian Skirrow, in *Studies in Entertainment: Critical Approaches to Mass Culture*, ed. Tania Modleski, Bloomington and Indiana, Indiana University Press, 1986, pp. 3–17.

'The practice of possibility', an interview with Terry Eagleton, *New Statesman*, 7 August 1987, pp. 19–21.
'People of the Black Mountains', John Barnie interviews Raymond Williams, *Planet 65* (October/November 1987), pp. 3–13.

13   Letters to newspapers

On railway accidents, letter to *The Times*, 28 July 1955.
On nationalized industries, letter to *The Times*, 30 November 1956.
On subsistence, letter to *The Times*, 5 July 1957.
On nuclear policy, letter to *The Times*, 10 September 1964.
On Vietnam, letter with others to *The Times*, 23 July 1966.
On National Extension College, letter with others to *The Times*, 28 December 1966.
On Pakistan guerrillas, letter to *The Times*, 3 November 1971.
On the future of the UN, letter with others from the Bertrand Russell Peace Foundation in *Manchester Guardian Weekly*, 11 January 1987, p. 2.

14   Williams as editor

Journals

Cambridge University Journal Student newspaper. Williams was editor from April to June 1940.
Outlook Published in Cambridge. Williams was an editor for 1941. Similar in format to *Penguin New Writing*.
Twentyone Weekly newspaper of the 21st Anti-Tank Regiment, Royal Artillery. Printed at Pinneberg, Germany. Williams was editor, April-October 1945.
The Critic
Politics & Letters
The Critical Quarterly
New Left Review
The Week Williams described as a 'sponsor'.
The Spokesman
Constituency bulletin for Cambridgeshire Labour Party. With Joy Williams. Some time between 1961 and 1966.
Literature and History Editorial advisor.
Media, Culture and Society Editorial board.

Books in series

The New Thinkers Library. Published in London by C. A. Watts & Co. Williams was General Editor 1962–1970.
Communications and Culture series. Macmillan. Editorial board.
Marxist Introductions. Oxford University Press.
English Literature in History series. General editor.
Communications series. Fontana.

Works about Raymond Williams

15 Select Bibliography on Williams

Amis, Kingsley, 'Martians Bearing Bursaries', *The Spectator*, 27 April 1962, pp. 554–5. Review of *Communications*.

Barnett, Anthony, 'Raymond Williams and Marxism: A Rejoinder to Terry Eagleton', *New Left Review*, no. 99 (1976), pp. 47–64.

Barnett, Anthony, 'Towards a theory', *New Society*, 21 July 1977, pp. 145–6. Review of *Marxism and Literature*.

Bateson, F. W., *Manchester Guardian Weekly*, 22 February 1976. Review of *Keywords*.

Bayley, J., *New York Review of Books*, 8 October 1970, p. 8. Review of *The English Novel*.

Berman, Marshall, *New York Times Book Review*, 15 July 1973, pp. 1, 26–30. Review of *The Country and the City*.

Blackburn, Robin, 'Raymond Williams and the Politics of a New Left', *New Left Review* 168 (March/April 1988), pp. 12–22.

Briggs, Asa, 'Creative Definitions', *New Statesman*, vol. 61, 10 March 1961, pp. 386–7.

Briggs, Asa, *Partisan Review*, vol. 45, no. 3 (1978). Review of *Television*.

Bryant, Anthony, 'The case of Raymond Williams', *The Insurgent Sociologist* 11 (Spring 1982), pp. 89–97. Review of *Politics and Letters*.

Bryant, Bernard Anthony David, 'The New Left in Britain: the dialectic of rationality and participation', Ph.D. dissertation, London School of Economics, 1981. Chapter Nine, 'Raymond Williams and New Leftism'.

Burchfield, R. W., 'A Case of Mistaken Identity: Keywords', *Encounter* 46 (June 1976), pp. 57–64. Review of *Keywords*.

Burgess, Anthony, 'A Very Tragic Business', *The Spectator*, 10 June 1966, p. 731. Review of *Modern Tragedy*.

Chanan, Michael, 'So that you can live (For Shirley)', *Framework* 18 (1982), pp. 7–8.

Christgau, Robert, 'Living in a Material World: Raymond Williams' Long Revolution', *The Village Voice Literary Supplement*, no. 34, April 1985, pp. 1, 12–18.

Clifford, James, 'On Ethnographic Allegory', in *Writing Culture: The Poetics and Politics of Ethnography*, ed. James Clifford and George E. Marcus, Berkeley, University of California Press, 1986, pp. 113–15.

Connolly, Cyril, 'Precious Land', *Sunday Times*, 8 April 1973, p. 38. Review of *The Country and the City*.

Corrigan, Maureen, 'Raymond Williams: Only Connect' *Village Voice*, 29 May 1984, p. 47. Review of *Towards 2000*.

Corrigan, Philip, *Media, Culture and Society* 2 (1980), pp. 87–91. Review of *Politics and Letters*.

Corrigan, Philip, *border/lines* 1 [Toronto] (1984), pp. 38–9. Review of *Towards 2000*.

Cowling, Maurice, 'Mr Raymond Williams', *The Cambridge Review*, 27 May 1961, pp. 546–51.

Davies, D. I., 'Pilgrim's Progress from Morris to Marx', *Canadian Forum*, August 1980, pp. 30–32. Review of *Politics and Letters*.

Davies, Ioan, *Stand* 5 (1961), pp. 61–4. Review of *The Long Revolution*.

Donoghue, Denis, 'Examples', *London Review of Books*, 2–15 February 1984, pp. 20–22. Review of *Towards 2000*.

Eagleton, Terry, 'The Idea of a Common Culture', in *From Culture to Revolution*, ed. Terry Eagleton and Brian Wicker, London, 1968, pp. 35–57.

Eagleton, Terry. 'The English Novel', *The Spokesman*, nos 15/16 (August/September 1971).

Eagleton, Terry, 'Criticism and Politics: The Work of Raymond Williams', *New Left Review*, no. 95 (1976), pp. 3–23. Reprinted in his *Criticism and Ideology: A Study in Marxist Literary Theory*, London, New Left Books, 1976, pp. 21–43.

Eagleton, Terry, *The Function of Criticism: From The Spectator to Post-Structuralism*, London, Verso, 1984, pp. 108–15.

Eagleton, Terry, 'Stepping Out', *New Statesman*, 27 January 1984, pp. 21–2. Review of *Writing in Society*.

Eagleton, Terry, 'Resources for a Journey of Hope: The Significance of Raymond Williams', *New Left Review* 168 (March/April 1988), pp. 3–11.

Empson, William, 'Compacted Doctrines', *The New York Review of Books*, 27 October 1977, pp. 21–2. Review of *Keywords*.

Fairlie, Henry, *Encounter*, August 1962. Review of *Communications*.

Franco, Jean, 'Go with the flow: books on television', *Tabloid* 3 (Winter 1981), pp. 35–41. Review of *Television*.

Friedman, Michael, H., *Science and Society* 41 (1977), pp. 221–4. Review of *Keywords*.

Garnham, Nicholas, 'Raymond Williams, 1921–1988: A Cultural Analyst, A Distinctive Tradition', *Journal of Communication* 38 (1988), pp. 123–31.

Giddens, Anthony, 'Raymond Williams' long revolution', *Times Higher Education Supplement*, 14 December 1979, pp. 11–12. Reprinted in his *Profiles and Critiques in Social Theory*, Berkeley and Los Angeles, University of California, 1982, pp. 133–43.

Giddens, Anthony, 'The state of sociology', *Times Literary Supplement*, 27 February 1981, p. 215. Review of *Culture*.

Green, Michael, 'Raymond Williams and Cultural Studies', *Cultural Studies* 6 (1975), pp. 31–48.

Gregor, Ian, *Essays in Criticism* 9 (1959), pp. 425–30. Review of *Culture and Society*.

Gross, John, *New Statesman*, 4 May 1962. Review of *Communications*.

Grossberg, Lawrence, 'Strategies of Marxist Cultural Interpretation', *Critical Studies in Mass Communication* 1 (1984), pp. 400–2.

Grundy, Bill, 'State papers?', *The Spectator*, 26 April 1968, pp. 560–61. Review of *Communications*.

Hall, Stuart, 'Some Notes on the Long Revolution and the Example of the 1840's', *Unveroffentlicht* (1970).

Hall, Stuart, 'Cultural Studies: two paradigms', *Media, Culture and Society* 2 (1980), pp. 57–72.

Hall, Stuart, 'The Williams Interviews', *Screen Education*, no. 34 (1980), pp. 94–104. Review of *Politics and Letters*.

Hall, Stuart, 'Only Connect: the life of Raymond Williams', *New Statesman*, 5 February 1988, pp. 20–21.

Hampshire, Stuart, 'Unhappy Families', *New Statesman*, 29 July 1966, pp. 169–70. Review of *Modern Tragedy*.

Harding, D. W., 'The Single Culture', *The Spectator*, 10 October 1958, pp. 495–6.

Review of *Culture and Society*.

Harrington, Michael, *Commonweal*, 4 December 1959, p. 294. Review of *Culture and Society*.

Hartley, Anthony, 'The Loaf and the Leaven', *Manchester Guardian*, 7 October 1958, p. 10. Review of *Culture and Society*.

Hartley, Anthony, 'Philistine to Philistine?', in *International Literary Annual 2*, ed. John Wain, London, John Calder, 1959, pp. 11–36.

Hartley, Anthony, 'The Intellectuals of England', *The Spectator*, 4 May 1962, pp. 577–81.

Heath, Stephen, 'Modern English Man', Presences series, *Times Higher Education Supplement*, 20 July 1984, p. 17.

Hewison, Robert, 'Collectively feeling', *Times Literary Supplement*, 27 February 1981, p. 239. Review of *Problems in Materialism and Culture*.

Hewison, Robert, *In Anger: British Culture in the Cold War 1945-60*, New York, Oxford University Press, 1981, pp. 160–200.

Hewison, Robert, *Too Much: Art and Society in the Sixties 1960-75*, London, Methuen, 1986, *passim*.

Higgins, John, 'Raymond Williams and the Problem of Ideology', in *Postmodernism and Politics*, ed. Jonathan Arac, Minneapolis, University of Minnesota Press, 1986, pp. 112–22. Reprinted from *Boundary 2*, 11 (Fall/Winter 1982/3), pp. 145–54.

Hill, Christopher, *New Society*, 5 February 1976. Review of *Keywords*.

Hoggart, Richard, 'An Important Book', *Essays in Criticism 9* (1959), pp. 171–9. Review of *Culture and Society*.

Hood, Stuart, *Guardian Weekly*, 8 June 1974, p. 21. Review of *Television*.

Hood, Stuart, 'In human contact', *Guardian Weekly*, 3 January 1982, p. 21. Review of *Contact*.

Hooker, Jeremy, 'A Dream of a Country: The Raymond Williams Trilogy', *Planet*, 49/50 (January 1980), pp. 53–61.

Howe, Irving, 'On Ideas of Culture', *The New Republic*, 2 February 1959, pp. 18–19; 9 February, pp. 23–4. Two-part review of *Culture and Society*.

Inglis, Fred, *Radical Earnestness: English Social Theory 1880-1980*, ch. 8, 'Culture and politics: Richard Hoggart, the *New Left Review* and Raymond Williams', Oxford, Martin Robertson, 1982.

Inglis, Fred, 'Innocent at home', *New Society*, 27 October 1983, pp. 158–60. Review of *Towards 2000*.

James, C. L. R., 'Marxism and the Intellectuals', in his *Spheres of Existence: Selected Writings*, Westport, Connecticut: Lawrence Hill and Co.; London: Allison and Busby, 1980, pp. 113–30. Originally written 1961.

Johnson, Richard, 'Three problematics: elements of a theory of Working-class culture', in *Working Class Culture: Studies in History and Theory*, ed. John Clarke et al., London, Hutchinson, 1979, pp. 201–37. For another version see his 'Histories of Culture/Theories of Ideology: Notes on an Impasse', in *Ideology and Cultural Production*, ed. Michele Barrett et al. London, Croom Helm, 1979.

Johnson, Richard, *Comment*, 15 September 1979. Review of *Politics and Letters*.

Kermode, Frank, *Encounter*, 12 (January 1959), pp. 86–8. Review of *Culture and Society*.

Kermode, Frank, *Partisan Review*, vol. 29, no. 3 (1962). Review of *Border Country*.

Kermode, Frank, 'Tragedy and Revolution', *Encounter* 27 (August 1966), pp. 83–5.

Review of *Modern Tragedy*.

Kettle, Arnold, 'Culture and Revolution: A Consideration of the Ideas of Raymond Williams and Others', *Marxism Today* 5 (1961), pp. 301–7.

Kettle, Arnold, *Red Letters* 6 (1977), pp. 71–3. Review of *Marxism and Literature*.

Kettle, Arnold, *Marxism Today* 23 (1979), pp. 28–9. Review of *Politics and Letters*.

Kettle, Arnold, 'Bernard Shaw and the New Spirit', in *Rebels and Their Causes*, ed. Maurice Cornford, Atlantic Highlands, N.J., Humanities Press, 1979, pp. 209–20.

Kiernan, V. G., 'Culture and Society', *New Reasoner* 9 (1959), pp. 74–83. Review of *Culture and Society*.

Klaus, Gustav H., 'Über Raymond Williams', in Raymond Williams, *Innovationen*, (1979), pp. 203–26.

Lange, Gerhard W, *Materialistische Kulturtheorie im Vergleich: Raymond Williams, Terry Eagleton und die deutsche Tradition*, Munster, Lit Verlag, 1984.

Leavis, F. R., *Nor Shall My Sword*, London, Chatto and Windus, 1972, pp. 150–1.

Lerner, Laurence, 'Beyond Literature: Social Criticism versus Aesthetics', *Encounter* 41 (July 1973), pp. 62–5. Review of *The Country and the City*.

Liljegren, S. B., *Studia Neophilologica* 25 (1952–3), pp. 180–1. Review of *Drama From Ibsen to Eliot*.

Lockwood, Bernard, 'Four Contemporary British Working-Class Novelists: A thematic and critical approach to the fiction of Raymond Williams, John Braine, David Storey and Alan Sillitoe', Ph.D. dissertation, University of Wisconsin, 1966.

Luckett, Richard, 'A Marxist in town and country', *The Spectator*, 5 May 1973, pp. 554–5. Review of *The Country and the City*.

Macdonald, Dwight, 'Looking Backward', *Encounter* 16 (June 1961), pp. 79–84.

MacCabe, Colin, 'The end of literary criticism', *Guardian*, 26 January 1984, p. 12. Review of *Writing in Society*.

MacCabe, Colin, 'Class of '68', in his *Theoretical Essays: Film, Linguistics, Literature*, Manchester, Manchester University Press, 1985, p. 20.

McGrath, John, 'The Theory and Practice of Political Theatre', *TQ (Theatre Quarterly)* 9 (1979), pp. 43–54.

McKeon, Michael, *Studies in Romanticism* 16 (Winter 1977), pp. 128–39. Review of *Keywords*.

Marcus, George E., 'Contemporary Problems of Ethnography in the Modern World System', in *Writing Culture: The Poetics and Politics of Ethnography*, ed. James Clifford and George E. Marcus, Berkeley, University of California Press, 1986, pp. 169–71.

Merrill, Michael, 'Raymond Williams and the Theory of English Marxism', *Radical History Review* 19 (1978–9), pp. 9–31.

Milner, Andrew, 'A Young Man's Death: Raymond Williams 1921–1988', *Thesis Eleven*, 20 (1988), pp. 106–18.

Morgan, Janet, 'Unquestioned questions', *Times Literary Supplement*, 4 November 1983, p. 1223. Review of *Towards 2000*.

Motterhead, Chris, *Screen Education* 14 (Spring 1975), pp. 35–8. Review of *Television*.

Mowat, C. L., 'The Education of Raymond Williams', *Critical Quarterly* 3 (1961), pp. 175–81. Review of *The Long Revolution* and *Border Country*.

Mulhern, Francis, 'Towards 2000, or News From You-know-where', *New Left Review*, no. 148 (November/December 1984), pp. 5–30. Review of *Towards 2000*.

Nairn, Tom, 'The Left Against Europe?', *New Left Review*, no. 75 (1972), pp. 106–8.

Nove, Alec, 'Struggling for the future', *Guardian*, 20 October 1983, p. 8. Review of *Towards 2000*.

O'Connor, Alan, 'Cultural Studies and Common Sense', *Canadian Journal of Political and Social Theory* 5 (1981), pp. 183–95.

O'Connor, Alan, 'Overlapping Worlds: The Circles of M. M. Bakhtin and Raymond Williams', in *Mikhail Mikhailovich Bakhtin: His Circle, His Influence,* papers presented at the International Colloquium, Queen's University, 7–9 October, 1983. Department of French Studies, Queen's University, Kingston, Ontario, Canada.

O'Connor, Alan, *Raymond Williams: Writing, Culture, Politics,* Oxford, New York, Basil Blackwell, 1989.

Parrinder, Patrick, *Literature and History* 7 (1981), pp. 124–6. Review of *Politics and Letters*.

Parrinder, Patrick, 'The accents of Raymond Williams', *Critical Quarterly* 26 (1984), pp. 47–57.

Parrinder, Patrick, 'Pamphleteer's Progress', review of *The Functions of Criticism,* by Terry Eagleton, *London Review of Books*, 7 February 1985, pp. 16–17.

Parrinder, Patrick, 'Culture and Society in the 1980's' and 'Utopia and negativity in Raymond Williams', in his *The Failure of Theory: Essays on Criticism and Contemporary Fiction*, Brighton, Harvester, 1987, pp. 58–71, 72–84.

Parrinder, Patrick, 'Diary', *The London Review of Books*, 12 February 1988, p. 25.

Pechey, Graham, '*Scrutiny,* English Marxism, and the Work of Raymond Williams', *Literature and History,* vol. 11, no. 1 (Spring 1985), pp. 65–76.

Pfeil, Fred, 'Towards a portable Marxist Criticism: A Critique and Suggestion', *College English* 41 (1980), pp. 753–68.

Pittock, Malcolm, *Essays in Criticism* 9 (1959), pp. 430–32. Review of *Culture and Society*.

Pittock, Malcolm, 'The Optimistic Revolution', *Essays in Criticism* 12 (1962), pp. 82–91. Review of *The Long Revolution*.

Potter, Dennis, 'Unknown Territory', *New Left Review* 7 (January-February 1961), pp. 63–5. Review of *Border Country*.

Quinton, Anthony, 'The Quality of Living', *The Spectator*, 26 May 1961, pp. 761–2.

Rosenberg, Harold, 'The Threat of Culture', *The Nation*, 7 February 1959, pp. 121–2. Review of *Culture and Society*.

Rowbotham, Sheila, 'Picking up the pieces', *New Socialist*, no. 31, October 1985, p. 49. Review of the paperback edn. of *Towards 2000*.

Ryan, Alan, 'Feudal lord of culture and society', *New Society*, 20 September 1979, pp. 628–9. Review of *Politics and Letters*.

Ryan, Kiernan, 'Socialist Fiction and the Education of Desire: Mervyn Jones, Raymond Williams and John Berger', in *The Socialist Novel in Britain: Towards the Recovery of a Tradition*, ed. H. Gustav Klaus, Brighton, Sussex, Harvester Press, 1982, pp. 166–85.

Said, Edward, *Orientalism*, New York, Vintage, 1979.

Said, Edward, 'Reflections on Recent American "Left" Literary Theory', *boundary 2*, 8 (Fall 1979), pp. 11–30.

Said, Edward, 'Traveling Theory', *Raritan* 1 (Winter 1982), pp. 41–67. Reprinted in his *The World, The Text, and The Critic,* Cambridge, Harvard University Press, 1983.

Said, Edward W., 'Raymond Williams, 1921-1988', *The Nation*, 5 March 1988, pp. 312,

314.

Sandall, Roger, 'When I hear the Word "Culture": From Arnold to Anthropology', *Encounter* 55 (October 1980), pp. 89–92. Review of *Politics and Letters*.

Scrivener, Michael, *Telos* 38 (Winter 1979–80), pp. 190–98. Review of *Marxism and Literature*.

Scruton, Roger, 'The Word in the World', *Times Literary Supplement*, 26 March 1976, p. 352. Review of *Keywords*.

Scruton, Roger, 'Raymond Williams', in his *Thinkers of the New Left*, London, Longman, 1985, pp. 54–65.

Sharratt, Bernard, 'Poisson: A modest review', in his *Reading Relations: Structures of Literary Production: A Dialectical Text/Book*, Brighton, Sussex, Harvester, 1982, pp. 35–40.

Siegmund-Schultze, Dorothea, 'Raymond Williams' Concept of Culture', *Zeitschrift fur Anglistik und Amerikanistik* 22 (1974), pp. 131–45.

Slater, David, 'Social Movements and a Recasting of the Political', in *New Social Movements and the State in Latin America*, ed. David Slater, Amsterdam, CEDLA, 1985, pp. 12–15.

Smith, Barry, 'A Historian's Comments upon *Culture and Society* and *The Long Revolution*', *The Melbourne Historical Journal* 8 (1969), p. 32.

Sparks, Colin, 'Raymond Williams, Culture and Marxism', *International Socialism* 9 (Summer 1980), pp. 131–44.

Spender, Stephen, *New York Review of Books*, 16 November 1972, p. 3. Review of *Orwell*.

Stedman Jones, Gareth, review of *Towards 2000* and *Wigan Pier Revisited*, by Beatrix Campbell, *Marxism Today*, July 1984, pp. 38–40.

Stein, Walter, 'Humanism and Tragic redemption', chapter 6 of *Criticism as Dialogue*, Cambridge, Cambridge University Press, 1969, pp. 183–246. *On Modern Tragedy*.

Thompson, E. P., 'The Long Revolution', *New Left Review*, no. 9 and no. 10 (May/June and July/August 1961), pp. 24–33, 34–9.

Thompson, E. P., 'A Nice Place to Visit', *New York Review of Books*, 6 February 1975, pp. 34–7. Review of *The Country and the City*.

Thompson, E. P., 'Last Dispatches from The Border Country', *The Nation*, 5 March 1988, pp. 310–12.

Thompson, John O., 'Tragic Flow: Raymond Williams on Drama', *Screen Education*, no. 34 (Summer 1980), pp. 45–58.

Times Literary Supplement, 'The Weight of an Abstraction', 26 September 1958, p. 548. Review of *Culture and Society*. See letter from Williams, 3 October 1958, p. 561.

Times Literary Supplement, 'Notes Towards the Definition of What?', 10 March 1961, p. 147. Review of *The Long Revolution*.

Times Literary Supplement, 'A Time for Tragedy?', 11 August 1966, pp. 717–18. Review of *Modern Tragedy*, possibly by George Steiner.

Wain, John, 'The Coronation of the Novel', *The Listener*, 4 June 1970, pp. 755–6. Review of *The English Novel*.

Ward, J. P., *Raymond Williams*, Writers of Wales Series, University of Wales Press for the Welsh Arts Council, 1981.

Watkins, Evan, 'Raymond Williams and Marxist Criticism', *boundary* 2, 4 (1975–6), pp. 933–46.

Watkins, Evan, *The Critical Act: Criticism and Community*, chapter 5, 'Raymond Williams and Marxist Literary Criticism', New Haven and London, Yale University Press, 1978.

Watkins, Evan, 'Conflict and Consensus in the History of Recent Criticism', *New Literary History* 12 (1981), pp. 345–65.

Williams, Merryn, 'Raymond Williams, 1921–88', *Planet* 68 (April/May 1988), pp. 3–6.

Wollheim, Richard, *Culture and Socialism*, Fabian Tract 331, London, The Fabian Society, 1961.

Wollheim, Richard, 'Definitions of Culture', *New Statesman*, 9 June 1961.

Wollheim, Richard, 'The English Dream', *The Spectator*, 10 March 1961, pp. 334–5. Review of *The Long Revolution*.

Woodcock, George, 'Half-Truths on Orwell', *The Nation*, 11 October 1971, pp. 341–2. Review of *Orwell*.

Woodcock, George, 'The Two Faces of Modern Marxism', *Sewanee Review* 86 (1978), pp. 588–94. Review of *Marxism and Literature*.

Zinman, Rosalind, 'Raymond Williams; towards a sociology of culture', Ph.D. dissertation, Concordia University, Montreal, 1984.

Index

Index by Mary Madden